‘AMALIYAT-E-JARĀḤIYA

(Operative Surgery)

——— A Comprehensive Book on ———

Unani Surgical Procedures

——— (General & Systemic) ———

Prof. Saiyad Shah Alam | Dr. Ansar Ahmad

Department of Ilmul Jarahat,

National Institute of Unani Medicine, Bengaluru

Dedication

To my parents,

who were my first teachers,

whose prayers, sacrifices, and

love have shaped my life.

And to all my teachers,

who have guided and inspired

me throughout my journey of learning.

This book is dedicated with

deep gratitude and respect to all of you.

Preface

The science of surgery has occupied a distinguished place in the history of Unani medicine since the earliest periods of medical scholarship. Classical physicians such as Hippocrates, Galen, Al-Rāzī, Ibn Sīnā, Al-Zahrāwī, and many other eminent scholars described numerous surgical procedures and operative techniques in their writings. Their contributions demonstrate that surgery was not merely an auxiliary practice but an essential component of the Unani system of medicine.

In Unani medicine, treatment is traditionally classified into three fundamental methods: *'Ilāj bi'l-Tadbīr* (regimenal therapy), *'Ilāj bi'l-Dawā'* (pharmacotherapy), and *'Ilāj bi'l-Yad* (surgical intervention). Among these, *'Ilāj bi'l-Yad* represents the practical application of surgical knowledge, where the physician intervenes directly through operative procedures to restore the natural state of the body. Over centuries, Unani scholars developed detailed descriptions of operative procedures

Despite this rich heritage, contemporary students and practitioners of Unani medicine often face difficulty in accessing clear and systematic material on operative surgery within the Unani framework. Much of the classical knowledge is scattered across numerous classical texts and is written in complex language, making it challenging for contemporary readers to understand and apply it in clinical practice. This situation created a need for a concise, well-organised book that clearly and accessibly presents the principles and procedures of Unani surgery.

The present book, *"Amaliyāt-e-Jarāḥiyya (Operative Surgery)"* has been written with this objective in mind. The primary purpose of this work is to compile, organize, and explain the fundamental principles of operative surgery as described in classical Unani literature while presenting them in a manner that is easier for modern readers to comprehend. This book attempts to bridge the gap between classical teachings and contemporary academic study.

Another important motivation for writing this book was the growing interest among students and scholars of Unani medicine in the surgical heritage of the system. Many postgraduate students, researchers, and practitioners wish to explore the operative aspects of Unani medicine, but often find limited structured material available for study. By compiling relevant concepts and procedures in a single volume, it is hoped that this book will serve as a useful reference for those who wish to understand the surgical dimension of Unani medicine more deeply.

This book is primarily intended for students of Unani medicine, postgraduate scholars, researchers, and practitioners, particularly those who wish to study the theoretical foundations and historical practices of Unani surgery. At the same time, it may also be beneficial for readers interested in the history of medicine and the development of surgical knowledge in traditional medical systems.

In preparing this work, careful effort has been made to remain faithful to the teachings of classical Unani physicians while presenting the material in a structured and coherent form. The discussions included in this book are based on the principles described in classical texts of Unani medicine and are organized systematically so that readers may understand both the theoretical basis and the practical aspects of surgical management.

Special attention has been given to explaining important topics such as the principles of operative treatment, the management of wounds and ulcers, haemorrhage control, abscess formation and drainage, inflammatory swellings, fistulae and sinuses, tumours, gangrene, and other surgical conditions described by classical physicians. Wherever necessary, the concepts have been clarified to help readers understand the underlying rationale of the procedures described in the Unani tradition.

It is hoped that this book will contribute, even in a modest way, to the preservation and dissemination of the surgical knowledge contained within the Unani system of medicine. The heritage of classical physicians represents a valuable intellectual tradition, and studying their work not only enriches our understanding of medical history but also strengthens the academic foundations of Unani medicine today.

No scholarly work is free from limitations, and it is possible that some shortcomings may remain despite sincere efforts. Constructive suggestions and corrections from readers, scholars, and colleagues will always be welcomed, as they will help improve future editions of this work.

Finally, I express my sincere gratitude to my respected teachers, mentors, and colleagues whose guidance and encouragement have always inspired my academic pursuits. I also remain deeply grateful to my parents and family members for their constant support and motivation throughout my educational journey. Without their encouragement, the completion of this work would not have been possible.

It is my sincere hope that this book will prove beneficial for students and scholars of Unani medicine and will encourage further study and research in the field of Unani surgery.

Prof. Saiyad Shah Alam

Dr. Ansar Ahmad

Department of Ilmul Jarahat,

NIUM, Bengaluru

Prologue

Surgery has always been an integral component of the medical sciences. From the earliest stages of human civilization, physicians recognized that certain diseases and pathological conditions could not be adequately treated by medicines alone. In such circumstances, manual intervention became necessary to restore the structure and function of the affected part of the body. Within the Unani system of medicine, this method of treatment is known as *'Ilāj bi'l-Yad,* or operative intervention, and it represents one of the three fundamental methods of therapy alongside *'Ilāj bi'l-Tadbīr* (regimenal therapy) and *'Ilāj bi'l-Dawā'* (pharmacotherapy).

The historical roots of operative surgery in Unani medicine are both deep and extensive. Classical physicians of the Greco-Arab medical tradition made remarkable contributions to the development of surgical knowledge. Early scholars such as Hippocrates and Galen laid the foundations of scientific surgery. Later, great physicians of the Islamic Golden Age—including Al-Rāzī (Rhazes), Ibn Sīnā (Avicenna), Al-Majūsī (Haly Abbas), Ibn Zuhr (Avenzoar), and Abū al-Qāsim Al-Zahrāwī (Albucasis)—expanded these foundations and produced detailed descriptions of surgical diseases and operative techniques.

Among these scholars, Abū al-Qāsim Al-Zahrāwī occupies a particularly distinguished position in the history of surgery. His monumental work on operative medicine described numerous surgical instruments, procedures, and methods of treatment that influenced medical practice for centuries. Classical Unani texts contain extensive discussions on the management of wounds, haemorrhage, abscesses, fistulae, tumours, fractures, dislocations, and many other conditions requiring surgical intervention. These writings demonstrate that surgery was not considered a secondary discipline but rather a systematic and scientifically developed branch of medicine.

Despite this rich surgical heritage, the study of operative surgery within the Unani system today presents certain challenges. Much of the classical knowledge is dispersed throughout numerous traditional texts, and the terminology used in those works is often complex for modern readers. Students and practitioners frequently find it difficult to access the operative aspects of Unani medicine in a structured and consolidated form. This situation highlights the need for a comprehensive work that organizes classical surgical knowledge in a systematic and accessible manner while preserving the authenticity of the original teachings.

The present book, *"Amaliyāt-e-Jarāḥiyya (Operative Surgery)",* has been written to present the principles and practices of surgery described in classical Unani literature in an organized and academically useful form. The material included in this work has been carefully compiled from classical Unani medical texts, and modern surgical procedures have deliberately not been included. The purpose of this approach is to preserve the original surgical concepts described by the classical physicians and to present them in a clear and systematic format for students and scholars of Unani medicine.

For the sake of clarity and systematic study, this book has been divided into two major sections: General Surgery and Systemic Surgery. Each section addresses specific aspects of surgical knowledge within the Unani framework.

The first section of the book deals with General Surgery, which focuses on the fundamental surgical conditions and principles that are applicable to many different parts of the body. This section includes topics such as pain management, haemorrhage, wounds and ulcers, gangrene, abscess formation, sinus and fistula, incision and drainage, various types of swellings, arterial surgeries, venous surgeries, and surgeries related to the hand and foot. These subjects form the basic foundation of operative surgery and provide essential knowledge required for understanding surgical diseases and their management.

The second section of the book addresses Systemic Surgery, which deals with surgical diseases related to specific organs and systems of the body. In this section, the surgical management of different anatomical regions and organ systems has been discussed. Topics included in this section are surgeries of the head, surgeries of the eye, surgeries of the ear, nose, and throat (ENT), surgeries of the pharynx, larynx, and trachea, breast surgeries, surgeries of gastrointestinal diseases, anorectal surgeries, urogenital surgeries, hernia, and obstetric and gynaecological surgeries. By presenting these topics in a systematic manner, this section provides a comprehensive overview of the surgical conditions affecting different body systems.

An important feature of this book is that all surgical discussions are derived exclusively from classical Unani medical texts. Modern surgical techniques and procedures have intentionally not been included in order to maintain the original perspective of Unani operative medicine. The objective is to present the classical understanding of surgical diseases and their management exactly as described by the traditional physicians.

To facilitate better understanding, the surgical conditions discussed in this book have been arranged in a clear and consistent format. Each topic generally begins with a general description of the disease, followed by its types or classifications. This is then followed by a discussion of the signs and symptoms of the condition, allowing the reader to understand its clinical presentation.

After the clinical description, the principles of management are explained according to the Unani theoretical framework. This is followed by a detailed explanation of the surgical management of the condition, including its indications and contraindications, as well as important aspects of pre-operative assessment, operative procedure, and post-operative care. Particular attention has also been given to post-operative wound management, which has always been regarded as an essential component of surgical treatment in the Unani tradition.

Another important feature of this work is the careful presentation of Unani medical terminology. The spelling and pronunciation of Unani terms have been verified and standardized with the help of authoritative dictionaries in order to ensure accuracy. Furthermore, wherever necessary, the corresponding modern medical terms have been provided in brackets to help readers understand the relationship between classical terminology and contemporary medical concepts.

It must be acknowledged that, despite the remarkable contributions of classical Unani physicians, certain limitations exist within the surgical literature of the tradition. Some surgical diseases are described only briefly in the classical texts, and in certain cases, detailed operative procedures are not available. Similarly, the surgical management of some diseases may appear limited when compared to modern surgical knowledge. Nevertheless, every effort has been made in this book to include all available information on these topics from classical sources so that readers may gain as complete an understanding as possible of the surgical knowledge preserved within the Unani tradition.

For this reason, a wide range of surgical diseases and procedures described in classical Unani literature have been incorporated into this work. It is hoped that only a very small number of Unani surgical topics, if any, remain outside the scope of this book. In this way, the present work attempts to serve as a comprehensive reference for the study of operative surgery in Unani medicine.

Ultimately, the study of these classical surgical texts not only enriches our understanding of the historical development of medical science but also highlights the intellectual achievements of the physicians who preserved and advanced surgical knowledge over many centuries. It is hoped that this book will encourage further study and research in the field of Unani operative surgery and contribute to the preservation of this important medical heritage.

Prof. Saiyad Shah Alam

Dr. Ansar Ahmad

Department of Ilmul Jarahat,

NIUM, Bengaluru

CONTENTS

GENERAL SURGERY
(JARĀḤAT 'UMŪMĪ)

Introduction and Principles in Operative Surgery

Principles of Treatment *(ʿIlāj)* in Unani Medicine

In the science of medicine (*Fann-e-Ṭibb*), there are three recognised methods of treatment.

First Method: *ʿIlāj bi'l Tadbīr*

This involves regulating the six essential factors (*Asbāb Sitta Ḍarūriyya*). It is applied both for maintaining health in healthy individuals and for treating patients whose temperament (*mizāj*) has deviated from its natural balance. These factors work to restore the body's temperament to its proper equilibrium. Diet (*Ghidhā'*) is considered one of these factors, and it must be used thoughtfully, paying attention to both its quality (*kayfiyat*) and quantity (*kammiyat*).

Second Method: *ʿIlāj bi'l Dawā'*

This is treatment with drugs (*ʿIlāj bi'l Dawā'*), in which medicines are administered orally or internally, or applied externally. Examples include plasters (*Ṭilā'*), poultices (*Ḍimādāt*), nasal medications, emetics, eye drops, gargles, and medicines applied by rubbing or sprinkling.

Third Method: *ʿIlāj bi'l Yad*

This is a procedural treatment (*ʿIlāj bi'l Yad*), or surgical intervention, where the physician performs actions with his hands. Examples include incising wounds, opening abscesses and swellings, cauterisation, and setting fractured bones.

Surgical Intervention in Unani Medicine *('Ilāj bi'l Yad)*

Definition of Surgery (*Jarāḥat*) According to Ibn al-Quff al-Masīḥī

Surgery (*Jarāḥat*) is a specialised branch of medicine that enables physicians to understand the conditions of the human body, especially those concerning tissue discontinuity (*Tafarruq e Ittiṣāl*) occurring at specific regions of the external body. It also equips the practitioner with knowledge of the appropriate interventions required once such tissue discontinuity occurs.

The ultimate goal of surgery is to restore the affected organ or tissue to its natural state (*ṭabī'ī ḥālat*), ensuring both structure and function are preserved or recovered.

Surgery (*'Ilāj bi'l Yad*)

Surgery *('Ilāj bi'l Yad)* is divided into three categories in Unani medicine:

1. vascular surgery *('Amal fil-'Urūq):* Surgical procedures involving vessels,
2. Soft Tissue Surgery *('Amal fil-Laḥm):* Surgical procedures involving muscles, soft tissues, and skin,
3. Orthopaedic surgery *('Amal fil-'Iẓām):* Manual operations performed on bones,

'Amal fil-'Urūq (Surgical Procedures on Vessels)

Surgical operations performed on vessels *('Urūq)* are of two types:

1. Procedures on static vessels *(al-'Urūq al-Sākina)* – also known as *Faṣd* (Venesection / Phlebotomy).
2. Procedures on pulsating vessels *(al-'Urūq al-Jahinda)* – which involve cutting or excising the arteries (Arteriotomy / Arteriectomy) and the treatment of vascular swellings, particularly aneurysms.

'Amal fil-Laḥm (Surgical procedures involving muscles, soft tissues, and skin)

Surgical operations performed on flesh *(laḥm)* are categorised into three types:

1. Identification of *Ḥijāma* (Cupping Therapy) – the recognition and precise application of cupping for therapeutic purposes.
2. Procedures of *'Amal-i-Baṭṭ* (Incision, Excision, and Suturing) – operative interventions involving cutting, excision of morbid tissue, and approximation of wound margins by sutures.
3. Procedure of *'Amal Kayy* (Cauterisation) – the deliberate application of heat or cauterising agents as a therapeutic measure to arrest bleeding, destroy diseased tissue, or prevent the progression of pathological conditions.

'Amal fil-'Iẓām (Surgical Procedures on Bones)

Surgical procedures related to bones *('Iẓām)* are of two types:

1. Surgical Procedure of *Kasr* (Fracture Reduction) – correction and anatomical alignment of fractured bones.
2. Surgical Procedure of *Khal'* (Dislocation Reduction) – repositioning of a dislocated bone to its normal site.

Taskīn-i-Alam
(Pain Management)

Sometimes, the patient experiences severe pain in the affected organ during treatment, which creates obstacles for the surgeon in the continuation of therapy. The cause of this pain may be either the pathological matter (*midda*) descending towards the organ, or trauma to the nerve (*'aṣab*), or injury to the membranous covering (*ghishā*) of the organ. At this stage, it becomes essential to alleviate the pain (*Taskīn-i-Alam*), so that the morbid matter (*midda*) may not be attracted towards the weakened organ *('uḍw ḍa'īf)*, as this can result in inflammation and subsequently weaken the vital strength (*quwwat*) upon which the success of treatment largely depends.

Pain may be relieved through two approaches

1. Real *(Ḥaqīqī)* Relief:
2. Non-Real *(Ghayr Ḥaqīqī)* Relief:

1. Real *(Ḥaqīqī)* Relief of Pain:

The real method of pain relief is to counteract its actual cause.
According to Jālīnūs, the cause of pain is *Tafarruq-i-Ittiṣāl* (discontinuity of tissue).
Ibn Sīnā considered both *Tafarruq-i-Ittiṣāl* and *Sū'-i-Mizāj* (dystemperament) as causes,
whereas *Fakhr al-Dīn al-Khaṭīb* and *Qāḍī Abū al-Walīd* Ibn Rushd thought that pain results solely from *sū' mizāj*.

General Management of Pain Based on Aetiology

If the cause of pain is *Tafarruq-i-Ittiṣāl* (discontinuity of tissue), the general management is directed towards promoting healing of the injured part.

If the cause is *Sū'-i-Mizāj Māddī* (material dystemperament), evacuation (*Istifrāgh*) of the offending matter is carried out under the advice of the physician. The mode of *Istifrāgh* varies according to the nature of the morbid matter (*midda*).

If the cause is *Sū'-i-Mizāj Sāda* (simple dystemperament), it is managed by employing its opposite (principle of contraries)

2. Non-Real (*Ghayr Ḥaqīqī*) Relief of Pain

The second form of pain relief, known as *Ghayr Ḥaqīqī*, is achieved through the use of *mukhaddirāt* (anodynes or sedatives)

The relief of pain through *Mukhaddirāt* (sedatives/anodynes) is explained on four grounds:

1. Due to their inherent coldness (*burūdat*), they constrict the pathways of the *rūḥ* (vital spirit) and prevent the sensory faculty (*quwwat ḥissiyya*) from penetrating. As a result, a negative state is produced, leading to diminished or absent perception of pain. In other words, pain in this context is nothing more than a negative perception rather than an independent entity.
2. Because of the *Burūdat* of *Adwiya Mukhaddira* (sedative drugs), the substance of *Rūḥ* becomes thickened (*ghalīẓ*), thereby obstructing its penetration and circulation through the pathways. Although the nerves (*a'ṣāb*) appear to lack visible passages,

Jālīnūs (Galen), in his work "*Kitāb al-'Ilal wa'l A'rāḍ,*" explained that these structures contain fine openings, similar to pores in hailstones, through which the *Rūḥ* usually flows. Sedatives obstruct this process, thus suppressing pain sensation.

3. Pain arises through sensation, heat (*ḥarārat*), and moisture (*ruṭūbaṭ*). The temperament (*Mizāj*) of sedatives is cold and dry (*bārid wa yābis*), which is opposite to the cause. By the principle of contrariety, the opposite weakens and breaks down the active faculty, thereby reducing pain perception.
4. Owing to their inherent toxicity, sedatives directly weaken the sensory faculty (*quwwat ḥissiyya*). When this faculty is debilitated, the perception of pain decreases, and consequently, the sensation of discomfort is diminished.

Note:

It must be emphasised that the real (*ḥaqīqī*) form of pain relief is the one truly beneficial and superior in its outcome. The other, namely the non-real (*ghayr ḥaqīqī*) form, although it provides temporary ease by lessening pain and thereby facilitating treatment, ultimately leads to weakening of the vital strength (*quwwat*). Moreover, the morbid matter (*midda*) that originally produces pain may become stagnant and lodged within the organ. For this reason, a surgeon should resort to such measures only in cases of absolute necessity.

Nazf al-Dam (Haemorrhage)

Concept and Management of Haemorrhage (*Nazf al-Dam*) in Unani Medicine

When a vein (*warīd*) or an artery (*shiryān*) is severed, profuse and rapid bleeding occurs. If the injury involves a vein, repair is often difficult; however, if it involves an artery, there remains a risk that it may not heal or rejoin at all.

Causes of Bleeding from Vessels

The causes of haemorrhage from the vessels (*'Urūq*) are either the opening of their orifices or rupture of their walls. The rupture of vessel walls may occur due to incision, tearing, crushing, or ulceration. The opening of their orifices results either from weakness of the vessels or from a sudden influx of blood in excess, which represents an acute condition imposed from outside.

The cause of blood oozing (*tarashshuḥ*) from the vessels is the dissolution or thinning of their walls, along with increased subtlety and dilution of the blood itself. This also occurs when the mouths of the smaller vessels become dilated.

Management and Haemostatic Measures

There are ten methods described for the control of haemorrhage:

1. **Diversion of the morbid matter (*Midda*)** – This is achieved either by applying cupping (*ḥijāma*) or by opening certain veins (*faṣd*) so that the blood is diverted to another site.
2. **Use of drugs that thicken the consistency of the matter** – Such medications cause coagulation and arrest bleeding at the site. Examples include *Khashkhāsh* (poppy seeds), *'Adas* (lentils), and *Unnāb* (jujube).
3. **Inducing sleep** – In some cases, sleep itself acts as a hemostatic measure. Even hypnotic drugs may be used, since during sleep the innate heat (*ḥarārat gharīziyya*) and the natural faculty (*quwwat ṭabī'iyya*) are drawn inward, which in turn pulls the *midda* away from the site of bleeding.
4. **Ligation of the bleeding vessel** – When a vein (*warīd*) or artery (*shiryān*) is severed, the affected vessel is exposed and tied with a

silk thread. In certain situations, the cut end of the vessel may even be inserted into the mouth of a large ant and then severed, as practised in abdominal wounds when the omentum protrudes, and its vessels are cut.

5. **Application of cold agents (*Adwiya Bārida*) directly over the site of bleeding** – For example, ice or hailstones may be applied. The intense cold thickens the blood, induces coagulation, and thereby seals the bleeding pathway
6. **Use of strong styptic agents** – Application of potent astringent drugs such as *Māzū* (Quercus infectoria), *Gulnār* (Pomegranate flower), and *Gandana* (Allium species) helps approximate the edges of the bleeding site, thereby arresting haemorrhage.
7. **Application of drying and absorbent substances** – Drugs that loosen and dilate the site while absorbing excess Discharge, such as *Safeda* (Lead carbonate) and *Bujhā hu'ā Chūnā* (Slaked lime), may be applied locally to control bleeding.
8. **Induction of eschar *(Khurand formation)*** – To occlude the bleeding pathway and prevent further discharge of blood, eschar-producing measures are employed. This may be achieved either through the use of caustic drugs (*kāwī adwiya*) or by the procedure of cauterisation.
9. **Proximal ligation** – Tying the site firmly above the point of bleeding can effectively arrest haemorrhage. For instance, in the case of accidental arterial incision during phlebotomy (*faṣd*) at the basilic vein, application of a tight bandage about four fingers above the elbow can stop further bleeding.
10. **Application of specific styptic agents** – Direct placement of special hemostatic substances at the bleeding site, such as a ball of rabbit's hair, or filings of *Ānbūs* (Lead oxide), proves effective in controlling haemorrhage.

Principles of Internal Haemorrhage

1. In cases of internal haemorrhage, the recommended approach is either:
   - to divert the blood towards the opposite direction,
   - or to transfer it to a nearby organ,

- or to manage it through cooling and astringent foods and drinks.

2. The treatment differs according to the organ involved, since therapeutic agents are directed towards specific organs in proportion to their suitability and affinity.
3. For example:
   - In uterine disorders, medicines are delivered through injections *(ḥuqna)*.
   - In intestinal conditions, remedies are administered via enemas.
   - In urethral and bladder diseases, therapeutic agents are introduced through catheters *(al-qāthāṭīr)*.

Jurūḥ-o-Indimāl-i-Jurūḥ
(Wounds and Wound Healing)

Fatal and Non-Fatal Wounds According to Organs

Hippocrates on Fatal Wounds

According to Hippocrates, rupture (*Kharq / Shigaf*) of vital organs such as the shoulder, brain, heart, kidney, small intestine, stomach, or liver is generally fatal. Survival is extremely rare. Wounds reaching the heart invariably lead to death, while those involving other organs may heal if superficial. The term *Kharq* denotes a deep penetrating wound that passes entirely through an organ, such as perforation of the bladder, diaphragm, or intestine, where natural union is impossible.

Rhazes on Brain and Vital Organ Injuries

Al-Rāzī observed that brain wounds are not always fatal, noting rare cases of healing even in deep lesions. However, when the wound becomes a true *Kharq* (complete rupture), death is inevitable, especially if it penetrates the brain cavities.

Brain Membrane (Meninges)

When a wound reaches the meningeal covering, relaxation (*Istirakhā*) occurs on the same side, and convulsions (*tashannuj*) on the opposite.

Stomach *(Mi'da)*

Perforation (*Kharq*) of the stomach is rarely survivable, though some authorities report occasional recovery.

Stomach Walls

Stomach wounds occur frequently due to their fleshy nature. These are usually not very deep and tend to heal more quickly.
But if the wound penetrates the cavity of the stomach, healing is rare.[4]

Liver (*Kabid*)

Superficial liver wounds may heal; however, deep injuries involving large vessels cause fatal haemorrhage. Some physicians noted that appendages of the liver may be removed surgically with recovery.

Heart, Diaphragm, and Bladder

Wounds of the heart and diaphragm are rare due to constant motion. The bladder, being *'Aṣabī* and relatively bloodless, heals rapidly after incision (as in lithotomy) due to its soft, fleshy nature.

Colon *(Qūlūn):*

Perforation of the colon *(shaqq al qūlūn)* generally heals easily, provided it does not recur frequently.
The colon's structure and function allow relatively better healing compared to other visceral organs.

Uterus *(Raḥim):*

In contrast, when perforation occurs in the uterus *(Shaqq al-Raḥim),* the prognosis is poor and healing becomes difficult.
This is due to the uterus's delicate structure, vascularity, and its association with reproductive function

Eyelids and Ear:

If a rupture occurs on the inner side of the eyelid, draining the abscess allows it to heal quickly through the outer rupture.
Even if the entire eyelid is split, healing still occurs, and there is no need to fear.

Nervous Organs *(A'ḍā' 'Aṣabiyya):*

Abscesses in nervous organs are typically very painful. It should be treated with warming *(musakhkhin)* and drying *(mujaffif)* medicines.

Soft tissue abscesses heal well; hard tissue abscesses are more dangerous.

Bone, Cartilage, Nerves, Jaw, and Prepuce:

Wounds here seldom heal. (Hippocrates)

Rāzī's Significant View on Wound Healing

In *Istisqā'* (Ascites) and moist temperaments, wounds heal slowly due to excess Discharge; in dry temperaments, healing is rapid. Elderly patients exhibit delayed recovery due to *qillat al-dam* (blood deficiency).

- Wounds causing *tashannuj* (tetanus) usually lack pus and heal poorly.
- Suppuration (*Ṣadīd*) signifies safety and a favourable prognosis, while its absence indicates danger.
- If ulcers with *Intifākh* occur anteriorly, complications like *Junūn* (madness), side pain, or bloody diarrhoea may follow.

General Prognostic and Environmental Factors

- Hot and moist climates, especially southern winds, aggravate wounds and promote putrid ulcers (*qurūḥ mu'taffina*).
- Loss of hair around ulcer margins signifies necrosis of adjacent tissues and malignancy due to *akhlāṭ fāsida*.
- Suppurating abscesses heal faster than non-suppurating ones.

Wound Management According to Rāzī' (Rhazes)

Small and Large Wounds

Displaced wound edges should be approximated by bandaging or suturing, depending on the gap size. Large wounds require both sutures and a supportive bandage.

Longitudinal vs. Transverse Wounds

Longitudinal wounds heal with bandaging alone; transverse wounds need suturing proportional to wound depth.

Puncture and Deep Wounds

Puncture wounds pose the risk of superficial closure while leaving deeper tissues unhealed. This prevents pus drainage and restricts medication penetration, resulting in severe pain.

In such cases, an additional incision is necessary to ensure adequate drainage and healing.

Swollen or Suppurating Wounds

Bandaging is contraindicated in wounds that are swollen or when suppuration is imminent.

Once pus has formed, bandaging may be used selectively—to keep the wound clean or to facilitate granulation. When bandaging is applied, it should be performed carefully so that the wound edges are brought into alignment.

Bandaging of wounds

Purpose defines technique:

- For Union (Iltihām) and closure: Firm approximation.
- For Granulation: Loose wrapping to allow blood flow.
- For Debridement or Medication: Pressure or retention dressings as required.

Bandaging technique

Bandaging in Fresh Abscesses

In newly developed abscesses, firm bandaging is essential to secure the affected site. The bandage should be gradually extended upwards to prevent downward accumulation of material.

In abscesses requiring cleansing, the bandage should be applied to pressure at the edges to prevent contamination.

Bandaging to Promote Granulation

Where granulation and tissue regeneration are desired, the bandage should be applied loosely, especially from the wound base upwards, to allow unobstructed blood flow. Impaired circulation weakens the organ, while contraction during granulation also hinders healing. The wound margins should be approximated each day gradually until complete closure occurs.

Wound Positioning for Drainage

The wound should face downward for natural drainage; if not possible, an incision may be made.

Rhazes records cases of large wounds—for example, one with depth at the knee but an opening at the thigh—that were managed by repositioning the limb so that the wound opening faced downward, thereby avoiding additional incisions. Similar approaches were applied to wounds of the arm and palm.

Qurūḥ al-'Aḍla
(Wound of Muscle)

Management of *Qurūḥ al-'Aḍla* According to Rhazes

Types of Muscle Wound Based on Orientation

1. Transverse Muscle Wound *('Arḍ al-'Aḍlah)*

- When an ulcer occurs across the breadth of a muscle, the edges remain widely separated.
- Sutures are required to approximate the margins.
- After suturing, a wooden splint should be applied to maintain support and prevent movement

2. Longitudinal Muscle Wound *(Ṭūl al-'Aḍlah)*

- A wound running along the muscle length can be managed by tight bandaging from both sides.
- Sutures or external supports are generally not required.

3. Large and Extensive Wound

- Extensive wounds require the use of desiccant drugs (*adwiya mujaffifah*) to dry excessive discharge.
- Bandaging should be performed carefully to approximate the ulcer margins.

4. Deep Muscle Wound

- In deep wounds, suturing at the base is essential, along with firm bandaging from both ends.
- Strong desiccant drugs are used to manage depth and control exudation.

Principles of Medicinal Management in Muscle Wound

1. Deep Wound Requiring Flesh Regeneration

- Require medicines with gradual desiccant *(mujaffif)* and moderate caustic *(muḥarriq)* properties to stimulate tissue growth.

2. Wound Requiring Adhesion *(Iltiḥām)*

- Treated with medicines that are more drying *(mujaffif)* than flesh-generating drugs *(munbit),*
- Mildly astringent *(qābiḍ)* but without causticity.

3. Wound Requiring Complete Healing *(Indimāl Kamil)*

- Managed with powerful desiccant *(mujaffif qawī)* and strong astringent drugs, more potent than wound-healing *(mudammil)* agents.

4. Wound with Excess Flesh *(Laḥm Zā'id)*

- Require strong caustic drugs *(adwiya ḥādda akkāla),* usually hot and dry in temperament, to burn away redundant tissue.

5. Wound with Secondary Complications

- If associated with another disorder, treat that underlying cause first.

6. Wound with Debris or Foreign Material

Use detergent medicines *(adwiya jālīya)* and cleansing agents (AdwiyaMuqalli'ah) to remove debris and pus.

7. Wound with Excess Discharge *(Ruṭūbat)*

- Strong desiccant medicines are essential to dry the ulcer and promote healing.

Management of Blood Coagulation in Surrounding Tissues

- In cases where blood coagulates between layers of skin, it must be resolved with softening agents *(adwiya murakhkhiya)* that possess strong desiccant properties without irritating.
- When coagulated blood is deeper in tissues, stronger dissolving and cutting drugs *(adwiya qawiyya muqaṭṭi'a)* are required.
- After dissolution, wound-healing medicines *(adwiya mudammila)* and appropriate dressings should be applied.
- If extravasated blood resolves quickly, the lacerated tissue heals rapidly.
- If dissolution is delayed, healing is prolonged, as accumulated debris obstructs proper tissue union.

Qurūḥ 'Asīr al-Indimāl (Non-Healing Ulcer / Chronic Ulcer)

Aetiology and Pathogenesis

According to *Kitāb Ikhtisār Ḥīlah al-Bir'*, wounds fail to heal when accompanied by other pathological conditions. Granulation tissue (*inbāt al-laḥm al-jadīd*) does not form until those underlying disorders are corrected. Putrified ulcers cannot heal until cleansed, and ulcers linked with *waram* (inflammation), *su'-i-mizāj* (deranged temperament), *qillat al-dam* (anaemia), or *rada'at al-dam* (blood morbidity) also resist healing.

Three main causes delaying ulcer healing are:

1. **Tissue Discontinuity and Infection:** Discontinuity of flesh (*Tafarruq-i-Ittiṣāl al-Laḥm*) and Putrefaction (*Fasād)* hinder adhesion.

2. **Impaired Blood Quality *(Raddī Dam):*** Impure blood fails to nourish and warm the tissue. granulation and healing are obstructed.

3. **Abnormal Tissue Growth:** Excessive or defective flesh causes chronic ulcers, even when the blood quantity is sufficient.[4]

Clinical Features and Prognosis

Chronic ulcers commonly affect persons with pale or freckled complexion, often with freckles or skin blemishes. and poor blood quality. Such ulcers appear whitish-yellow and fail to produce healthy granulation. They require *munbit laḥm* and blood-attracting medicines.

According to *Kitāb Abiẓīmiyā'*, ulcers accompanied by pale-yellow complexion indicate hepatic disease, whereas patchy or blemished-skin ulcers suggest *Sawdāwī* (melancholic) blood, both poor prognostic signs. Sometimes, splenic dysfunction is also associated.

Hard ulcers (*Qurūḥ Ṣulba*) with greenish or black discolouration are fatal, representing conversion of blood into *Khilṭ aswad* (black bile). Soft, hot, yellow discharging ulcers (*qurūḥ rikhwa*) spread rapidly, causing destruction of tissue and loss of surrounding hair. All ulcers require rest and protection from irritation for healing.

In elderly patients, ulcers heal slowly due to *qillat al-dam* (blood deficiency) and poor granulation.

Role of Pus in Ulcer Prognosis

Ulcers producing pus (*ṣadīd*) are considered safe and non-malignant, while those lacking pus, such as *Qurūḥ Ākila* (Ulcerative/erosive ulcers), *Saraṭānīya* (Cancerous ulcers), *Qurūḥ Khayrūnīya* and *Tilāfiyūn*, are dangerous and resistant to healing.

Ulcers and Associated Convulsions

Kitab Abiẓīmiyā records: When an ulcer occurs with soft swelling (*Waram Layyin*), it does not cause *tashannuj* (tetanus) or *junūn* (madness), but if associated with *waram damawī* (sanguine swelling), convulsions may occur.

Principles of Ulcer (Qurūḥ) Management

Several factors hinder granulation (growth of flesh), union *(iltihām)*, and cicatrization *(indimāl)* in ulcers:

1. Treatment according to Causes Hindering Healing

- **Hot Inflammation *(Waram Ḥārr):*** The most common barrier to healing. No adhesion, granulation, or drug penetration occurs until inflammation subsides. Thus, treatment must first resolve *Waram*, then the ulcer itself.

- **Altered Temperament of flesh *(Su'-i-Mizāj al-Laḥm):*** Requires antagonistic medicines to restore natural temperament.

- **Morbid Humours *(Kaymūs Radi'):*** Chronic ulcers (*'Asīr al-Indimāl*) may result from discharge of putrid humours from nearby organs (e.g., liver, spleen). Management requires general correction and diversion of these discharges.

- **Callous Surface:** A hardened crust must be excised to allow drug absorption.

- **Induration of Edges *(Ṣulba Hawashi):*** Hard ulcer margins require softening (emollient drugs) or surgical removal.

- **Black or Gangrenous Changes:** Dead tissue should be excised and treated with *muḥallil ḍimād* (resolvent plasters).

2. **Treatment according to Types of Morbid matter**

- **Local Morbid matter:** Managed with strong desiccants (*mujaffif qawī*). If ineffective, excision is necessary.
- **Systemic / Humoral Morbid matter:** Correct blood (*Iṣlāḥ al-Dam*) and prevent diseased discharge from reaching the ulcer.
- **Combined Morbid matter (both ulcer flesh and body humours are diseased):** Requires simultaneous local and systemic treatment.

3. **Difficult-to-Heal Ulcers *(Qurūḥ 'Asīr al-Indimāl)***

- These ulcers result from *Khilṭ lāḥij* (stagnant humour), *safrā'* or *sawdā'* Morbid matter, or weak penetration of medicines. In such cases, excision of diseased tissue is essential, followed by cautery (*amal-i-kayy*) or application of caustic drugs (*adwiya muḥarriqa*).[4]

4. **Specific Ulcer and Treatment**

- **Ulcers with Blood Deficiency:** Require rubefacients (stimulating ointments) and local stimulation to attract blood.
- **Ulcers with Excess Discharge:** Apply strong desiccants that do not cause irritation.
- **Ulcers with Excess Dryness:** Remove crust, irrigate with Waram water, and apply *marham bāsalīqūn*.

5. **Treatment of Simple Ulcer *(Qarḥa Basita)* and Compound Ulcer *(Qarḥa Murakkaba)***

- Treatment of small ulcers with suturing, bandaging, and protection of edges
- Treatment of large ulcers with cavities and discharge, Use of desiccative medicines *(mujaffif),* flesh-generating agents *(munbit laḥm),* and healing medicines *(adwiya mundamila)*

6. **Tissue Loss and Corresponding Treatment**

- When only skin is destroyed → use of healing agents *(adwiya mundamila)*
- When only flesh is destroyed → use of flesh-producing medicines *(munbit laḥm)*
- When both flesh and skin are destroyed → combined treatment with tissue-generating and healing agents.

Qurūḥ Khabītha (Malignant Ulcers / Ulcerative Carcinoma / Rodent Ulcers)

Definition

Qurūḥ Khabīthah (Malignant ulcers), also termed *Qurūḥ Ākilah* (Corrosive or Devouring Ulcers), are characterised by putrefaction, foul odour, and necrosis of the affected tissue.

Principles of Treatment

Excision of Diseased Tissue

- The affected part must be completely excised from the organ involved.
- Excision should extend to healthy tissue to ensure total removal of necrotic and putrefied matter.
- If the ulcer originates within a relatively healthy structure, all diseased portions must still be removed from the root to prevent recurrence.
- Surgical Treatment should only be undertaken in patients of adequate physical strength capable of enduring the procedure.
- In debilitated individuals, extensive excision or cauterisation should be avoided.

Post-Excision Management

After thorough removal, the ulcer bed should be treated with suitable medications possessing desiccant, detergent, healing (*mudammil*), and tissue-regenerating (*munabbit al-laḥm*) properties.

Ghānghārānā / Qaṭ'al-A'ḍā' (Gangrene and Amputation)

Amputation (*Qaṭ' al-A'ḍā'*) was acknowledged in Unani surgery as a crucial life-saving procedure when *'Ufūnat* (putrefaction or severe infection) made a limb beyond recovery through medicinal means. Classical physicians emphasised that if a gangrenous or decaying organ were left untreated, the Morbid matter could extend to adjoining tissues, leading to systemic poisoning and death. In such cases, the removal of the affected part was regarded as the only rational treatment to halt the progression of putrefaction and preserve the remaining healthy body.

According to Abū Al-Qāsim Al-Zahrāwī, gangrene of the extremities may arise from either internal or external causes. When all medicinal and topical measures fail, and the spread of disease becomes apparent, amputation becomes obligatory. The procedure should be carried out precisely at the junction where the diseased tissue ends, thereby preventing further extension of infection and saving the patient's life.

Causes *(Asbāb)*:

As described in *Kāmil al-Ṣinā'a al-Ṭibbiyya*, gangrene may develop due to a severe internal illness in which the *Ṭabī'at* (vital force) drives putrefactive matter toward the extremities—particularly the feet and ankles—causing black discolouration. It may also result from fractures or ulcers that undergo Morbid matter and necrosis. When such decay appears, surgical removal of the affected limb becomes essential to stop the spread of putrefaction to vital parts.

Signs and Symptoms:

The condition manifests as blackening of the affected limb, resembling tissue burnt by fire. Gradually, putrefaction spreads to surrounding structures, producing foul odour and loss of sensation. If not arrested, systemic sepsis follows, making urgent surgical amputation imperative for preserving the patient's life.

Surgical Intervention in Gangrene and Amputation

When medicinal treatment fails, and the condition becomes irreversible, amputation *(qaṭ' al-a'ḍā')* must be performed with precision to prevent the spread of *'ufūnat* (putrefaction). The procedure begins with the exposure of the bone at the healthy margin, ensuring complete removal of necrotic tissue while preserving viable structures. The vitality of tissue is judged by its firm adherence to bone and the presence of pain upon palpation—indicating intact vascularity.

Guidelines by Abū al-Qāsim Al-Zahrāwī (Albucasis, 936–1013 CE)

Al-Zahrāwī classified amputation levels based on disease progression. In cases of localised gangrene or venomous bites:

- If limited to a finger or toe, excision should be done at the interphalangeal joint.
- If extended to the hand or foot, removal should occur at the wrist or tarsal joint, respectively.
- If the infection reaches the forearm or leg, amputation must be performed at the elbow or knee joint.
- However, when the disease progresses beyond these levels—reaching the shoulder or thigh—surgery is no longer advisable, as the outcome is invariably fatal. In such cases, supportive management is preferred.

Operative Technique by Al-Zahrāwī

Zahrāwī's operative technique involved applying ligatures both proximal and distal to the intended amputation site. Assistants were instructed to retract these ligatures in opposite directions to clearly expose the surgical field. The surgeon then dissected the intervening soft tissues using a broad scalpel until the bone was completely denuded, after which the bone was sawn swiftly and cleanly. Linen cloths were placed around the site to prevent trauma to surrounding tissues, and haemorrhage was controlled immediately through cauterisation or styptic applications. The wound was then dressed and regularly managed until full healing was achieved.

Operative Technique According to Al-Majūsī (Haly Abbas, 930–994 CE)

In *Kāmil al-Ṣinā'a al-Ṭibbiyya*, Al-Majūsī emphasised performing amputation sequentially to minimise haemorrhage and patient mortality. The surgeon was instructed first to remove superficial diseased tissue before exposing the bone, avoiding total excision at once to prevent excessive bleeding. Once the bone was reached, it was to be sawn rapidly after protecting adjacent muscles with linen cloths, thus preventing injury and severe pain. After bone removal, all remaining necrotic tissue was carefully excised to ensure the wound remained clean and viable.

Cauterisation Following Amputation

After excision of gangrenous tissue, classical surgeons recommended cauterisation with boiling oil to seal blood vessels, prevent haemorrhage, and neutralise infection. This process also facilitated the formation of healthy granulation-like tissue, thereby promoting wound healing and preventing septic complications.

Note on Surgical Risk

Unani surgeons advised that if the danger of amputation outweighs its potential benefit, the procedure should be avoided, as surgical interference in advanced gangrene often hastens death. In such situations, only supportive and conservative measures should be adopted.

'Amal-i-Baṭṭ / Baṭṭ al-Khurāj (Incision and Drainage)

Types of *'Amal-i-Baṭṭ*

'Amal-i-Baṭṭ is of two kinds: Natural *(Baṭṭ-e-Ṭabī'ī)* and Artificial *(Baṭṭ-e-Maṣnū'ī)*.

1. ***Baṭṭ-e-Ṭabī'ī*** **(Natural 'Amal-i-Baṭṭ):**

   This occurs when the body's innate power (*quwwat-e-ṭabī'iyya*) expels pus naturally. It is considered a sign of strong vitality (*ṭabī'at*). However, excessive discharge of pus should be avoided as it may weaken the body and lead to debility.

2. ***Baṭṭ-e-Maṣnū'ī*** **(Artificial 'Amal-i-Baṭṭ):**

   This involves surgical incision with instruments (*ālāt al-jarāḥiyya*) and should only be performed when the abscess has reached complete maturation (*nuḍj-e-kāmil)* and the matter is ready for expulsion.

Principles and Timing of Incision *(Shigāf)*

When signs of maturation—such as softening, relief in pain, subsidence of fever, and heaviness—are evident, incision becomes necessary. The softest part of the abscess is selected for incision, ideally at the lower portion to facilitate natural drainage.

According to Abū Bakr Al-Rāzī

Premature incision before full maturation delays healing and results in persistent, foul drainage. Matured abscesses, once opened, dry and heal rapidly. However, if the abscess is near a joint or vital organ, early surgical intervention is justified to prevent complications.

Method of Performing Incision

Incision may be carried out using a surgical instrument *(ālāt al-jarāḥiyya)* or medicated eruptives *(adwiya mufajjira)*. The latter is used when the patient cannot tolerate operative pain or when the abscess lies close to a joint or vital structure. If the pus is thick or *ḥarārat gharīziyya* (innate heat) is weak, a surgical incision is preferred for effective drainage.

Size and Direction of Incision *(Shigāf):*

The incision should correspond to the size of the abscess, the softness of the site, and the organ involved.

- Large abscess → long and wide incision.
- Small abscess → short incision.
- Soft sites → longitudinal incision *(Shigāf-e-Ṭūlī).*
- Always incise at the lowest dependent part for proper drainage.

Operative Technique by Classical Surgeons

According to Jālīnūs (Galen):

The incision should be made at the most prominent, soft area, allowing pus to flow downward. After incision, absorbent (*jādhib*) non-irritant drugs should be applied, and any necrotic tissue excised. Near the groin or axilla, the incision should follow the skin lines, and powdered *kundur* should be applied.

According to Al-Zahrāwī:

The correct time for incision is when pain and redness subside, throbbing (*dafaq*) diminishes, and the head of the abscess (*ra's-e-khurāj*) wrinkles—indicating complete maturation. Incision should be made at the lower part of the swelling for easy drainage, or at the thinnest prominent site if that is not possible.

Nature of Incision According to Organs *(A'ḍā')*

The direction of incision differs according to the anatomical site:

- **Head:** Transverse incision.
- **Forehead:** Vertical incision to prevent eyelid obstruction.
- **Near eyes:** Crescent-shaped incision (*Shigāf-e-Hilālī*).

- **Nose:** Longitudinal direction.
- **Behind ears, jaws, breasts, elbows, wrists, fingers:** Longitudinal incision (*Shigāf-e-Ṭūlī*).
- **Abdomen:** Slightly away from the Rectus muscle (*'Aḍal al-Baṭn*).
- **Axilla, thighs:** Transverse incision (*Shigāf-e-'Arḍī*).
- **Flank, back, thighs, leg, penis, testes:** Longitudinal incision.

Incision in Muscular Regions

When abscesses occur within muscle bellies (e.g., biceps or gastrocnemius), two parallel incisions should be made on either side, overlapping slightly without cutting through muscle fibres. This preserves muscular function and prevents necrosis. The cavity is then gently packed, drained, and dressed for healing.

Quantity of Pus to be Evacuated *(Miqdār-e-Ṣadīd)*

The amount of pus (*ṣadīd / midda*) removed depends on its quality:

- ***Ṣadīd-e-Jayyid* (Good quality pus):** Whitish, moderately thick, and mildly odorous — should be drained fully.
- ***Ṣadīd-e-Raddi* (Poor quality pus):** Evacuate partially to prevent debility.
- Excessive pus indicates tissue liquefaction; insufficient pus signifies incomplete maturation.

Indications for Incision of Abscesses

1. **In Muscular Regions *('Aḍalāt):***

   Incision should be delayed until *Nuḍj-e-Kāmil* (complete maturation) is achieved. Premature incision leads to persistent discharge and delayed healing.

2. **Near Joints or Ligaments:**

   Immediate incision is required to prevent putrefaction of ligaments, joint structures, or muscles, and to preserve function.

Surgical Principles of Abscess Incision and Perforation

(According to Abū al-Qāsim Al-Zahrāwī and ʿAlī ibn al-ʿAbbās Al-Majūsī)

Classification and Surgical Criteria

Abū Al-Qāsim Al-Zahrāwī classified swellings (*Waram*) into types requiring either incision *(ʿamal al-shaqq)* or perforation *(ʿamal al-baṭṭ)*. The surgical approach depends on:

1. The nature of the swelling and the type of humour or pus involved.
2. The anatomical site of the lesion.

He emphasised that:

- Abscesses on the head differ in treatment from those on the posterior.
- Lesions in fleshy parts require a different intervention than those near joints or ligaments.
- Mature abscesses should be opened after complete *Nuḍj*, while those near joints or vital organs require early incision to prevent putrefaction and functional loss.
- Perianal abscesses must be incised before maturation to prevent fistula formation.

Types of Incisions for Abscess Drainage

According to Abū al-Qāsim Al-Zahrāwī, the choice of incision or perforation (*ʿamal al-shaqq / ʿamal al-baṭṭ*) depends on the location, size, and nature of the abscess:

- **Longitudinal Incision *(Shigāf-e-Ṭūlī):*** For hands, feet, joints, tendons, nerves, arteries, and all flat regions.
- **Curved or Crescent Incision *(Shigāf-e-Hilālī):*** To follow body curvature, especially near the groin or axilla.
- **Latitudinal Incision *(Shigāf-e-'Arḍī):*** Applied when anatomy demands horizontal drainage.

- **Circular or Lunate Incision:** For abscesses where the overlying skin has become necrotic.
- **Triangular or Myrtle-Leaf Incision:** Used for inguinal swellings.
- **Single or Multiple Openings:** Based on abscess size—single for small, multiple for large.
- **Fleshy Parts:** Delay incision until pus matures to avoid prolonged discharge and induration.

Operative Technique of Incision and Drainage

The procedure of incision *('amal al-shaqq)* begins by placing the surgical instrument (such as a lancet or bistoury) on the healthy margin of the abscess and cutting across to the opposite healthy side. All pus, putrid blood, and necrotic matter should be completely evacuated.

Wound Packing and Dressing

After evacuation, the cavity should be filled with linen or cotton to occupy empty spaces and dressed with a bandage.

The next day, inspect the abscess:

- If partially clean, apply cotton soaked in Rose oil *(Ravghan-e-Gul).*
- If contaminated, use cotton dipped in ghee (clarified butter) until the cavity is clean.
- Once free from pus, apply healing ointments to promote granulation and closure.

Precautions for Large Abscesses

Both Al-Zahrāwī and Al-Majūsī emphasised gradual evacuation of pus in large abscesses to prevent collapse of *Rūḥ-e-Ḥaywānī* (vital spirits):

- Evacuate partially on the first day, then bandage and continue draining gradually over the next two days.
- This method is crucial for weak patients, children, pregnant women, and the elderly.

- Sudden, complete evacuation may cause syncope or death due to loss of vitality.

Post-Incision Care

After incision:

- Cleanse the wound thoroughly.
- Insert swabs of lint or cotton in small openings, or one in each incision for large, multiple abscesses, so they meet internally.
- Pack the cavity with dry cotton or plucked linen, then apply a firm bandage until the third day.
- Remove packing and continue local treatment with suitable ointments to complete healing.

Khurāj and *Dubayla* (Abscess and Cold Abscess)

Definition

An *Abscess (Khurāj)* is a large, hot swelling in which *Ṣadīd* (pus), or both *Dam* (blood) and *Ṣadīd,* accumulate.

A *Cold Abscess (Dubayla)* is a deep-seated swelling containing various *akhlaṭ* (humours), such as blood and viscid phlegm (*Balgham Laẓij*), and sometimes lime-like, sandy, or hair-like substances.

Opinion of Zakariyyā Al-Rāzī

According to Al-Rāzī, the best *Khurāj* are those that incline outward with a pointed apex, as they mature rapidly.

Broad abscesses, formed by cold and viscid humours, mature slowly and tend toward putrefaction. Internal abscesses that are entirely directed inward are also considered better than those partially connected to the surface.

Clinical Features

In the initial stage, the swelling increases in size, feels hot and tense, and is associated with severe pain and throbbing (*dafaq*).

During *Nuḍj* (maturation), the pain subsides, and the site becomes soft.

Good-quality pus (*Ṣadīd-e-Jayyid*) is white, smooth, moderately thick, and with little or no odour, indicating proper maturation.

Surgical Management

Ibn Zuhr's View

When medical therapy fails, and *Khurāj* ripens fully, incision (*shaqq*) becomes necessary. The abscess may open naturally or require intervention using a sharp instrument, cautery, or caustic drugs (*adwiya kāwiya*).

Al-Rāzī's Guidelines

If *Nuḍj* occurs in a hot swelling (*waram ḥārr*), with throbbing pain and redness, appropriate resolvent drugs (*Adwiya Muḥallila*) may be applied.

For surgical opening, the incision should begin at the most prominent, thinnest area of the skin and extend downward to allow proper drainage. In rounded or depressed regions, the incision should run parallel to the tension of the skin.

Ibn Hubal Baghdādī's Guidelines

If the *Midda* (morbid matter) is excessive, or if *Nuḍj* is difficult due to patient weakness or thick skin, early incision is advised to prevent deeper spread.

When the swelling does not rupture after maturation, incision should be performed at the site of pus collection, ideally in the lower dependent part, to ensure complete evacuation and to avoid injury to vessels (*'urūq*) or nerves (*'aṣab*), especially near joints.

Jayb, Mukhabbi / Nāṣūr (Sinus and Fistula)

Sinus (*Jayb, Mukhabbi*)

A *sinus* is formed when an abscess develops in any fleshy part, becomes chronic, and accumulates pus. Upon rupture or perforation, the pus discharges, leaving a hollow cavity resembling a vessel, with overlying skin becoming thin and rag-like. As long as the suppuration does not involve deeper structures like bone, tendon, or ligament, the condition is termed a *sinus* and not a fistula.

A fistula *(nāṣūr)* occurs when the disease extends to deeper structures, forming an abnormal tract involving bone or tendons.

Surgical Management of Sinus According to Al-Zahrāwī

The management of a sinus depends on the condition of the overlying skin and the extent of suppuration.

Excision of Diseased Skin:

If the skin is excessively thinned, rag-like, and Morbid, it should be excised through a circular incision around the sinus.

Irrigation When Skin is Viable:

If the skin retains thickness and shows potential for adhesion, medicinal irrigation is performed instead of excision. For large sinuses with foul-smelling discharge, irrigation with *Marham-e-Miṣrī* (Egyptian ointment) is recommended.

Irrigation Technique:

The solution is introduced into the *sinus* opening, which is then bound for about two hours and pressed out afterwards. The process is repeated for several days until the *sinus* becomes clean and odourless.

After cleansing, medicines that promote granulation are applied, such as palm ointment dissolved in rose oil or other suitable agents.

Management of Narrow or Wide Openings:

If the opening is too narrow for the syringe, it should be slightly widened using a knife or a pad soaked in *Marham-e-Miṣrī*.

If the opening is wide, the edges should be approximated with sutures, leaving enough space for irrigation.

Management of Elevated Sinus Openings:

If the opening lies higher than the lowest part, an incision should be made at the lower point to allow drainage. If not possible, the affected part should be positioned to facilitate discharge.

External Application and Dressing:

An ointment is spread on lint covering the *sinus*, with a hole slightly larger than the opening. A second lint piece with softening ointment is placed over it, keeping space for pus discharge. The larger dressing remains for several days, while the smaller one is changed frequently to permit discharge observation and assess the healing process.

Signs of Healing:

When discharge becomes scanty and superficial, healing is near. The dressing may be changed every one to three days and continued until closure. Healing time varies among individuals; some recover quickly, while others heal slowly.

Fistula (*Nāṣūr*)

Definition and Clinical Features

A *fistula (Nāṣūr)* is any chronic wound or swelling that turns into a non-healing ulcer discharging pus continuously, regardless of its site. In Unani terminology, it is also called *Deftuxion*.

A true *fistula* presents as a compact, hard, white, and painless induration with a central hollow resembling a bird's quill, hence the name "quill." The discharge may vary in amount and quality, sometimes moist and continuous, at other times scant or intermittent.

Classical Unani Concept of Non-Healing Ulcers

According to classical surgeons like Ibn Zuhr and Al-Zahrāwī, ulcers that fail to heal are caused by:

1. **Lack of Blood or Nutrition**, leading to poor granulation.
2. **Hardness of Ulcer Edges**, preventing new tissue growth.
3. **Abundance of Putrefied Matter (*Midda Fāsida*)**, delaying repair.
4. **Necrosis or Foul Discharge** from the ulcer.
5. **Inappropriate Remedies**, which hinder recovery.
6. **Environmental or Local Morbid matter**, affecting healing.
7. **Regional Predisposition** to chronic ulcers.
8. **Involvement of the bone**, which prolongs the disease.

Operative Treatment of Fistula (*Nāṣūr*)

Fistulae may occur in any region of the body. Those involving deep structures such as great vessels, nerves, intestines, bladder, ribs, or major joints are difficult or incurable. Superficial or limited fistulae, however, can be treated surgically after proper evaluation.

Exploration and Preoperative Assessment

- **Straight Fistula:** Explore using a bronze or iron probe.
- **Tortuous Fistula:** Use a flexible lead probe to trace its course.
- **Multiple Openings:** Inject fluid into one and observe its exit from others to identify interconnections.

Preoperatively, assess the depth, direction, and relation to vital structures. Only after complete knowledge of the tract should surgery be attempted.

Accessible and Harmless Fistulae

When located away from joints, arteries, tendons, or vital organs:

- Lay open the fistula, excise all granulation and diseased tissue, and dress regularly until healing occurs.

Deep or Straight Fistulae

For deep or straight tracts:

- Incise the tract fully, remove all diseased tissue, and apply caustic medicaments to destroy residual infection.
- Follow with *Marham* (healing ointments) to promote granulation.
- If healing fails, *Kayy* (cauterisation) may be required.

Fistulae Caused by Bone

If the *Nāṣūr* is due to diseased bone:

- Open and inspect the site; if bone is blackened, scrape off Morbid portions and dress to encourage healing.
- Persistent pus discharge indicates incomplete removal; repeat cleaning as needed.
- If the infection is deep and inaccessible, further surgical intervention is avoided.

Management of Fistula Involving Bone

Extraction of Small Bones:

Remove affected small bones with fine forceps. If several are involved, extract all carefully. If ligaments obstruct access, they may be incised when safe.

Delayed Extraction:

If immediate removal is difficult, induce suppuration with medicated dressings (sulphur with olive oil or *marham-e-miṣrī*) to soften ligaments and facilitate later extraction. Maintain incision patency until the bone loosens and crumbles for removal.

Management of Large Bones:

In large bones (e.g., tibia, femur), scrape away all blackened or necrotic areas. If the Morbid matter reaches the marrow, saw off the affected portion entirely and manage the wound with dressings until complete healing.

Awrām (Swelling)

Definition

Waram (swelling) is defined as the enlargement of a body part caused either by the influx of morbid matter or by the generation of matter within the part itself.

Etiology

The principal causes of *waram* include:

1. The four humours (*Dam, Ṣafrā', Balgham, Sawdā'*).
2. Abnormal gases (*Riyāḥ*).
3. Watery fluids (*Mā'iyyat*).

External factors such as injury, wound, crushing trauma, fracture, dislocation, or sprain can also cause *waram* by weakening the part and allowing morbid matter to accumulate. A general plethora of humours in the body further predisposes to swelling.

Types of Swellings (Classification)

According to Unani physicians:

- *Damawī* (Sanguineous) → Phlegmonous *(Phlegmoni)* swelling.
- *Ṣafrāwī* (Bilious) → *Namla* or *Ḥumra* (erysipelatous).
- *Sawdāwī* (Melancholic) → *Saqeerus* (hard, indurated).
- *Balghamī* (Phlegmatic) → *Waram Rikhw* (oedematous swelling) caused by *Riyāḥ* or *Mā'iyyat*; *Tahabbuj* (diffuse oedema) also belongs to this type.

Swelling may arise from a single humour or a combination of several.

- *Ḥādd* (Hot, Acute) swellings result from sanguineous or bilious matter.
- *Bārid* (Cold, Chronic) swellings arise from phlegmatic or

melancholic matter, including *Waram Rīḥī*, *Waram Mā'ī*, and *Tahabbuj*.

General Treatment of Inflammations (*Waram*)

The treatment of inflammation is approached from four perspectives:

1. According to the causes
2. According to the material (matter) involved
3. According to the site (location) of the inflammation
4. According to the evacuating (expelling) agents of the matter.

1. Treatment According to Causes

A. External Causes

When due to trauma or injury:

- Apply *Murakhkhi* (emollient) and *Muḥallil* (resolvent) medicines to soften and disperse matter at the site.
- Use *Rādi*ʿ (repellent) drugs around, but not directly over, the wound to prevent obstruction of natural drainage.
- When matter accumulates, evacuate it by incision or other suitable means.

B. Internal Causes

When *Waram* develops from internal factors:

- Avoid premature use of *Rādi*ʿ or *Murakhkhi* medicines at the initial stage, as both may aggravate inflammation.
- Perform *Faṣd* (venesection) or *Hijāma* (cupping) for evacuation, considering the patient's strength.
- Subsequently, apply *Murakhkhi* over the site and *Rādi*ʿ around it.

A. Treatment of Inflammations Due to Internal Causes

When inflammation arises due to internal causes, it results from the influx of either hot *(ḥārr)* or cold (bārid) matter.

1. If the Matter is Hot *(Ḥārr)*

- Begin with *Faṣd* or *Hijāma* to reduce excess.
- Administer a *Mushil* (purgative) if indicated.
- Apply *Rādi'* to prevent further influx and *Muqawwī* to strengthen the organ, ensuring vital structures are protected.

During the stage of increase *(Zamāna'-i-Tazayyud),* combine *Rādi'* and *Murakhkhi* medicines.

During the stage of peak (*Zamāna'-i-Intihā'*), discontinue *Rādi'* and continue *Murakhkhi* with *Muḥallil.*

During the stage of decline (*Zamāna'-i-Inḥiṭāṭ*), use *Muḥallil* alone to assist *Ṭabī'at* in resolving matters.

If the inflammation occurs in a vital organ, combine *Qābiḍ* (astringent) and *Mufarriḥ* (aromatic) drugs instead of using *Muḥallil* alone, to preserve the strength and vitality (*arwāḥ*) of the organ.

2. If the Matter is Cold *(Bārid)*

- Use *Murakhkhi* (emollient) + *Muḥallil* (resolvent)
- Avoid excessive *Rādi'* (risk of hardening).
- Adjust medicines according to mizāj (temperament):

  Children → More *Murakhkhi*

  Elderly → More *Rādi'*

  Middle age → Balanced use

B. Treatment According to the Nature of Matter *(Mādda)*

According to *Ibn Hubal Baghdādī*, inflammation (*Waram*) varies according to the type of matter *(mādda)* responsible for its formation. Six principal types are identified, each requiring a specific therapeutic approach:

1. The Four Humours (*Dam, Ṣafrā', Balgham, Sawdā'*)

2. Watery Matter (*Mā'ī*)
3. Gaseous Matter (*Rīḥī*)

1. Sanguine Swelling (*Waram Damawī*)

- Example: *Phlegmonous Swelling (Waram Falgmūnī).*
- Treatment: Managed by following the standard therapeutic protocol for *Waram Falgmūnī*, which includes moderation of heat and evacuation of excess blood through *Faṣd* or *Hijāmah*, followed by *Murakhkhī* (emollient) and *Muḥallil* (resolvent) applications.

2. Bilious Swelling (*Waram Ṣafrāwī*)

- Examples: *Ḥumra* and *Namla.*
- Treatment: Requires stronger *Rādi'* (repellent) medicines than *Waram Damawī* due to intense heat.
- If ulceration develops, treat the local lesion first using *Mujaffif* (drying) agents to absorb excess *ruṭūbāt* (Discharge) and promote healing.

3. Phlegmatic Swelling *(Waram Balghamī)*

- **Early Stage (*Zamāna'-i-Ibtidā'*):** Use a balanced combination of *Rādi'* (repellent) and *Murakhkhī* (emollient) medicines.
- Sole *Rādi'* may harden matter; sole *Murakhkhī* may soften excessively and aggravate swelling.
- **According to Temperament (*Mizāj*):**
- Moist temperament (children): Use more *Murakhkhī,* less *Rādi'*.
- Dry temperament (elderly): Use more *Rādi',* less *Murakhkhī.*
- Moderate temperament: Apply both in balanced proportion.

4. Melancholic Swelling *(Waram Sawdāwī)*

- Begin treatment with *Murakhkhī* medicines combined with a small quantity of *Rādi'*.

- Administer *Munḍijāt Sawdā'* (concoctives of black bile) to ripen the matter.
- Complete therapy with purgatives (*istifrāgh*) for the elimination of *Sawdāwī* matter.

5. Gaseous Swelling *(Waram Rīḥī)*

- Treatment focuses on dispersing trapped gases using *Muḥallil Rīyāḥ* (carminative resolvents) and Warm fomentations (*nuṭūlāt*).

6. Watery Swelling *(Waram Mā'ī)*

- Initially administer medicines that open pores and help expel the watery content.
- Follow with *Mujaffif* (drying) agents to consolidate and strengthen the affected part.

C. Treatment According to the Site of Organs

1. Classification of Organs

Organs are classified into two major types:

- Concave (*Muqā'ar*) organs
- Non-concave (*Ghayr Muqā'ar*) organs

Each type is further divided into:

- Vital (*Ra'īsa*) organs
- Non-vital (*Ghayr Ra'īsa*) organs

Concave Organs (*A'ḍā' Muqā'ara*)

Examples:

Behind the ear, axilla, and inguinal glands.

Principle of Treatment:

- In Swelling of concave organs—whether *ḥārr* (hot) or *bārid* (cold)—the use of *Rādi'* (repellent) medicines is strictly prohibited. Because *Rādi'* agents may divert *mādda* (morbid matter) inward toward *a'ḍā' ra'īsa* (vital organs), which can endanger life.

- Preferred Approach: Apply *Murakhkhi* (emollient, softening) medicines that disperse matter safely and relieve tension without risk to vital structures.

Non-Concave Organs (*A'ḍā' Ghayr Muqā'ar*)

These organs are classified into vital (*A'ḍā' Ra'īsa*) and non-vital (*A'ḍā' Ghayr Ra'īsa*) types.

In inflammations of vital organs—such as the brain, heart, and liver—strong *Rādi'* or *Muḥallil* medicines should be avoided. Instead, *Qābiḍ* (astringent) and *Mufarriḥ* (aromatic, strengthening) agents are used to preserve structure and protect the *arwāḥ* (vital spirits).

In non-vital organs, general principles of *ḥārr* (hot) and *bārid* (cold) inflammations are followed. *Rādi'*, *Murakhkhi*, and *Muḥallil* medicines may be applied more freely, as there is no danger of diversion toward vital parts.

Treatment According to the Expulsion (*Daf'*) of Matter

When the *mādda* (morbid matter) is being expelled naturally by a *'Uḍw Ra'īs* (vital organ) or through *al-Ṭabī'a al-Mudabbira li'l-Badan* (the governing faculty of the body), *Rādi'* (repellent) medicines should not be used during the initial stage (*Zamāna-i-Ibtidā'*). Because repelling the matter in such cases may obstruct the body's natural evacuation process and interfere with the inherent wisdom of *Ṭabī'a*, potentially worsening the condition.

Treatment of Cold, Soft, Hard, and Other Types of Swelling (*Awrām*)

1. Cold Swelling (*Awrām Bārida*)

In the early stage, apply *Rādi'* medicines combined with mild *Muḥarrik* (heating) and *Qābiḍ* (astringent) agents to stimulate circulation and strengthen tissues.

2. Soft Swelling (*Awrām Layyina*)

Use *Muḥallil* (resolvent) and *Mujaffif* (drying) medicines to disperse matter and restore tone to the affected area.

3. Hard Swelling (*Awrām Ṣulba*)

Treat with *Muḥallil* agents, but avoid rapid dissolution without softening. Combine *Nuḍj* (maturation) with *Taḥlīl* (resolution) to prevent hardening of residual matter.

4. Flatulent Swelling (*Awrām Rīyāḥiyya*)

Provide gentle heat (*ḥarārat laṭīfa*) to disperse *riyāḥ ghalīẓa* (thick gases) and open *masām al-jild* (cutaneous pores) for evacuation.

5. Hot Swelling (*Awrām Ḥārra*)

Avoid dense or sticky *ṭilāʾ* (pastes) that block pores and drive the matter inward. Apply *Hijāma* (cupping) to draw the inflammation toward the surface and prevent deeper spread.

6. Inflammations of the Viscera (*Awrām al-Aḥshāʾ*)

Initially, use *Mubarrid* (cooling) and *Rādiʿ* drugs. During resolution (*taḥallul*), add *Qābiḍ* and *Mufarriḥ* medicines to strengthen the organ's faculty—especially in the stomach and liver. Early treatment may also include *Faṣd* (venesection) and mild purgation.

General Therapeutic Principle

All inflammations benefit from *Istifrāgh* (evacuation of matter) and a light, restricted diet to support *Ṭabīʿa* in restoring equilibrium.

Inflammatory Swelling due to Blood

Falghamūnī (*Phlegmon*)

Definition

According to Jālīnūs (Galen*)* in *Aghlūqan*, Phlegmon originally referred to any inflammation, whether from *sū'-mizāj* or hot substances. Later, physicians restricted it to swelling arising specifically from blood (*dam*), usually large in size.

Description by Ibn Hubal Al-Baghdādī

Ibn Hubal Al-Baghdādī describes *Falghamūnī* as a hot, inflammatory swelling originating from bloody matter accumulated in an organ's cavities, affecting either superficial or deep tissues. It may be caused by thick (*dam ghalīẓ*) or thin (*dam raqīq*) blood, rarely by pure blood alone—when it occurs, it is called *pure phlegmon*.

If the organ has a strong sensation, pain is severe; when arteries are abundant, throbbing and pricking pain predominate. Jālīnūs notes that redness and burning may occur even without material accumulation.

Causes

Internal: Fullness of blood (*Imtilā'-i-Dam*) and its local accumulation.

External: Trauma (*Ḍarba*), falls (*Saqṭa*), or wounds.

Excessive intake of putrefying foods (meat, wine, dates), lack of exercise, or habitual stoppage of bleeding (e.g., *bawāsīr*, interrupted *faṣd*) may also cause it.

The *Asbāb Fā'iliyya* (efficient cause) is *Dam* mixed with *Ṣafrā'*, producing *Hiddat* (heat) or agitation.

Types and Clinical Features

Two types are noted:

1. Redness appearing in discontinuous lines.
2. Redness appearing in continuous bands.

Signs: Red or dark hue, tense skin, severe pain, throbbing, and heat. The swelling does not pit on pressure, and fever may accompany advanced stages.

Treatment

Falghamūnī is treated similarly to *Namla* (Erysipelas), though more vigorously due to greater heat and size.

Treatment of External Causes (*Asbāb Khārijiyya*)

In fullness of body (*Imtilā' al-Badan*), perform *Faṣd* from the vein on the side opposite to the lesion—right if swelling is on the left, and vice versa—removing blood according to tolerance.

Treatment of Internal Causes (*Asbāb Badaniyya*)

When the cause is internal, and *Imtilā'* exists without natural evacuation, *Faṣd* should be done followed by *Rādi'* (refrigerant) and mildly *Murakhkhi* (relaxing) local applications.

General Therapeutic Principles

If inflammation affects the upper body, bleed from the opposite side. Apply *Ḍimād Bārid* (cold poultices) early. Persistent pain or throbbing indicates abscess formation; discontinue excessive cooling and shift to *Muḥallil* (resolvent) and *Murakhkhi* (relaxant) measures.

Abscess Formation (*Khurāj*) in *Falghamūnī*

When *Waram Falghamūnī* progresses to *Khurāj*, fever, pain, and heat intensify, marking the transformation of *midda* into pus (*qayḥ*). During this stage, rest, a light diet, and minimal exertion are essential until resolution occurs. When pain and fever subside, and appetite improves, incision (*al-shaqq*) may be performed for drainage.

If the abscess shows thinning skin and peripheral itching, incise at that site; otherwise, choose a thinner area away from vital structures (*A'ṣāb, Awtār, Ribāṭāt*). Pus evacuation must match patient strength—gradual if weak, complete if strong.

Surgical Management After Incision (*Al-Shaqq*)

1. **Drainage:** Press gently to remove pus; insert a *Fatīla* (wick) if continuous discharge is needed, using absorbent medicated dressings (*adwiya jādhiba*).
2. **Depth of Incision:** Jālīnūs advised deep incisions for complete evacuation, avoiding superficial cuts that may cause *Fasād* (putrefaction).
3. **Severe Morbid matter and Gangrene (*Ghāngharānā*):**

   If sensation persists, excise necrotic tissue and cauterise (*'ilāj bil-ḥadīd*).
   If sensation is lost, indicating death of the part, scrape diseased bone until healthy tissue appears.
4. **Bone Sawing (*Nashr al-'Iẓām*):** The saw's teeth should face one direction, applied downward repeatedly—never dragged to prevent splintering.
5. **Protection of Bone Marrow (*Maghz-i-'Iẓām*):** After cutting, apply medicated dressings to promote granulation until *Ṭabī'at Mudabbira-e-Badan* restores the surface.

Swelling from Phlegmatic Humour (*Balgham*)

Sal'a (Tumour)

Definition of *Sal'a*

Sal'a refers to an abnormal tissue growth (*neoplasm*).

Phlegmatic Tumours (*Sal'a Balghamiyya)*

These swellings contain putrefied phlegmatic material enclosed in a capsule, mobile under the skin, and distinct from the underlying organ. Their size may range from that of a chickpea to a small melon.

Classical Description

Ibn Hubal Al-Baghdādī:

The swelling consists of phlegmatic matter confined within a sac. The contents may be thick and fleshy or fluid, often resembling honey. The mass is freely movable and painless.

Al-Ṭabarī:

Non-inflammatory viscid phlegm solidifies within an organ, forming a soft, grape-like mass (*Sal'a*), deriving nourishment from humours and impeding organ function.

Ibn Zuhr (Avenzoar):

Caused by extremely thick, cold phlegm; *Sal'a* is painless, non-suppurative, and slowly enlarges as it draws sustenance from similar humours.

Classification of *Sal'a*

General Types:

1. *Sal'a Salīma* (Benign)
2. *Sal'a Khabītha* (Malignant / *Saraṭān*)

Usually, *Sal'a* denotes the benign type.

Subtypes of *Sal'a*

1. ***Sal'a Shaḥmiyya* (Lipoma/Fatty type)**_Fatty type; thick phlegmatic matter, firm, minimal sensation, non-depressible.
2. ***Sal'a 'Asaliyya* (Soft Tumour/Honey-like type)**– Honey-like consistency; thinner phlegm, depressible, resembling a honey-filled sac.
3. ***Sal'a Ardahāliyya* (Semolina-like type)**– Semolina-like; mixed consistency, moderately soft, intermediate between *'Asaliyya* and *Shaḥmiyya.*
4. ***Sal'a Shīrāziyya* (Milk-curd type)**– Milk-curd type; thinnest phlegm, softest and easily depressible swelling.

Treatment of *Sal'a* (Tumour)

Medical Management

At the onset, medical therapy should precede surgery:

- Avoid phlegm-producing foods.
- Give a heating diet (*Mussakhkhin Ghidhā'*).
- For *Sal'a 'Asaliyya* (Honey-like type):
- Apply local medicines; if *Taḥlīl (dissolution)* occurs, surgery is avoided.
- If unresolved, use *Adwiya Muḥarriqa* (caustics); persistent cases require surgery.

Surgical Management of *Sal'a*

General Principles

Surgical procedures such as excision of *Sal'a*, incision of abscesses, and treatment of *Khanāzīr* (Scrofula) by instruments (*'amal bi'l ḥadīd*) should be performed only after *Faṣd* (venesection), *Istifrāgh* (evacuation), and dietary regulation, when *Mizāj* (temperament) is balanced. Neglecting these prerequisites is discouraged.

Role of Surgery

Except for *Sal'a 'Asaliyya*, most types of *Sal'a* require surgical removal after *Tanqiya'-i-Badan* (purification).

Surgical Technique:

The assistant stretches the *Sal'a* downward; a careful incision is made until the capsule is reached and opened for removal. The skin is lifted with hooks (*Ṣunnāra*) and separated without rupturing the capsule.

Precautions:

Make a cruciform incision, lift the skin with hooks, grasp the capsule using *Qamadīn*, and avoid vascular injury. If the capsule tears, remove all remnants to prevent recurrence.

Management of Large Tumour *(Sal'a)*

After evacuation, excise the capsule and suture. Any remaining part should be removed with forceps and, if necessary, cauterised using *dawā-e-ḥārr* (caustic agent); apply old ghee to aid healing.

Alternative Management When Surgery is Not Possible

If surgery or cauterisation is contraindicated:

Perform *Baṭṭ* to mature (*Nuḍj*) the swelling until suppuration occurs, then incise to evacuate pus while keeping the capsule intact. Fill with old ghee to promote decay and manage as an ulcer until healed.

Methods by Abū al-Ḥasan Aḥmad bin Muḥammad Raban Ṭabarī

1. **Medicinal Ointments:**

   Apply *Marham Isranj* to soften and *Marham Dakhiliyun* to liquefy contents. If fluid, it may resolve; otherwise, rupture and discharge, then use *Marham Rāl wa Kundur* to heal.

2. **Seton Technique:**

   Incise the lower part using *Warda*; insert a wick, enlarging it daily until full drainage occurs. Remove the capsule and apply healing ointments if putrefaction develops.

3. **Surgical Excision:**

   Assess duration, site, and patient fitness before excision. Remove the capsule intact and apply soothing ointments to relieve pain and promote granulation.

Views of Ibn Zuhr and Al-Rāzī

Ibn Zuhr (Avenzoar, 1091–1162 CE):

For small *Sal'a*, prescribe light, digestible food and *Sikanjabin 'Unṣulī*; apply *Ushq* with vinegar. If large, excision by a skilled surgeon is required.

Zakariyyā Al-Rāzī (Rhazes, 865–925 CE):

Before excision, inspect the site for major vessels. Keep *Dawā' Jālīnūs*, egg white, rabbit fur, or feathers ready for haemostasis. If a vessel is injured, apply pressure or cauterise with *al-mikwā*.

Khanāzīr (Scrofula)

Definition

Khanāzīr (Scrofula) is a type of tumour similar to *Sal'a* (Tumour), but differs in that it remains attached to the underlying tissue rather than being separated. It commonly affects glandular regions, particularly the neck.

Types

1. **Painful Type** – caused by thin fluid that does not block sensory pathways.
2. **Painless Type** – produced by thick, viscous humour that obstructs sensation.

   It is more prevalent in individuals with short necks and Balghamī *(phlegmatic)* temperaments.

Surgical Management by Ibn al-Quff

When indicated, a longitudinal incision is made—without extending into the tumour. The skin is lifted with *Ṣunnāra* (hook) and separated from the mass. Surrounding healthy tissue is dissected, and the entire tumour excised, following the method of *Sal'a* removal.

For large *Khanāzīr*, retractors help elevate and detach it carefully from adjacent structures, avoiding injury to vessels and nerves. Any accidentally cut vessel should be ligated with silk *(silk)*. After complete removal, local cleansing (*Tanqiya'*) is done, redundant skin trimmed, sutures applied, and the site dusted with *dharūr aṣfar* before treating it as an ulcer.

Surgical Management According to 'Alī ibn 'Abbās Al-Majūsī

Surgical Technique :

- Make a longitudinal incision over the swelling, avoiding entry into the mass.
- Retract both flaps with forceps and separate the surrounding swollen tissue.
- Excise the *Khanāzīr* gradually in small sections (*Baṭṭ wārī* technique).
- For large masses, lift the tumour with forceps and detach it carefully.
- Avoid injury to arteries and muscles; ligate any vessel before division.
- After removal, palpate the cavity for remnants and excise any residual growth to prevent recurrence.

Closure and Dressing:

The cavity is clean, approximate and suture the skin flaps. If excess skin remains, trim it before closure. Finally, dust the site with *dharūr aṣfar* for healing.

Tha'ālīl (Warts) and *Masāmīr* (Corns)

Description in Unani Texts

Tha'ālīl (Warts) are hard skin projections; if their edges are irregular, they are termed *Qurun*.

Masāmīr (Corns) are round, nail-shaped growths causing pain on pressure or movement.

Al-Zahrāwī's Description:

Warts are small, rough, rounded elevations on the skin, commonly seen on hands, while corns appear on soles and toes, resembling nail heads and causing pain during walking.

Etiology

Both *Tha'ālīl* and *Masāmīr* arise from thick, viscous *Balghamī* (phlegmatic) matter.

Medical Treatment

- If associated with *ghalaba'-i-dam (sanguineous dominance)* → perform *Faṣd* (venesection), followed by *Mushil-i-Sawdā'* (purgatives of black bile).
- If not sanguineous → evacuate *Sawdā'* without *Faṣd.*
- Before evacuation, administer *Munḍij* (concoctives) for *Balgham* and *Sawdā'*.

Surgical Management by Al-Zahrāwī, Al-Majūsī, and Ibn al Quff

When medicinal therapy fails, surgical intervention is performed. Classical Unani surgeons (Al-Zahrāwī, Al-Majūsī, Ibn Zuhr) describe three main methods—cauterisation, excision, and ligation.

1. Cauterisation *('Amal Kayy)*

A metallic tube (iron or silver) equal to the wart's thickness is heated and applied to burn the lesion. *Ghee* (Clarified butter) is applied to soften the crust. The wart is extracted with *Mithqās* (forceps), and

Marham-e-Zangār (copper ointment) is applied to the root.

Healing is aided by *Mudammil* and *Munbit Laḥm* medicines.

2. Excision with Ligation and Cauterisation

A ligature (*Silk thread*) is tied around the base of the wart, then the lesion is cut off from below using *Mithqās* or *ʿAmādein* (surgical scalpel). The root is cauterised with *Mikwā* (gold cautery) or caustic drugs to prevent recurrence.

This method ensures complete removal and rapid healing.

3. Simple Ligation *(Kharam Method)*

A thick hair or silk thread is tightly tied at the wart's base and gradually tightened over several days until it separates.

Although effective, it is slower and less reliable compared to excision and cauterisation.

Surgical Management of Corns *(Masāmīr)*

For corns, the surgeon cuts around the lesion, grasps it with forceps or a hook, and removes it completely from the root, followed by cauterisation to prevent recurrence.

Swelling from Black Bile *(Sawdā')*

Saraṭān (Cancer)

Nature and Pathogenesis

Sawdā' (Melancholic humour) is of two types:

- *Ṭabī'ī Sawdā' (Natural)* → causes induration (*Saqīrūs*).
- *Muḥtariq Sawdā' (Burnt)* → leads to *Saraṭān (Cancer)*.

Saraṭān is an ulcerative tumour with crab-like vascular extensions due to *Imtilā'-i-'Urūq (engorgement of vessels)*.

According to Ibn Zuhr, such swellings are known as *Saraṭān* and are extremely difficult to cure.

Classical Descriptions

Ibn Hubal Baghdādī:

Described *Saraṭān* as a fatal disease; early intervention may delay its progress, but death is inevitable. The tumour is hard, deeply rooted, and surrounded by greenish veins. It begins small but enlarges progressively, often causing severe pain and warmth. Occasionally, indolent forms cease progressing.

Jālīnūs (Galen):

In his treatise *"al- Mirra al- Sawdā'"* (On Black Bile), he attributed cancer to *Muḥtariq Sawdā'* and described abnormal vessel proliferation within the tumour. It usually arises in *A'ḍā' Raṭba (Moist Organs)*—especially the breast, uterus, glands, and intestines. Jālīnūs warned against surgical interference except in dire necessity.

Ibn Zuhr

Such swellings (tumours) develop in the body, which people recognise by the name of *cancer (saraṭān)*. This type of swelling is *'asīr al-shifā'* (difficult to cure), and recovery from it is extremely difficult.

Difference between *Saraṭān* and *Saqīrūs*

1. **Form:** Cancer shows engorged vessels filled with *sawdāwī* matter.
2. **Pain:** Constant in cancer; minimal in *Saqīrūs*.
3. **Ulceration:** Present in cancer, absent in *Saqīrūs*.
4. **Origin:** Cancer is primary; *Saqīrūs* is often secondary.

Etymology

The term *Saraṭān* (Cancer) derives from its crab-like form and vascular extensions resembling crab legs gripping tissue — a view shared with modern Latin *"Cancer"* and Greek *"Karkinos"*.

Al-Ṭabarī added that its name reflects both its nature (burnt, earthy matter) and shape (crab-like with branching veins).

Prognosis and General Treatment

Hippocrates:

Advised against treating *hidden (Khafī)* cancers; intervention shortens life, whereas non-interference prolongs it. Hidden cancers may be early-stage or internal (e.g., uterus, rectum, nostrils).

Jālīnūs (Galen) & Hippocrates:

Emphasised cautious management—preferring *tanqiya* (purification), *faṣd (venesection)*, purgation, and dietary control over surgery in internal or advanced cases.

Ibn Zuhr:

Confirmed the rarity of recovery and severe prognosis.

Medical and Surgical Approach of Saraṭān (Cancer)

In *Saraṭān*, whether internal or external, medical treatment may be beneficial, especially in early or localised stages. However, in the initial phase, complete surgical removal is difficult because the root lies deep within the connected vessels.

After excision, recurrence may occur since *sawdāwī (melancholic)* blood often remains within the vessels. Surgical procedures also cause intense pain that may exceed the patient's tolerance.

Conversely, in advanced and externally developed cancers, surgical excision produces little or no pain, as the diseased tissue has already lost local sensation due to morbid matter of humours.

Surgical Management of *Saraṭān*

Indications:
Surgery is advised only for small, localised, and accessible tumours (e.g., breast, thigh). Extensive or nerve-invading cancers should not be operated.

Preoperative Care:

- *Tanqiya'-i-Badan (purification of body)* by repeated purgation and *Faṣd.*
- Avoid strong heating or irritant drugs.

Operative Procedure by Al-Zahrāwī, Ibn al-Quff, and Al-Majūsī

- The patient is positioned, and the tumour is hooked and elevated.
- A circular incision is made around the mass, excising skin and tumour completely to its root.
- Bloodletting is allowed to continue naturally to expel *sawdāwī* blood.
- Surrounding vessels are pressed to drain residual morbid matter.
- In case of haemorrhage, cauterisation (*Kayy*) is done on the bleeding vessel.
- Apply ointments used for ulcers to promote healing.

This technique was endorsed by Al-Zahrāwī, Ibn al-Quff, and Al-Majūsī.

Caution and Prognosis

Surgery is prohibited when cancer occurs near vital organs (uterus, arteries, nerves). In such cases, medical management—*Faṣd*, purgation, and dietary moderation—is preferred. Even after excision, recurrence is common due to residual *sawdāwī* blood.

Saqīrūs

(Scirrhous)

Definition

Saqīrūs refers to a hard, indurated swelling, which may occur independently or as a sequela of other swellings.

Causes

1. **Excessive Use of *Muḥallilāt* (Resolvent Agents):**

   Overuse dissolves only the subtle part of the humour, leaving the coarse matter behind, which coagulates and hardens—especially when derived from *Dam* (blood), due to its hot and moist temperament.

2. **Excessive Use of *Mubarridāt* (Refrigerant Agents):**

   These congeal the humour, thickening it into a solid mass. This form often results from *Balghamī* (phlegmatic) matter due to its inherent viscosity.

Classical Descriptions

Abū al-Ḥasan Raban Ṭabarī:

Described *Saqīrūs* or *Waram Ṣulb* as a firm swelling arising from *Khilṭ Ghalīẓ Sawdāwī* (thick melancholic humour*)* containing moisture. The humour infiltrates the organ, expanding its tissues and solidifying due to its dense nature.

Ibn Hubal Baghdādī:

Defined *Saqīrūs* as any *hard swelling without pain*, usually produced by *Sawdāwī* (melancholic) or *Balghamī* (phlegmatic) residues.

- If caused by *Sawdā'*, the colour appears dark or dusky.
- If caused by *Balgham*, it grows slowly and resists resolution.

- Hard swellings of internal organs (*Aḥshā'*) arise from unresolved *Waram Ḥārr* (hot inflammations) or frequent use of mucilaginous and cold drugs, leading to solidification.

Types and Characteristics

- **Primary Saqīrūs:** develops directly from inherently dense matter.
- **Secondary Saqīrūs:** results from the transformation of other swellings.
- **Pure Saqīrūs:** firm, painless, insensitive.
- **Impure Saqīrūs:** painful, discoloured, and irregular.
- ***Saqīrūs Sawdāwī*:** turns the skin dark or lead-coloured, whereas *Saqīrūs Balghamī* does not alter the skin's colour.

Treatment and Prognosis

Early-stage *Saqīrūs* is curable if treated before the loss of sensation of the organ occurs.

Once the hardness becomes extreme and sensation is lost—indicating obstruction of the *Rūḥ Ḥayawānī (vital spirit)*—recovery is extremely difficult, resembling paralysis or senile degeneration.

Ghudda wa Sal'a Ghuddiyya

(Glandular Nodules and Masses)

Description and Classification

Glands are of two types:

- **Natural Glands:** Located beneath both palates, at the roots of the ears, in the axillae, near the ureters, and inside the thighs.
- **Accessory Glands:** Formed from thick, superfluous humours that coagulate due to coldness.

Small, hard, painless glandular nodules commonly occur on the head, hands, feet, and muscular areas.

Etiology

These swellings originate from melancholic humour *(Sawdā')* and coldness, which cause solidification of body fluids (humours).

When they enlarge, they are termed *Ghudda-e-Sal'a*; if static, *Sal'a Ghuddiyya*.

Ibn Hubal Al-Baghdādī attributed them to indigestion combined with physical exertion during gastric fullness.

Surgical Management

Indications:

If nodules remain static and painless, excision is unnecessary. When progressive or painful, surgical removal is advised—except when beneath bone, major vessels, or muscles without a capsule. In *Sal'a*-like nodules, excision or local resolvent applications may be used.

Al-Majūsī's Surgical Technique:

- Make a careful skin incision without injuring the capsule. Elevate and dissect the capsule intact using forceps. If rupture occurs, allow it to slough out completely; remnants are destroyed by caustic drugs.
- Postoperatively, treat the wound as a surgical ulcer.
- Firm, non-cystic indurations are managed conservatively with *Marham Dakhliyūn* or other softening applications.

Ibn Hubal Al-Baghdādī's Method:

For *Baṭṭūrīyah* (cystic swelling), incision and excision are performed as in *Sal'a*.

Kays /Akyās (Cyst)

Definition & Types

A cyst *(Kays)* is a closed sac-like structure enclosed by a distinct membranous capsule, flesh-coloured, initially pea-sized, and may enlarge to the size of a melon.

Types:

1. **Fatty cysts** – containing solid, fatty matter.
2. **Fluid-filled cysts** – containing fluids of varying colour and consistency.

Difference Between Cyst and Abscess

- **Abscess:** Associated with heat, fever, and *pain* until the accumulated matter ripens and discharges, after which symptoms subside.
- **Cyst:** Painless, without heat or fever, enclosed in a capsule with a smooth, flesh-like appearance. It enlarges gradually and may contain either fatty or fluid matter.

Surgical Management

Preoperative Assessment:

An explorer *(Al-Midass)* is used to determine the cyst type.

- Fluid discharge → fluid-filled cyst.
- No discharge → *fatty cyst.*

Operative Steps:

- Fluid cyst: Make a simple incision.
- Fatty cyst: Make a cruciform incision and retract skin with hooks.

Capsule Removal:

- Excise the capsule completely and intact.
- If torn, remove in fragments; any remnant may cause recurrence.

Residual Capsule Management:

- For incomplete excision, apply caustic powder and soothing dressings until healing completes.

Ganglion Cyst

(Swelling Arising from the Twisting of a Tendon)

Definition

A ganglion cyst is a firm, rounded swelling originating from a tendon, often caused by trauma, excessive strain, or mechanical stress. Similar to vascular swellings, it may also occur along tendinous sheaths.

Common Sites

- Dorsum of the wrist (most frequent), Heel region, Areas of articular movement (joints)

Clinical Features

- Hard, flesh-coloured, subcutaneous swelling
- Usually painless; pressure may cause numbness
- Freely movable laterally, but fixed anteroposteriorly
- Swellings over joints should not be incised, as it may cause palsy *(fālij)*

Surgical Management

For Small Swellings (Head/Forehead):

- Make a skin incision, grasp the swelling with forceps, and excise completely from the root

For Larger Swellings:

- Elevate with a hook, dissect carefully to remove entirely
- Close incision with sutures and apply dressing until healed.

Surgeries in Arterial Diseases

Sudda-e-Sharāyīn wa Awrida

(Vascular Obstructions)

Introduction

Sudda (obstruction) occurring in vessels, especially arteries, is among the most serious types due to its effect on circulation and organ perfusion. When it affects *vital organs (A'ḍā' Ra'īsa)* such as the heart, liver, or brain, it becomes highly critical.

Etiology *(Asbāb-e-Sudda)*

Obstruction arises in two main ways:

1. **Excessive Accumulation *(Imtilā' Kathīr)*:** Abnormal buildup of humours within vessels.
2. **Viscosity and Stickiness *(Ghilẓat wa Lazūjat)*:** Thick, adhesive humours adhering to vessel walls.

Modern Correlation:

The Unani concept of *Sudda* parallels conditions like Atherosclerosis, Ischemic Heart Disease, Cerebrovascular Stroke, and Hepatic Obstruction (Portal Hypertension).

Principles of Management

1. Deobstruent Drugs *(Mufattiḥ-i-Sudad Adwiya):*

Act by penetrating and clearing vessel lumina (*Tajāvīf al-'Urūq*) and expelling morbid matter.

2. Role of Attenuants *(Mulaṭṭif)* and Resolvers *(Muḥallil)*:

Used when obstruction is due to viscosity (*Ghilẓat*).

- Excessively strong drugs dissolve only subtle components, hardening the rest; thus, they are combined with *Murakhkhī* (softening) and *Mulayyin* (moistening) agents.

- Weak drugs merely loosen matter, worsening the blockage.

3. Obstruction Due to Lazūjat (Stickiness):

Requires drugs that detach the humour from organ tissue (*Jirm-e ʿUḍw*) to facilitate expulsion.

4. Obstruction Due to *Imtilā'* (Excess Accumulation):

Managed by *istifrāgh* (evacuation) through *faṣd* (bloodletting), purgation, or diuresis.

5. Obstructions in Vital Organs *(Aʿḍā' Ra'īsa):*

Strong *Mufattiḥ* and *Muḥallil* drugs are used cautiously with *Qābiḍ* (astringent), *Mufarriḥ* (aromatic), and *Muqawwī* (organ-strengthening) agents.

6. Obstructions with Coldness and Viscosity *(Burūdat wa Ghilẓat):*

Initially treated with *Mufattiḥ* and *Muḥallil Adwiya*.

If *ʿUfūnat* (putrefaction) develops, use *Jālī* (detergent) and *Muddir-i-Bawl* (diuretic) agents instead of hot deobstruents.

7. Hepatic Obstructions *(Sudda al-Kabid):*

Topical *Ḍimādāt* (poultices) combining *Mufattiḥ*, *Muḥallil*, and mild *Qābiḍ* drugs are effective for strengthening the liver and maintaining its *Quwwat* (vital power).

Aneurysmā / Umm al-Dam / Jarāḥat al-Shiryān

(Aneurysm)

Classical Definitions

Ibn al-Quff:

Describes *Aneurysmā* as a vascular swelling caused by rupture of an artery after trauma or incision, wherein the vessel remains adherent to the skin without forming a crust.

Al-Majūsī(Haly Abbas):

Defines it as a localised arterial swelling arising from rupture (*Al-Shaqq*) within an artery, without breach of the overlying skin.

Ibn Hubal Al-Baghdādī:

Notes that injury to an artery during *Faṣd* (phlebotomy) may lead to subcutaneous blood collection or *Waram*. Due to the cartilaginous (*Ghuḍrūfī*) nature of arteries, spontaneous healing rarely occurs; repair depends on surrounding tissue consolidation.

Clinical Features

- Characterized by pulsation (*Ḥarakāt-e-Shiryān*) felt on palpation; pressure temporarily reduces swelling.
- **Arterial swelling:** deep, pulsatile, elongated.
- **Venous swelling:** superficial, rounded, non-pulsatile.

Management

Ibn al-Quff

- **Major arteries *(Shiryān Kabīr):*** Surgical excision avoided due to fatal haemorrhage. *Faṣd* (venesection) on the opposite side for controlled evacuation (*Istifrāgh al-Dam*). Apply a lead plate *(Asrab)* to compress and prevent bleeding.
- **Minor arteries *(Shiryān Ṣaghīr):*** Longitudinal incision for evacuation; artery sutured on both sides with silk thread. Postoperative dressing with vinegar and rose oil; apply *Mudammil* and *Mulaḥḥim Dharūr* to promote healing.

Ibn Hubal Al-Baghdādī

- **Large arteries:** Avoid surgery; prefer pharmacological management.
- **Small arteries:** Expose and ligate both ends with silk thread soaked in astringent wine. Apply *Mudammil Dharūr* for hemostasis—e.g., *Aylwā* (Aloes), *Kundar* (Olibanum), *Anzarūt*

(Gum ammoniac), *Dam al-Akhawain* (Dragon's blood).

- Cautery *(Āla al-Kayy)* may be used cautiously for haemorrhage control.

Al-Majūsī

- **Contraindications:** Avoid surgery in major arteries (axilla, thigh, neck).
- **Small vessels:** Longitudinal incision, evacuation of blood, elevation of the artery using *Zanbūr (hook)*, and double ligation with silk thread. Apply dressing to promote healing.

Management of Ruptured Arteries

- The swelling is grasped between the fingers along with the overlying skin.
- A Silk-thread ligature is applied at one end.
- The swelling is incised, blood expressed completely, and the skin compressed to expel remaining blood.
- A dressing is applied to ensure hemostasis and promote healing.

Abū Al-Qāsim Al-Zahrāwī (Albucasis)

(a) Arterial Aneurysm:

- **Contraindication:** Avoid incision in major sites (axilla, groin, neck, head).
- **Surgical Technique:**
- Longitudinal incision and careful exposure of the artery.
- Double ligature below and above rupture.
- Incise between ligatures to evacuate blood.
- Dress to allow suppuration until ligatures detach naturally; apply healing ointments afterwards.

(b) Venous Aneurysm:

- Grasp the swelling along with the overlying skin.
- Pass a needle threaded with a double ligature applied crosswise to form four secure knots.
- Central incision for drainage; excise excess skin and dress with wine and oil until healing completes.

Qaṭ' al-Shiryān

(Rupture of the Artery)

Definition

Qaṭ' al-Shiryān denotes complete or partial rupture of an artery, commonly occurring during *Faṣd* (venesection). It presents with sudden, profuse, and forceful bleeding that fails to stop spontaneously.[3]

Etiology *(Asbāb)*

Most frequent during venesection of the *Warīd Basalīq* (Basilic vein) when the lancet pierces too deeply and injures the arterial wall.[3]

Clinical Signs *('Alāmāt)*

- Profuse, spurting haemorrhage.
- Bright red, oxygenated blood indicating arterial origin.

Management

Initial Measures

- Application of *Adwiya Qābiḍa* (styptic/astringent drugs) and *Adwiya Muḥarriqa* (cauterising agents) to arrest bleeding.
- If bleeding persists, surgical intervention is indicated.

Surgical Management

Step 1: Exposure: Incise the overlying skin and carefully dissect the surrounding tissues to reach the artery.

Step 2: Elevation: Elevate the artery with *Zanbūr* (hook) or *Mūchna* (forceps).

Step 3: Ligation: Ligate both ends of the ruptured artery with Silk sutures. The injured arterial segment is divided to prevent re-bleeding; the ligated ends are approximated for closure.

Step 4: Wound Care: Apply *Adwiya Mulahhima* (cicatrising agents) such as *Ṣibr* (Aloes), *Kundar* (Olibanum), *Anzarūt* (Gum ammoniac), and *Dam al-Akhawain* (Dragon's blood). Dress and bandage firmly to maintain hemostasis and aid healing.

Qaṭ' al-Shiryān Khalf al-'Uḍwn

(Transection of the Post-Auricular Arteries)

Therapeutic Indications

Transection of the two pulsating arteries behind the ear is recommended for:

- *Sa'fah* (dry neuralgia or chronic neuralgic pain)
- Certain ophthalmic disorders
- Chronic chest ailments

Operative Technique

Preparation: Shave the area behind the ear. Palpate and mark the arterial pulsation with ink.

Incision: Make a small incision down to the bone to transect the artery. Keep the incision minimal to avoid excess trauma.

- **In Absence of Palpation:** If pulsation is not palpable, make a transverse incision about three finger-breadths behind the ear root, cutting until blood spurts and reaches the bone.

Evacuation and Scraping: Allow moderate bleeding for therapeutic effect. Incise the membrane over the bone and lightly scrape the bone surface to prevent *Waram Ḥārr* (hot inflammatory swelling).

Dressing and Aftercare: Bind the site firmly with cloth strips. Treat the wound as other surgical injuries using standard dressings and *Mudammil* (healing) medications.

Sill al-Shiryān fī al-Ṣudghayn

(Ligation of the Superficial Temporal Artery)

Meaning of *Sill*

In Unani surgery, *Sill* denotes making a longitudinal incision over an artery, elevating the skin with a hook to expose the vessel for ligation or excision.

Therapeutic Indications

Ligation of temporal arteries is indicated in chronic and refractory conditions such as:

- *Shiqīqa* (migraine)
- Persistent ocular and nasal disorders
- *Waram Ḥārr* (inflammatory swelling) of the temporal muscles.

Operative Technique

Preparation

- Shave the temporal region and palpate arterial pulsation.
- If not palpable, apply hot fomentation or tie a firm neck band to increase arterial prominence.
- Mark the site with ink.

Incision and Exposure

- The assistant elevates the skin; the surgeon makes a longitudinal incision.
- Retract wound edges with forceps and expose the artery carefully.

Management of Thin Arteries

- Elevate with forceps and excise a segment about three finger-breadths long.

- Apply *Marham* and healing ointments.

Management of Large Arteries

- Excise the desired portion and ligate both ends with *Silk* sutures, maintaining a three-finger-breadth gap.
- Sprinkle *Dharūr Aṣfar* (yellow healing powder) for cicatrization.

Surgeries in Venous Diseases

Dawālī (Varicose Veins)

Definition

Dawālī are abnormally enlarged, twisted veins engorged with *Sawdāwī* matter (melancholic humour), most often found in the legs of those engaged in strenuous labour, such as porters and ploughmen.

Causes *(Asbāb)*

Thickening and accumulation of *Khilṭ-i Sawdāwī,* causing venous engorgement and loss of elasticity.

Etymology

The name *Dawālī* derives from the crab-like appearance of engorged veins, resembling *Saraṭān* (cancer), which also displays radiating vein-like structures.

Surgical Management of Varicose Veins

Preoperative Preparation

Faṣd (venesection) of *Warīd Bāsalīq* and strong purgation (*Isḥāl Qawī*) to eliminate *Sawdāwī* matter.

Three Main Surgical Procedures by Al-Zahrāwī (Albucasis, 936–1013 CE)

1. Incision and Evacuation of Black Blood

- Foment the leg with hot water and bandage tightly.
- Make one or more incisions over the vein and express thick blood by pressure.
- Bind firmly after evacuation and avoid *Sawdā*-producing foods.
- Repeat when veins refill.

2. Excision of the Vein

- After shaving and heating/exercising the limb, make a longitudinal incision near the knee or ankle.
- Retract with *Zanbūr* (hooks), the vein. The vein is dissected free from surrounding tissues and exposed, and elevated with a blunt hook.
- then remove it segment by segment (either upward or downward).
- If resistance occurs, pass a Silk ligature beneath and twist until extraction is complete.
- Dress with wool soaked in wine and rose or olive oil until healing.[5]

3. Excision of Tortuous Varices

- For irregular veins, make incisions along both sides, elevate, and excise completely with caution to prevent rupture.

Surgical Technique by Al Majusi

- Incise affected veins, ligate both proximal and distal healthy segments with firm *Silk* sutures, then excise the diseased portion between them.
- The method resembles that used for arterial surgery in the temporal region.

Surgeries of Nerves, Muscles

Injuries of the Nerve

Management

Avoidance of Cold Applications

Cold applications should be strictly avoided near an injured *ʿAṣāb (nerve)*, as they aggravate the condition and delay recovery.

Wound Management

- The wound should be kept open; premature closure may lead to *Waram* (inflammation), *ʿUfūnat* (putrefaction), and possible fatality.
- If the opening is narrow, surgical enlargement is necessary to prevent early healing and pus accumulation.

Local Fomentation

Fomentation with a cloth dipped in lukewarm, raw olive oil is beneficial for maintaining Warmth and circulation.

Prevention of Suppuration

Formation of pus should be prevented by frequent use of *Mujaffif* (drying) and *Jādhib* (absorbent) medicines to reduce Discharge and infection risk.

Pharmacological Remedy

Gum Buṭm (Pistacia terebinthus) is regarded as one of the most effective treatments for nerve injuries.

Jurḥ , Tafarruq-i-Ittiṣāl

(Injuries of Muscles)

Definition

Disruption or separation of soft tissues (*Tafarruq-i-Ittiṣāl al-Laḥm*) is termed *Jurḥ* (wound).

Management According to Size and Depth

Small Wounds

If the wound is minor, approximate the edges carefully and adhere them together. ensuring no oil, hair, or foreign matter enters.

After proper alignment, wrap gently with a clean bandage — it usually heals within three days.

Large Wounds

When approximation is not possible, apply sutures (*Khayṭ*) and sprinkle *Mudammil (healing)* medicines to promote recovery.

Deep Wounds

If a wound (*Jurḥ*) is deep but not extensive, wound-filling medications should not be applied immediately, as this may close the wound opening and cause pus accumulation.

Introduce medicine into the deeper layers and keep the opening patent with cotton soaked in ghee or oil.

Wide and Deep Wounds

Apply firm sutures in depth, with gentle closure at the surface. Keep the limb positioned downward for drainage.

If pus accumulates, make a lower incision for continuous evacuation.

Complications and Critical Wounds

Wounds of muscular ends are serious; nerve or artery injury may cause bleeding or spasms.

In hand spasm, cut the affected tendon to prevent contracture.

Management of Discontinuity (*Tafarruq-e-Ittisāl*)

The management of Discontinuity (*Tafarruq-e-Ittisāl*) in soft tissues requires careful attention to three main aspects:

- **Debridement and Clearance:** Removal of necrotic or harmful material and redirection of any substances moving toward the wound (*Jurḥ*).
- **Wound Filling and Nutritional Support:** Filling of the wound with appropriate agents while ensuring that the patient receives proper nutrition to aid recovery.
- **Prevention of Infection and Removal of Gangrenous Tissue:** Prevention of local infection and excision of necrotic tissue, separating it from healthy structures.

Persistent and Complicated Wounds

- A chronic wound (*Jurḥ*) suggests infection (*ʿUfūnat*) reaching bone; open surgically, cleanse, and remove splinters or fragments.
- When a wound (*Jurḥ*) is associated with swelling (*Waram*), the swelling should be treated first.
- This is because *Waram* obstructs the normal process of wound healing.
- Patients with *Sill* (TB), *Istisqāʾ* (Ascites), or *Judhām* (Leprosy) heal poorly due to deficiency of *Ṣāliḥ Akhlāṭ* (healthy humours).

Surgeries of Hand and Foot

Al-Iṣba' al-Zā'ida / Iltiḥām al-Aṣābi'

(Polydactyly and Syndactyly)

Clinical Description of Supernumerary Digits ***(Al-Iṣba' al-Zā'ida)***

Morphological Types:

Supernumerary digits appear in various anatomical forms:

- *Laḥmī* (soft tissue) – composed of flesh only.easily mobile
- *'Aṣabī* (neural) – containing nerves.
- *Salāmiyāt* (osseous) – with phalanges, contains bone and sometimes nail, usually immobile.
- With or without nails; *Mutaḥarrik* (mobile) or *Ghayr Mutaḥarrik* (immobile).

Site of origin:

- From the base of the finger → sometimes mobile, difficult to remove.
- From the phalanges → immobile, requiring bone surgery.

Common Locations:

Usually found near the little finger (ulnar side), rarely near the thumb (radial side). Digits with bones may originate from the articulation of adjacent joints or accessory phalanges.

Surgical Management of Supernumerary Digits

Qaṭ' al-Iṣba' al-Zā'ida **(Amputation of extra finger)**

1. ***Laḥmī / 'Aṣabī*** **(Soft Tissue or Neural Type)**

- Simple excision (*Qaṭ'*) is performed with cosmetic care.
- Apply *Adwiya Ḥābis al-Dam* (styptics) and *Adwiya Mulḥimah* (cicatrising agents).

- If bleeding persists, use *'Amal al-Kayy* (cauterisation).

2. Digits with Phalanges (Osseous Type)

- **Mobile** ***(Mutaḥarrik):*** Excise at the joint *(al-mafṣil),* followed by hemostatic and healing therapy.
- **Immobile** ***(Ghayr Mutaḥarrik):*** Excision is more complex due to bony involvement. Excise soft tissue, then resect bone with a surgical saw.

Surgical Challenges and Techniques

Description by Al-Majūsī (Haly Abbas)

When Arising from Joints *(Al-Majūsī):*

- Excise the surrounding flesh (*Laḥm*) of the extra digit in a circular manner (like peeling sugarcane).
- Resect the osseous structure using a surgical saw and smooth the surface to prevent irregularities or sharp projections that may hinder healing.
- Apply ulcer-healing drugs for *Inbāt al-Laḥm* (tissue regeneration) and *Tajfīf* (drying).

Description by Al-Zahrāwī:

- *Laḥmī* digits → simple base excision with a broad scalpel.
- *Osseous* digits → A circular incision is made through the surrounding soft tissue until the bone is exposed. The bone is divided with a surgical saw.
- Digits at the root of a normal finger are difficult and should be avoided if risky.

Iltiḥām al-Aṣābi' (Syndactyly)

Definition and Aetiology

Fusion and adhesion of two or more digits (*Iltiḥām al-Aṣābi'*).

- *Khilqī* (Congenital): Due to defective embryonic separation.during intrauterine development.
- *Iktisābī* (Acquired): Secondary to ulceration *(Qarḥa),* wounds (*Jarāḥat*), or burns.

Classical Unani Surgical Approach

Surgical Technique for Acquired Syndactyly by Ibn al-Quff:

- A surgical incision is made to separate the adhered digits
- After separation, place a cloth soaked in *Ravghan-e-Gul* (rose oil) between them to prevent re-adhesion.
- Apply *Ḥābis al-Dam Adwiya* if bleeding occurs.

Surgical Technique by Al-Zahrāwī:

- The web between the digits is carefully excised to restore normal anatomical separation.
- Interpose rose oil–soaked dressing or thin metal sheet (lead) to prevent fusion until complete healing.
- If the adhesion involves a digit attached to the palm, the incision must follow the plane of adhesion, preserving the natural contour and functional integrity of the hand.

Surgeries of Nails

Dākhis (Paronychia)

Definition and Clinical Features

Dākhis is an abnormal overgrowth of soft tissue beneath the nail, commonly affecting the thumb or great toe, though other digits may be involved.

If untreated, it may progress to:

- Abscess formation and pus discharge
- Tissue necrosis and erosion of the nail root
- Destruction of the nail or underlying bone in advanced stages
- Foul-smelling discharge with livid discolouration and broadening of the fingertip.

Surgical Treatment by Al-Zahrāwī:

Excision and Cauterisation

- Excise all redundant and superfluous tissue and apply cautery for better outcomes.

If Bone and Nail are Healthy

- When the ingrown edge pierces the surrounding flesh:
- Insert a fine probe beneath the margin to lift it.
- Excise impinging tissue.
- Apply caustic agent and suitable ointment dressings until healed.

If Bone is Diseased

- Excise the necrotic bone, as healing does not occur until all dead tissue is removed.

If Extensive Infection

- If infection spreads deeply, perform amputation at the nearest joint, followed by routine postoperative care.

Jurūḥ al-Aẓfār

(Broken Nails / Nail Injuries)

Clinical Features

Injuries to the nail may occur as:

- *Lacerations*
- *Crushing injuries*
- *Bruising with severe pain*

Surgical Management

1. Phlebotomy (Faṣd)

Performed initially to reduce local inflammation and congestion.

2. Excision of the Nail

- The damaged nail is removed with a sharp scalpel through a longitudinal incision.
- Care is taken not to injure the nail bed, as this may cause intense pain and lead to *Laḥm Zā'id* (abnormal granulation tissue).

3. Postoperative Care

- The exposed nail bed is dressed with *Mudammilāt* (healing) and *Musakkina* (sedative, cooling) applications to promote comfort and recovery.

Ṣufra al-Aẓfār

(Yellow Discolouration of Nails)

Aetiology (Asbāb)

- Caused by excessive growth of flesh (*Laḥm Zā'id*) partially covering the nail.
- Common in the great toe due to accumulation of dust and dirt; in hands, it usually follows inflammation of the nail-bed (*Basahrī*).
- Often associated with *Waram Ḥārr* (hot swelling) or accumulation of *Mādda Ḥādda* (acrid morbid matter) leading to *'Ufunah* (infection).

Clinical Features ('Alāmāt)

- Retention of pus and morbid matter beneath the nail, causing decay of the root.
- Infection extends to the entire nail and nail-bed, producing foul odour and discolouration.
- Advanced cases involve the underlying bone, resulting in a livid hue and broadening of the fingertip.

Surgical Management

1. Excision and Cauterisation (for Severe Cases)

- Excise the adherent or infected tissue, followed by cauterisation.
- *Ṣufra al-Aẓfār* belongs to the *Akkāl (corrosive)* category; thus, cauterisation prevents gangrene and finger necrosis.

2. Conservative Management (When Nail and Bone Are Intact)

- If only excess flesh (*Laḥm Zā'id*) causes pricking pain from *waram ḥārr,* insert a fine probe or fine-tipped nail-cutter under the nail corner, trim the edge, and the cut edge of the nail should then be slightly elevated and repositioned over the overgrown flesh, so that it gradually suppresses and eliminates it

- This non-invasive method yields excellent results in mild cases.

3. Excision of Excess Flesh

- In extensive overgrowth, surgically remove the excess flesh and apply *Adwiya Mulahhima (wound-healing drugs)* to aid recovery.

SYSTEMIC SURGERY

(JARĀḤAT NIẒĀMĪ)

SURGERIES OF THE HEAD

Mā' al-Ra's (Hydrocephalus)

Definition

Hydrocephalus is a pathological condition characterised by abnormal accumulation of fluid within or around the cranial cavity. In Unani medicine, it is referred to as *Ijtimā' al-Mā' fī al-Ra's*.

Types of Hydrocephalus

Classical Unani physicians describe three distinct types:

1. **Subcutaneous Collection** – Fluid between the skin and periosteum (*Simḥāq*).
2. **Subpericranial Collection** – Fluid between the *Simḥāq* and cranial bone.
3. **Subdural Collection** – Fluid between cranial bone and dura mater (*Umm Jāfiya*).

Etiology (Asbāb)

The main causes include:

- **Severe cranial pressure**–Intense external pressure on the head may lead to inflammation (*Waram*) as a defensive response, resulting in fluid retention.
- **Birth trauma** → fall or pressure during delivery leads to accumulation of fluids (*Ruṭūbā)t* in weak tissues.
- **Head injury** → rupture of vessels (*'Urūq*) causes extravasation that later forms into a raw humour material (*Mādda Khām)*.

Observation by Al-Zahrāwī (Albucasis, 936–1013 CE)

According to Al-Zahrāwī, hydrocephalus occurs most frequently in newborns, often when the midwife exerts excessive pressure on the infant's head during delivery. In some cases, the cause remains concealed and idiopathic.

Observation by Al-Majūsī (Haly Abbas, 930–994 CE)

The disease is predominantly seen in infants. It may arise from rough handling during delivery or from internal causes such as rupture of cranial vessels (*'Urūq*) and alteration (*Taghayyur*) of extravasated blood without *nuḍj* (maturation) or *taḥallul ilā ṣadīd* (suppuration). In such cases, the cranial region becomes porous, and *Ruṭūbāt* stagnate beneath the skin and periosteum (*Simaḥāq*).

Clinical Features (*'Alāmāt*) of Hydrocephalus

First Type – Accumulation of Fluid between Skin and Periosteum *(Simḥāq)*

Soft, compressible swelling with mild pain; subsides easily, though the skin colour appears altered.

Second Type – Accumulation of Fluid between Periosteum *(Simḥāq)* and Cranial Bone ('Aẓm al-Qiḥf)

Firm, non-compressible swelling with severe pain and slight discolouration; resolution is slow due to tissue thickness.

Third Type – Accumulation of Fluid between Cranial Bone ('Aẓm al-Qiḥf) and Dura Mater (Umm Jāfiya)

Severe pain without softness; pressure causes inward displacement of fluid. The forehead protrudes, eyes remain closed and stony, and excessive tearing occurs, though the skin appears normal.

Clinical Observation by Al-Majūsī (Haly Abbas)

When fluid collects between the cranial bone and thick meningeal membrane (*Umm Ghalīẓa*), the swelling is non-compressible and persistent. In infants, the skull may sink inward due to soft bones and the separation of sutures.

Characteristic signs:

- Separation of cranial bones
- Prominent forehead
- Fixed, stony eyes

- Excessive tearing

The prognosis is poor, and treatment is generally discouraged due to the delicacy of the condition.

Surgical Management of Hydrocephalus (*Ijtimāʿ al-Māʾ fī al-Raʾs*)

General Principles

- The main principle of treatment in hydrocephalus is surgical intervention (*ʿAmal bi-Ḥadīd*), particularly in the first and second varieties.
- Objective: gradual evacuation of accumulated fluid (*Ruṭūbāt*) while preventing sudden collapse.
- Proper postoperative wound care and a balanced dietary regimen are essential to maintain strength.
- Surgery is contraindicated in the third type due to poor prognosis and high risk.

First Type – Accumulation of Fluid between Skin and Periosteum *(Simaḥāq)*

Site and Direction of Incision *(Shigāf):*

A transverse incision, about two thumb-joints in width, is made at the swelling site. The fluid should drain gradually to avoid shock or weakness.

Postoperative Dressing:

After incision, cover with clean linen (*Katān*) and bandage firmly. The dressing is removed after three days, residual fluid gently expressed, and re-dressed for another three days.

Second Type – Accumulation of Fluid between Periosteum *(Simaḥāq)* and Cranial Bone *(ʻAẓm al-Qiḥf)*

Type of Incision:

Two intersecting incisions at right angles forming a cruciform (*Taqāṭuʿ Ṣulībī*) are made to ensure adequate drainage by creating multiple drainage channels.

Post-surgical Management:

Same regimen as in the first type—bandaging, gradual expression, and redressing at intervals.

Third Type – Accumulation of Fluid between Cranial Bone *('Aẓm al-Qiḥf)* and Dura Mater *(Umm Jāfiya)*

Surgical procedures are generally avoided due to grave risks. But if the infant is robust and the matter tends outward, it may be treated like the second type with caution.

Dietary and Supportive Regimen

A light, dry diet with restricted fluids is advised to maintain strength and prevent recurrence.

Surgical Technique by Al-Zahrāwī in Hydrocephalus

Indications:

Fluid may collect either between the skin and bone or beneath the bone.

Small Swelling (Single Incision):

A single transverse incision, two thumb-joints long, at the head's centre.

Large Swelling (Cross Incision):

Two intersecting incisions for better drainage.

Sub-bone Accumulation *(Taḥt al-ʿAẓm):*

Characterised by suture separation and fluid fluctuation on pressure.

Three midline Intersecting incisions allow complete evacuation of the fluid.

Dressing Regimen:

Apply a bandage and fomentation with wine and oil for five days, then shift to a lighter dressing with lint and ointments.

Surgical Technique by Al-Majūsī in Hydrocephalus

Fluid between the Scalp and Periosteum :

- In moderate swellings, two intersecting incisions at the centre are made.
- For larger swellings, three incisions shaped like the Greek letter Tau (T) ensure thorough evacuation.

After drainage, the cavity is filled with medicated preparations for three days. If granulation is delayed, slight bone scraping promotes healing.

General surgical care with dressings, ointments, and wound-healing measures is continued.

Sal'āt / Rasūlī (Tumours) and *Ghudūd* (Glandular Swellings) of the Head

Definition

A *Sal'a* / *Rasūlī* (tumour) is a dense, immovable swelling that develops beneath the skin and remains fixed in position.

Ghudūd (glandular swellings), though firm, are movable within their confined anatomical boundaries.

Etiopathogenesis

The formation of *Sal'a* and *Ghudūd* in the head is primarily due to the accumulation of thick vapours (*Bukhārāt Ghalīẓa*).

- When these vapours ascend toward the scalp, they strike the skin and air beneath it, becoming trapped.
- Due to their dense quality (*Kayfiyat Ghalīẓa*), the skin pores (*Masāmāt*) are occluded, leading to retention and gradual hardening.
- Over time, this condensed matter transforms into *Sal'a* or *Ghudūd*.

Management

Evacuation and Purification *(Tanqiya 'al-Badan)*

Initial therapy involves phlebotomy (*Faṣd*) and purgation (*Istifrāgh*) to expel morbid matter (*Tanqiya' al-Badan*).

Surgical Excision

- At a suitable season, cruciform (*Ṣalībī*) or longitudinal (*Ṭūlī*) incisions are made over the swelling.
- The root is completely excised using a *Ṣunnāra* (curved hook) or *Mishrāṭ* (scalpel) to prevent recurrence.
- Care must be taken near vital structures such as the *Yafūkh* (palate) and ears to avoid injury to arteries (*Shiryān*). If an artery is accidentally cut, immediate cauterisation is essential.

Postoperative Care

- Healing is supported with medicated ointments containing *Ṣamgh Ṣanawbar* (pine resin) and *Kundar* (frankincense).
- Alternatively, topical powders (*Dharūr*) such as *Sar Qūlūn* are applied to promote cicatrization.

Jurūḥ al-Ra's

(Cranial Wounds)

Classification

According to Unani physicians, cranial wounds are classified into six distinct categories:

1. ***Qāshirā*** – Derived from *Qishr* (peel/skin). It involves only the superficial layer of the scalp, without deeper extension.
2. ***Mulḥima*** – Derived from *Laḥm* (flesh). It extends through both skin and underlying flesh *(Laḥm)*.
3. ***Mūḍiḥa*** – Derived from *Waḍḥ* (to make clear). It reaches up to the cranial bone (*Aẓm al-Qiḥf*), exposing it without fracture.
4. ***Hāshima*** – Derived from *Hashm* (to crush or break). It fractures the bone into pieces (*Hashm*) without displacement.
5. ***Nāqila*** –Derived from *Naql* (to displace). A fragment of bone is displaced (*Naql*) from its original site.
6. ***Māmūṭa*** – Derived from *Umm* (mother). It penetrates as deep as the *Umm al-Dimāgh* (meningeal covering).

These six represent the classical types of *Jurūḥ al-Raʾs*.

General Management

- If the wound is wide and the margins do not approximate naturally, a dressing (*Rifāda*) is used for approximation.
- If edges can be joined, suturing (*Khiyāṭa*) is performed, alternating stitches at right angles.
- After suturing, A *Dharūr* (dusting powder) is applied longitudinally over the wound.

Specific Management According to Type

1–2. *Qāshirā and Mulḥima*

Treatment follows general principles. In *Mulḥima*, since flesh is involved, the use of *Marham, Khiyāṭa* (suturing) may be unnecessary. If healing delays, resin-based (*Ṣamagh*) ointments that stimulate granulation are applied.

3. *Mūḍiḥa*

When the wound exposes the bone, it must be protected from air. *Ravghan Zayt* (olive oil) or old animal fat is applied until fibrous tissue covers the exposed skull. Contamination must be avoided, as infection halts healing.

4. *Hāshima*

In bone fractures without displacement, fragments should be carefully repositioned and treated as in *Mūḍiḥa*.

5. *Nāqilah*

When bone fragments (*Shaẓāyā*) are displaced, none should be left inside the wound. Thorough cleansing is essential, followed by ointments that promote granulation and tissue regeneration.

6. *Māmūṭa*

This deepest and most dangerous wound reaches the *Umm al-Raʾs* (meninges). Protection from air is crucial to prevent *Tashannuj* (convulsions) and *Junūn* (mania).

The surgeon must avoid probing with a *Mishraṭ* (scalpel) or finger to prevent fatal complications such as *Sakta* (collapse or stroke).

Management of Head Injuries According to Al-Zahrāwī

Head Wounds Without Bone Fracture

In superficial wounds caused by stones or blunt objects, where only the skin is affected:

- To prevent abscess formation, perform venesection (*Faṣd*)—preferably from the cephalic vein opposite the injury. If bloodletting is not feasible, maintain a light diet, avoiding meat, wine, and heavy food.
- If inflammation occurs → apply cotton soaked in rose oil or rose oil with astringent wine.
- If no inflammation and the wound is fresh → apply healing powder.
- If the wound is altered or exposed to air → use ointments that promote pus discharge, continuing dressings until recovery.

Severe Head Wounds (Sword Cut or Similar)

- If the wound is large and the dressing cannot close the margins → perform suturing (*Khiyāṭa*).
- If skin remains attached by a thin strip → excise the loosened part and apply medicines that generate firm flesh to cover the bone.
- If skin becomes necrotic → remove all diseased tissue before applying healing agents.

Haemorrhage in Wounds

If arterial or venous bleeding persists and medicines fail:

- Examine the vessel; if partially cut → divide completely and ligate.
- If bleeding continues, → cauterize the site until haemorrhage stops.

Shaqīqa (Migraine)

Etymology

The term *Shaqīqa* (hemicrania) derives from *Shiqq* (half), as the pain affects one side of the head rather than the entire cranium.

Aetiology and Pathogenesis

The disease arises from the accumulation of morbid matter in limited quantity within the cranial arteries.

- This matter, deficient in nutritive transformation (*Istiḥāla*), remains as waste, causing localised obstruction and pain.
- The cranial arteries, receiving minimal nutritive supply from the heart, retain residual humoral impurities leading to *Shaqīqa*.

Types according to Temperament

1. *Shaqīqa Ḥārra* (Hot Type):

- Caused by *ḥārr* and *ḥād* (acrid) humours.
- Produces severe, pulsating pain and inflammation.

2. *Shaqīqa Bārida* (Cold Type):

- Arises from *bārid* and *rutubat ghayr Naḍīja* (cold, moist, raw humours).
- The pain is dull and persistent, resistant to resolution.

Therapeutic Principles

Treatment corresponds to temperament:

- In *bārid* types → use warming and resolving measures to dissipate cold, moist humours.
- In *ḥār* types → employ cooling, sedative, and anti-inflammatory therapy to neutralise *ḥād* humours.

If pain resolves with *tanqiya'* (evacuation), *istifrāgh* (purification), and dietary regulation, no surgical intervention is required.

Surgical Management in *Shaqīqa* (Migraine)

When medical measures fail, surgical attention is directed toward the temporal arteries (*Shiryān al-Ṣudghayn*) and posterior auricular arteries.

The principal operation is *"Batr"* (arterial incision followed by cauterisation,

An alternative, *Sal* (longitudinal incision of the artery), sometimes followed by cauterisation.

Classical physicians generally preferred *Batr* with cauterisation as a safer and more effective method.

Cauterisation and Arterial Transection in the Management of *Shaqīqa*

Indications

Cauterisation (*Kayy*) or arterial cutting (*Batr*) should not be performed unless:

- The patient possesses adequate physical strength.
- The temperament is pure.
- The season and external environment are moderate.

ʿAmal al-Kayy (Cauterisation)

Cauterisation is recommended for chronic migraine (*Shaqīqa Muzmina*), severe catarrh (*Nazla Ḥādda*), or persistent headache (*Ṣudāʿ Shadīd*) unresponsive to medical treatment.

1. The cautery iron (*Mikwā*) is applied down to the bone to divide the artery ends completely.
2. Double-bladed cauteries are preferred for even, gradual division and better hemostasis, and eliminating *ruṭūbāt* (humours) and preventing recurrence.

Types of Arterial Transection *(Qaṭʿ al-Shiryān)*

1. *ʿAmal al-Sall* (Longitudinal Incision)

- The skin over the temporal artery is incised longitudinally to relieve local congestion.Then the vessel is cut (*Batr*).
- In some cases, mild cauterisation may follow to prevent recurrence.
- This method, though simpler, was less preferred due to higher chances of relapse.

2. *ʿAmal al-Batr* (Arterial Transection with Cauterisation)

Direct Method:

- The artery is exposed by a small incision, then cut (*Batr*). Both ends are cauterised immediately to stop bleeding and prevent reformation of humours.

Protected Method With *Ṣunnāra and Miṣṭāḥa*:

- The artery is lifted with a hook (*Ṣunnāra*). A flat metallic plate (*Miṣṭāḥa*) is placed beneath the vessel to protect deeper tissues. Cauterisation is then applied, and the artery is divided.
- The *Miṣṭāḥa* prevents the cautery heat from damaging cranial membranes (*Ghishāʾ al-Qiḥf*), thereby avoiding complications such as convulsions (*Tashannuj*).

Operative Steps:

1. The temporal hair is shaved, and the pulsating artery is located by palpation or by applying heat and neck compression to make it prominent.
2. The skin is scraped with a scalpel (*Al-Mibḍaʿ*) until the artery is reached and isolated with a hook (*Ṣunnāra*).

If thin, the artery is twisted with the hook-tip and divided; if large, it is ligated at two points with strong double threads, preferably of silk or lute-string and the middle portion excised.

Hemostasis and Postoperative Care

- Bleeding is controlled by immediate cauterization, application of powdered *Zāj* (vitriol) with compression, or manual pressure until clotting occurs.
- The wound is then packed with teased cotton, covered with dry

Mudammil and *mujaffif* agents, and bandaged firmly. A light, dry diet is advised, avoiding Discharge until healing is complete.

Surgeries of the Eye

Diseases of the Eyelids

Sha'īra, Gahanjanī

(Stye/Hordeolum)

Definition

Sha'īra is a pustular swelling develops on the upper or lower eyelid, resembling a small boil. It closely resembles *'Arūs*—a term used for swellings in the axilla.

Difference between Sha'īra and 'Arūs:

- In *Sha'īra*, the pustule is firm, gland-like, and may persist for years. Its colour resembles that of the eyelid.
- In *'Arūs*, the swelling is reddish, soft, and tender, often arising from over-eating, and subsides with fasting or simple hot fomentation.

Observation by Ibn Hubal Al-Baghdādī

Sha'īra is a small, elongated swelling at the eyelid margin caused by the accumulation of *mādda ghalīẓa* (thick morbid matter) that hardens into a firm nodule.

Surgical Management

- If *Sha'īra* resolves with medicinal therapy, no surgical procedure is required. If persistent, extraction becomes necessary.
- Make a longitudinal incision (*qaṭ' ṭūlī*) over the swelling. And carefully extract the gland using the nail or the edge of a scalpel (*mishraṭ*), avoiding injury to surrounding tissues.

Post-Operative Care

After removal:

Apply a mixture prepared from *lubb rummān* (pulp of pomegranate) macerated in *sirka* (vinegar) and *duhn ward* (rose oil) externally over the eyelid to promote healing and reduce inflammation.

Sharnāq

(Xanthelasma / Hydatid of the Upper Lid)

Definition

According to Ibn Hubal Al-Baghdādī, *Sharnāq* is a cystic or fatty swelling that develops in the upper eyelid, often causing difficulty in elevating the lid. It adheres to the upper portion of the eye and contains a viscid, fatty substance composed of nervous and membranous tissues.

Al-Rāzī adds that *Sharnāq* is a type of *Sal'a'* (cystic tumour) that arises in the upper eyelid and prevents its elevation.

Clinical Description According to Al-Rāzī, Ibn Hubal, Al-Majūsī, and Al-Zahrāwī

Al-Rāzī, Al-Baghdādī, Al-Majūsī, and Abū Al-Qāsim Al-Zahrāwī collectively describe *Sharnāq* as a fatty, cystic lesion of the upper eyelid that restricts its movement and commonly affects children or individuals with predominance of *Ruṭūbat*.

Clinical features:

- A cystic or gland-like swelling beneath the skin of the upper lid that remains fixed in position.
- Contains viscid fatty material derived from nerves and membranes.
- Lid appears moist (*Marṭūb*), flaccid (*Mustarkhī*), and heavy, hindering elevation.
- Associated symptoms include *Nazla* (catarrh), *Dhalka* (laxity of eyelids), *Dama'* (excessive tearing), and *Ashūb al-'Ayn* (ophthalmia).
- Patients, especially children, experience intolerance to sunlight, frequent lacrimation, and a tendency to lie face-down due to ocular discomfort.
- On palpation, a soft, fatty mass is felt beneath the upper eyelid folds.

Abū Al-Ḥasan Aḥmad Ibn Muḥammad Al-Ṭabarī

According to *Al-Ṭabarī*, *Sharnāq* results from *Ghilẓat* (thickening) of the eyelids, causing difficulty and pain during blinking.

Surgical Management of *Sharnāq*

Preoperative Preparation

According to Al-Rāzī, Ibn Hubal Al-Baghdādī, and Al-Majūsī

- The patient is seated upright or kneeling. An assistant supports the head from behind and restrains the hands if necessary.
- The eyelid is drawn downward by the surgeon, while the assistant elevates the eyebrow region to make the *Sharnāq* prominent.
- If the lesion is small or hidden, gentle pressure or a thread tied at the eyelid root helps localise the swelling.

Exposure and Localisation of the Lesion

- The eyelid is held between the index and middle fingers.
- Pressure is applied gently until the viscid matter (*Ruṭūbat*) collects beneath the fingers. *Sharnāq* becomes visible and palpable as a rounded swelling.

Incision Technique

Type and Direction:

- A transverse incision (*Qaṭ' 'Arḍī*) is preferred, slightly longer than a venesection wound. In cases with deeper or extensive lesions, a longitudinal incision (*Qaṭ' Ṭūlī*) may be used (as suggested by Jālīnūs and Al-Rāzī).
- Depth must be adequate to expose the lesion but should not injure the cartilage or muscle of the eyelid.

Instruments Used:

- A rounded scalpel (*Mishraṭ*) or lancet is used to make the incision.
- In *Al-Zahrāwī's* method, a circular linen pad is placed around the lesion for stabilisation before incision.

Extraction of the Lesion

- After incision, the *Sharnāq* (hydatid cyst) appears as a white fatty mass. It is gently mobilised right, left, upward, and downward using fingers wrapped in linen or a small cloth to avoid slippage.
- The mass is gradually lifted and extracted intact without rupturing the capsule.
- Extreme care is taken to avoid injury to the ocular surface *(Ṣifāq al-ʿAyn)* or removal of eyelid muscle.

If the lesion adheres to the ocular membrane:

- Only the free portion is excised. and the adherent part is treated by applying powdered salt *(Milḥ)* to destroy it gradually.

Management of Residual Tissue and Hemostasis

- If remnants remain, powdered salt or vinegar-water *(Āb Sirka)* compresses are applied to dissolve fatty residue. Some surgeons recommend using vinegar-water–soaked cloths immediately after extraction to ensure dissolution and prevent reformation.
- In case of bleeding, gentle pressure or light cauterisation may be performed.

Postoperative Care

Day 1: Apply compresses of vinegar-water over the incision site.

Day 2: If there is no *Waram Ḥārr* (inflammatory swelling) → apply Marham prepared with *Rasūt* and *Shiyāf Māmīthā*.

If swelling or heat is present → use cooling agents *(Mubarridāt)* such as *Sandal*, *Fūfal*, or *Gul-e-Armanī* mixed in *Āb Kāsnī Sabz* or *Āb Kishnīz Sabz*.

Apply Dharūr Aṣfar or medicated ointments to promote healing. And protect the wound with linen bandaging *(Rifāda)* until full recovery.

Complications and Precautions According to Jālīnūs, Al-Rāzī

Avoid deep excision, as it may damage the eyelid muscle or ocular membrane.

- Excessive removal can lead to weakness of lid elevation and protrusion of fat, causing pain and swelling.
- Gradual excision in small portions is advised to ensure safe removal of the fatty mass.
- Use of longitudinal incision is permissible when the lesion is deep or extensive.

Barada

(Chalazion /Tarsal / Meibomian Cyst)

Definition and Description

According to Al-Rāzī, Al-Majūsī, and Ibn Hubal Al-Baghdādī, *Barada* is described as a small, hard, rectangular swelling usually occurring on the upper eyelid, occasionally on the inner surface or at the roots of eyelashes. It arises from thick, viscid humour *(Mādda Ghalīẓa)* that solidifies within the eyelid, resembling a hailstone *(Barad)* in texture.

Classical physicians agree that it results from condensed white humour, which becomes firm and encapsulated inside the tarsal plate or lid margin.

Surgical Management

Indication for Surgery

When *Barada* fails to respond to medical therapy, surgical excision is indicated.

Patient Preparation and Exposure

- The patient is seated upright before the surgeon. and the eyelid is grasped firmly between the thumb and index finger and everted to expose the swelling. If the *Barada* lies on the inner surface, eversion of the lid is essential for proper access.

Incision Technique

- A transverse incision *(Qaṭ' 'Arḍī)* is made over the cyst using a blunt-ended scalpel (*Mishraṭ*).
- The incision depth should be sufficient to open the cyst but not deep enough to injure the cartilage or lid margin.

Extraction of the Mass

- The congealed mass is gently removed using the tip of a fine instrument or nail-cutter.
- Care must be taken to remove the entire cystic content to prevent recurrence.
- In deeper lesions, the surgeon should avoid injuring the tarsal plate or muscle beneath.

Suturing and Dressing

- If the incision is wide with loose edges → suturing is recommended.
- If small, suturing is unnecessary — instead, apply Dharūr Aṣfar (yellow dusting powder) and bandage the eyelid gently.
- The wound should remain clean and protected from dust or rubbing.

Postoperative Care

- Local applications: Patients may chew powdered cumin *(Zīra)* and salt *(Milḥ),* use their extract as eye drops to cleanse the area.
- Compresses: Apply cold or lukewarm compresses and maintain light bandaging until healing completes.
- Observation: Monitor for inflammation (*Waram-e-Ḥārr*); if present, apply cooling agents *(Mubarridāt).*

Iltizāq al-Jafn / Iltiṣāq al-Jafn (Symblepharon)

Definition

Iltizāq al-Jafn refers to the adhesion of one eyelid to another, or to the conjunctiva *(Ṭabaqa Multaḥima)*, cornea *(Ṭabaqa Qarniyya),* or both.

The adhesion may occur near the canthus (corner of the eye) or in the middle of the eyelid.

Etiology

1. Traumatic Causes

- Injury to the ocular surface, forming an adhesion when the eyelid closes over it.
- Scratching or rubbing of the eye with fingernails.

2. Post-Inflammatory Causes

- Improperly treated *Jāla* (pterygium-like opacity) leading to adhesion.

3. Post-Surgical Causes

- Adhesion to the sclera or cornea after ulceration or excision of pterygium *(Qaṭ' al-Ẓafara).*
- Adhesion within the eyelid margins following excision of *Sal'a'* (tumour) and faulty closure.

Clinical Features

- Fusion of the eyelid with the ocular surface.
- Restricted eyelid movement.
- Possible corneal damage or opacity if adhesion involves the cornea.

Surgical Management

The objective is to separate the adhesion mechanically while preventing injury to the cornea and re-adhesion during healing.

Mechanical Separation

According to Al-Zahrāwī, Ibn Hubal, and Al-Majūsī

- A probe *(Al-Misbār),* nail-cutter *(Naqsh),* or scissors *(Qamādīn)* is gently inserted between the eyelid and ocular surface to free the adhesion.
- Dissection should be gradual and controlled, avoiding damage to the *Ṭabaqa Qarniyya* or prolapse of the iris (*Ṭabaqa 'Inabiyya*).

Operative Technique According to Al-Zahrāwī

- A blunt probe (*Al-Misbār*) or hook (*Al-Mirwad*) is gently inserted beneath the eyelid and raised to expose the adhesion.
- A scalpel *(Mibḍa')* with a slightly blunt edge is used to peel the adhesion gradually — avoiding deep cutting. Dissection continues until the eyelid regains its natural position and full mobility.

Surgical Method According to Ibn Hubal Al-Baghdādī

- In *Iltizāq* near the inner canthus, a small needle incision is made to create an opening.
- A *Qamādīn* or fistula-cutting instrument is inserted to divide the adhesion.
- Cotton soaked in rose oil and copper oxide or *Safaida Kāshghārī* is placed between the eyelid and eye to prevent recurrence. *Kuḥl-e-Raushnā'ī* (lamp-black collyrium) and *Mīl Tāmba* (copper oxide)are applied regularly post-surgery.

According to Al-Majūsī

- If incision extends to the *Ṭabaqa Qarniyya*, the patient should chew cumin *(Zira)* and salt *(Milḥ);* their extract is instilled into the eye. And soft linen cloth (Katān) is placed over the eyelid to prevent re-adhesion.
- The dressing is soaked with egg yolk *(Zardī Bayḍa)* and rose oil *(Ravghan Gul)* and kept for three days. Later, Shiyāf Abyaḍ (white eye suppository) is instilled to promote healing.

Post-Operative Care

Immediate Care: If corneal rupture occurs → apply cotton soaked in rose oil *(Ravghan Gul)* and egg white *(Safīdi Bayḍa)*.

Second Day: Instil cumin–salt water *(Āb Zīra o Milḥ)* as eye drops.

Third Day: Insert *Shiyāf* (eye suppository) and apply cooling ointments if inflammation appears.

Preventive Measures After Surgery

- Place soft linen pads *(Kharqa)* between the eyelid and eyeball to avoid recurrence.
- Use mild collyria *(Akwāḥ Shāfiya)* with verdigris (*Zanjār*) and saline washing *(Mā' al-Milḥ)* to cleanse and strengthen the ocular tissues. And avoid direct exposure to heat or dust during recovery.

Istirkhā' al-Jafn

(Ptosis, Blepharoptosis)

Definition

Istirkhā' al-Jafn refers to the drooping of the upper eyelid resulting from relaxation of the muscles responsible for its elevation.

It occurs due to the predominance of moist humours *(Ghalaba'-i-Ruṭūbat),* which weaken the eyelid tissues, rendering the patient unable to lift the lid.

Clinical Association

At times, *Istirkhā' al-Jafn* appears in association with Ophthalmia *(Āshūb al-'Ayn)*.

Drooping may involve the entire eyelid, from eyelashes to the eyebrow, or only the posterior portion of the eyelid.

Surgical Management

Treatment of Underlying Causes

If *Istirkhā'* arises secondary to paralysis or facial palsy, treatment should target the primary systemic condition first. As the neurological or humoral imbalance improves, eyelid drooping gradually resolves.

'Amal-e-Tashmīr (Blepharoplasty)

When the eyelid remains persistently lax, obstructing vision, a corrective surgical procedure termed *Tashmīr (Blepharoplasty)* is performed.

Operative Steps:

- A small segment of the upper eyelid is excised according to the degree of laxity. And the edges are sutured to shorten and tighten the lid.
- This restores eyelid tone and elevation, allowing the eye to open normally.

Shatra Dākhiliyya, Shatra Khārijiyya (Entropion and Ectropion)

Definition

Entropion ***(Shatra Dākhiliyya):*** Inward turning of the eyelid margin—usually the lower lid—causing eyelashes to rub against the globe.

Ectropion ***(Shatra Khārijiyya):*** Outward turning of the eyelid margin, exposing the conjunctiva and preventing complete closure of the eyelid.

Entropion *(Shatra Dākhiliyya)*

Etiology

According to Abū Al-Qāsim Al-Zahrāwī, inversion of the lower eyelid may be:

1. **Congenital** – present from birth.
2. **Acquired** – following injury, incision, cauterisation, or surgical error.

Surgical Management

General Principles

- The surgical plan should correspond to the form and severity of inversion.

- The skilled surgeon modifies incision and suturing technique according to each case.
- In many instances, the morphology of the lid itself guides the operative approach.

Operative Techniques by Al-Zahrāwī

1. Primary Method

- A curved needle with double wool is passed from the inner to the outer canthus, both ends fixed in the lid. And the eyelid is stretched upward, followed by a broad transverse incision.
- If the lid resumes its normal position, the operation is complete. If not, a probe *(Misbār)* is applied to assist inversion correction.

2. Lambda-Shaped Excision *(Qaṭ' al-Lambdā)*

- Two oblique incisions are made on the inner surface, meeting at an angle like the Greek letter λ (lambda), and the triangular tissue between them is excised.
- Edges are approximated with two wool sutures, and relaxing medicaments (adwiya murakhkhiya) are applied postoperatively.

3. Secondary Type (Acquired Entropion)

- When caused by prior incision or cauterisation, a linear incision below the eyelashes is made.
- Wound edges are separated, and soft packing is inserted to maintain spacing until healing occurs.

Ectropion *(Shatra Khārijiyya)*

Etiology

Shatra Khārijiyya occurs due to:

- Improper suturing by an inexperienced surgeon.or forceful eversion during surgery.
- Scarring or contraction after ulceration.

Surgical Management According to Al-Zahrāwī and Al-Majūsī

1. Primary Technique

- A curved needle with double silk suture is passed through the everted lid tissue—from inner to outer canthus and ends are pulled upward, and redundant tissue is excised with a scalpel *(mishraṭ)*.
- If the eyelid returns to normal alignment, no further step is required.

2. Secondary Correction (Lambda Technique)

- If eversion persists, two converging incisions are made, forming a λ-shaped angle.
- The triangular segment of tissue is excised. And edges are sutured with double silk, restoring the natural contour of the lid.

3. Ectropion from Faulty Suturing or Cautery

- A fresh incision is made below the eyelashes, avoiding old scar tissue. A medicated wick or cotton pad is inserted between the old and new wound to prevent re-adhesion.
- Regular dressing and mild cooling agents are used to reduce inflammation.

Postoperative Care

- Instil drops made from cumin and salt chewed together. and apply a pledget dressing *(Rifāda)* and secure with a bandage.
- Next day, remove the bandage and assess for inflammation *(Āshūb al-'Ayn)*. If inflammation occurs → treat as per ophthalmic guidelines. And if absent → apply *Shiyāf Aḥmar* (red suppository) or *Dharūr Aṣfar Ṣaghīr* (yellow styptic powder) to promote healing and prevent recurrence.

Shatrah-Ayn-'Arnabiyyah

(Lagophthalmos)

Definition

Shatrah-Ayn-'Arnabiyyah **(Lagophthalmos):** Failure of complete eyelid closure, resembling the rabbit's eye; due to shortening/retraction of lids, leaving the globe uncovered.

Aetiology (concise):

- **Congenital:** tissue deficiency of the eyelid → incurable.
- **Acquired**: cicatrization after ulcer/injury, postoperative scarring (e.g., after epilation procedures); faulty suturing/excess traction; cauterisation/incision scars.

Ibn Hubal's description aligns with upper-lid shortness, causing non-closure.

General Management Principles:

- If due to suturing/scar contracture → release/excise scar to restore lid mobility.
- If due to muscular spasm → *murakhkhī* (relaxing) measures.
- Avoid styptic/drying agents that worsen contracture and recurrence.

Surgical Procedure (Lagophthalmos/Entropion correction/Eyelid Inversion)

According to Al-Majūsī& Al-Zahrāwī

Goal: lengthen/release contracted lid and prevent re-cicatrization in faulty position.

Steps:

- **Exposure & Assessment:** Healthy eye covered; affected lid everted and scar band identified.
- **Incision/Excision:** Make a precise incision over the cicatrix or excise the thickened band to release contracture (avoid lid margin notching).
- **Edge Separation:** Bluntly separate wound edges to create a controlled gap; do not over-resect.
- **Packing/Spacer:** Insert fine linen strips/pledgets impregnated with

marham Munbit-i-Laḥm (flesh-generating ointment) between edges to maintain length and contour.

- **Bandaging:** Apply a firm, well-moulded bandage; keep both eyes relatively at rest. Adjunct Emollients (post-op): Poultices (fenugreek), fomentation with mallow + linseed water; diachylon plaster softened with oils on linen packs. Avoid styptics/driers.
- **Follow-up:** Maintain spacers until supple healing; monitor for inversion/ectropion; gentle lid exercises when epithelialized.

Prognosis: Correction of inversion/lagophthalmos is achievable by release and emollient healing; complete cosmetic restoration is not guaranteed; success hinges on preventing re-contracture.

Sha'r Zā'id
(Dystichiasis, Extra or Misdirected Eyelashes)

Definition

Growth of eyelashes outside their natural site, causing irritation or injury to the eye surface.

Etiology (*Asbāb*)

- Excess growth due to thick morbid humour (*Ghalīẓ wa Fasid Mādda*) producing superfluous hair.
- May follow chronic inflammation, trauma, or repeated epilation.

Clinical Features (*'Alāmāt*)

- Visible abnormal lashes emerging outside the natural margin.
- Continuous friction over the cornea and conjunctiva, leading to irritation, watering, or ulceration.

Surgical Management

Classical Opinions by Al-Rāzī, Al-Majūsī, Al-Zahrāwī, Al-Ṭabarī

Four principal classical methods are described; later, Unani surgeons combined or modified them according to severity.

1. *Ilzāq* (Adhesion / Sticking Method)

- Adhesive substances are applied to the eyelid margin to seal follicles and prevent regrowth of extra lashes.
- Used for mild, early cases.

2. *Kayy* (Cauterisation) by Al-Rāzī and Al-Majūsī

- Abnormal hair first plucked; root then touched with heated *Mikwā* (cautery needle). Cautery destroys the follicle permanently.
- Treat 1 – 2 lashes per sitting only to avoid thermal injury. In extensive cases, repeat after complete healing.

- Eye protected by pulling lid away or covering with *Madda Samaghiyya* (gum barrier).

3. Pruning / Stitching Method *(Qadḥ Sha'r Zā'id)* by Al-Zahrāwī and Al-Majūsī

- Needle with thread passed through eyelid margin → controlled eversion of lid.a linear incision (from *Āmāq to Āmāq*) made along abnormal follicles.
- Three sutures applied (central + angles).
- Only the skin of the eyelid incised— deeper tissues spared.

Post-operative dressing:

Dust *Dharūr Aṣfar* (yellow powder), and cover with vinegar-water compress to prevent Waram (swelling). healing within ≈ 3 days.

Outcome: shortens eyelid and corrects inturned lashes.

4. *Taqṣīr Al-Ajfān* (Shortening of Eyelid)

For multiple or diffuse lash rows.

- Eyelid muscle fixed between two wooden splints and tied until controlled necrosis (≈ 10 days).
- If excessive shortening → apply *Murakhkhiyāt* (relaxants); if laxity persists → use *Qābiḍāt* (astringents).

Thread-Insertion / Pirōnā Technique (Al-Rāzī, Al-Ṭabarī)

A minimally invasive Unani method for misdirected eyelashes *(Dystichiasis)*.

Instruments & Materials

- Fine sewing needle.
- Human hair thread → coated with wax for strength and smooth passage.

Technique

- Fold hair, insert both ends into the needle eye, forming a loop.

- Evert eyelid; pass the needle from the conjunctival to the cutaneous side.
- Draw looped hair through tissue; trim ends flush.
- If breakage occurs, retrieve the remnant gently; avoid reusing the same tract.
- Reinforce with wax coating × 7 times for fixation.

Precautions

- Handle delicately to prevent tissue trauma or Waram.
- Use a new puncture for repeat, never the same site.

Therapeutic Principles & Post-operative Care

- Use relaxing *(Murakhkhiyāt)* or mild astringent *(Qābiḍāt)* agents based on lid tone after healing, and avoid harsh or styptic substances that induce contraction.
- Maintain ocular hygiene; apply rose oil + egg yolk dressings if irritation occurs.
- Follow with gentle fomentation using mallow and linseed water. And protect eyes from wind and sunlight until full epithelial recovery.

ʿAmal-e-Tashmīr

Definition & Indication

ʿAmal-e-Tashmīr refers to the surgical elevation and excision of the eyelid skin to correct abnormal eyelash growth *(Shaʿr Zāʾid)* or misdirected lashes (Trichiasis / Distichiasis) causing corneal irritation, tearing, or ulceration.

Indicated when conservative measures—such as plucking *(Nazaʿ)*, adhesion *(Ilzāq)*, or cauterisation *(Kayy)*—fail to relieve symptoms.

Patient Position & Preparation

- Patient placed supine with head supported in the surgeon's lap, and the healthy eye is covered; the surgeon sits at the head-end.

- Long lashes are first epilated manually using mastagī (resin) to gather hairs for control.
- Small, subdermal lashes may be localised using a curved needle passed from the conjunctival surface to the skin surface.

Operative Technique by Al-Majūsī & Al-Zahrāwī

Step 1 – Eversion and Incision

- The upper eyelid is everted and stabilised with the left hand. And a fine lancet *(al-Mibḍa')* initiates a horizontal incision along the lash line—extending from the greater to the lesser tear canal *(al-kuway al-kabīr → al-kuway al-ṣaghīr).*
- The incision remains superficial, avoiding deep penetration to prevent hair root inversion or ocular injury.

Step 2 – Skin Elevation and Suturing

- Three sutures are placed through the incised skin. The threads are gently lifted by the assistant to elevate the lid margin away from the cornea.
- Elevation must be moderate—excessive traction may lead to ectropion (outward turning) or cosmetic deformity.

Step 3 – Excision of Redundant Skin

- The elevated fold of skin is excised with fine scissors *(Miqrāḍ),* and the two edges are reapproximated and sutured, using special knots where the suture enters internally and loops outward for firm closure.

Step 4 – Wound Management & Dressing

- Apply *Dharūr Aṣfar* (yellow antiseptic powder) over the incision.
- Traditional soothing: a mixture of salt and cumin saliva used as local eye fomentation. And covered with soft linen/gauze and bandaged.
- Suture Removal: After 2–3 days, threads are cut; healing ointment *(Marham Munbit-i-Laḥm)* is applied for tissue repair.

Alternative / Adjunct Techniques by Al-Zahrāwī and Al-Majūsī

A. Ischemic Compression *(Taqṭīr bil-Qaʿṣāb)*

- Target skin segment compressed between two wooden clamps to stop blood flow. Necrosed part dries, blackens, and sloughs off naturally; the site is then sutured and treated as above.

B. Myrtle Leaf Technique *(Waraq al-Ās)* by *Al-Zahrāwī*

- The inner eyelid is marked in a myrtle leaf shape (for accurate cosmetic contour).
- Skin within marking is excised via two parallel incisions, guided by anatomical symmetry.
- The flap is dissected using a hook *(Ṣunnāra),* sutured with woollen thread for aesthetic outcome.

C. Thread or Hook-Assisted Elevation

- If hooks are unavailable, three threads (central + two corners) are inserted under the eyelid.
- These threads are lifted together to expose and remove the redundant skin, then sutured as per standard technique.

Post-operative Management

- Treat mild *Waram* (inflammation) with wax-based *Musakkina* (soothing ointments).
- *Murakhkhiyāt* (relaxants) for tight lids; *Qābiḍāt* (astringents) if excessive laxity.
- Avoid dryness and irritation; maintain ocular hygiene and apply rose-oil poultices.
- Protect from sunlight, wind, and physical strain until complete healing (3–4 days).

Sha'r Munqalib

(Trichiasis, Inward-Growing Eyelashes)

Definition

Trichiasis (*Sha'r Munqalib*) refers to the inversion or inward curling of eyelashes, causing continuous friction over the cornea and conjunctiva. The condition results in pain, tearing, and may progress to corneal opacity (Bayāḍ al-'Ayn) or ulceration if untreated.

Indications for Surgery by Ibn Zuhr, Al-Rāzī, and Al-Zahrāwī

Surgical correction is advised when:

1. One or a few misdirected lashes irritate plucking or adhesion.
2. Multiple recurrent lashes or deeply rooted aberrant hairs resist conservative treatment.
3. Secondary complications such as ulceration, opacity, or chronic inflammation develop.

General Principles of Management

- Minor, isolated lashes → managed by epilation (Naza') or cauterisation (Kayy).
- Recurrent or multiple lashes → treated by surgical excision or reconstruction ('Amal al-Tashmīr / incision and suturing).
- Postoperative care aims to preserve eyelid contour and prevent recurrence.

I. Minor Procedures for Limited Trichiasis

Epilation and Adhesion Method

- Offending lash is plucked or adhered to adjacent lash using Lu'āb (saliva) or Mastagī (resin) to redirect it away from the globe.It is effective for one or two lashes only.

Cauterisation *(Kayy)*

- Following lash removal, the follicular root is touched with a heated fine needle *(Mikwāh)* to destroy the base and prevent regrowth.
- Treat only 1–2 lashes per sitting to avoid scarring.
- After cautery → apply Safīdī Bayḍa(White Egg) and Ravghan Gul (rose oil) for cooling and healing.

II. Extensive Trichiasis (Multiple or Recurrent Lashes)

Eyelid Margin Excision / ʿAmal al-Qadḥ al-Shaʿr

- The eyelid margin containing aberrant follicles is excised.
- Three sutures are applied—central and at both angles—to lift the margin and separate lashes from the cornea.
- Dressing with Dharūr Aṣfar (yellow antiseptic powder) and gentle bandaging until healing.

Excision and Suturing (*ʿAmal-e-Tashmīr*)

- For deep or multiple lashes, a horizontal incision is made along the lash line using *al-Mibḍaʿ* (surgical knife). The affected strip of tissue is removed, and the wound is sutured with fine silk or cotton thread.
- Caution: Incorrect depth may cause Shatra or lid deformity.
- Cooling agents (Araq-e-Gulāb) and soothing regimens maintain *Mizāj al-ʿAyn* (ocular temperament) post-surgery.

III. Thread-Loop Extraction Technique

For 1–3 misdirected lashes (*Shaʿr Zāʾid*), Al-Zahrāwī introduced a loop-thread surgical method, providing precise correction with minimal trauma.

Steps:

- A fine needle is threaded with smooth silk, forming a loop with a knot; a secondary inner loop may be added. The needle passes beneath the eyelid near the aberrant lash base and emerges through the skin margin.
- The misdirected lashes are inserted into the loop; gentle traction

draws them outward to align with natural lashes.

- The loop and thread are removed, the eyelid is bandaged for 2–3 days to allow tissue regeneration *(Inbat -e-Laḥm)* and fixation.

- For short lashes, attach longer natural hair to assist traction, or delay until hair growth allows secure looping.

Postoperative Regimen

- Maintain gentle ocular hygiene and avoid excessive rubbing or discharge exposure.
- Apply Ravghan Gul + Zardi-e-Bayḍa as emollient dressing.
- Monitor for Waram (inflammation); if present, use *Murakhkhiyāt* (relaxants) or *Qābiḍāt* (astringents) accordingly.
- Avoid exertion, anger, or exposure to sunlight until healing.

Prognosis & Therapeutic Principle

All classical Unani surgeons — Ibn Zuhr, Al-Rāzī, Al-Zahrāwī, and Al-Majūsī— emphasise that:

- Mild *trichiasis* responds to *Kayy* (cautery) or adhesion.
- Severe/recurrent forms require surgical excision (*ʿAmal al-Tashmīr*).

Aim: restore eyelid alignment, preserve corneal integrity, and prevent blindness.

- Aesthetic correction is secondary to functional preservation.

Diseases of the Lacrimal Apparatus

Gharab

(Lacrimal Fistula / Fistula lacrimalis)

Definition

Gharab: abscess at Āmāq-i-Akbar (medial canthus) with external or internal pus discharge; if neglected → nāsūr of lacrimal sac with chronic suppuration, soft-tissue loss, and possible nasal bone erosion.

The lesion lies between the medial canthus and lateral nasal wall; swelling may incline outward (visible oedema/fluctuance) or inward (concealed; harder to diagnose).

Nature of Discharge

In *Gharab*, the abscess may rupture spontaneously, releasing purulent material through different routes:

1. **External drainage** – pus discharges outward without tissue necrosis.
2. **Nasal drainage** – pus tracks into the nasal cavity, occasionally regurgitating into the conjunctival sac.
3. **Bidirectional flow** – discharge occurs both outwardly and inwardly at the same time.

Depth of Involvement

1. **Superficial discharge** – confined to the surface; bone remains unaffected.
2. **Deep-seated discharge** – penetrates deeply, causing bony destruction *(Fasād al-ʿAẓm);* neglected cases may lead to erosion of the nasal bone.

Prognostic Indicators

1. **Outward drainage** → usually easy to treat, especially once a

fistulous opening *(Nāsūr)* has formed.

2. **Inward or ocular drainage** → difficult to manage, marked by recurrent pain and persistent epiphora .

Surgical Management

Indications & Early Surgery

- Do not wait for full suppuration near *Āmāq;* early incision prevents rupture toward the eye and chronic fistulae.
- Operate for chronic fistulae, recurrent abscess, persistent epiphora, or suspected bony involvement.

Operative Options by Ibn Hubal, Al-Rāzī and Al-Zahrāwī

Excision / Curettage of Fistula (Primary method)

- Open the tract, evacuate pus; excise necrotic/hypertrophied tissue down to a healthy base.
- Assess bone with probe:
- Bone intact → manage with *adwiya munbit-i-laḥm* (granulation-promoters).
- Bone diseased (fasād al-ʿaẓm) → scrape/curette until sound bone appears.

Cauterisation *(Kayy)* vs Caustics *(Adwiya ḥādda)*

- If bone is necrotic or tract is stubborn: red-hot smooth cautery to carbonise and free crusts; eye protected with cold flour paste/linen or saline sponge.
- Caustic drugs are alternatives where cautery is unsuitable, but *kayy* preferred for reliability. Repeat 2–3 times until sloughs are shed.

Creation of Nasal Passage (rhinonasal drainage; Dacryocystorhinostomy)

- After debridement, perforate toward the nasal cavity—low and

toward the nasal cartilage *(ghuḍrūf al-Anf),* never the orbital side.

Success sign: bleeding from the nose/mouth. Then dilate/cauterise the tract to keep it wide and clean; pack with cotton + marham-i-zingār, or apply cooling distillates (*Shiyāf-i-Māmīthā, ʿArq-i-Kāsni, ʿArq-i-Makū, ʿArq-i-Sadābahār*). Do not leave the cavity empty.

- Some surgeons advocate thaqb routinely, Al-Rāzī often preferred definitive cautery alone unless drainage demanded.

Post-operative Care

- Repeated cleansing; pack with cotton soaked in *Āb-i-Kharnūb Nabṭī Raṭb* (fresh carob juice) to promote closure.
- Dress with *adwiya qābiḍa* (styptic/astringent);

Durable cure: cavity fills with granulation, discharge ceases, no recurrence for 40 days (Al-Zahrāwī).

Diseases of the Conjunctiva

Ẓafara , Nākhūna

Pterygium, Ungula

(Excrescence of Canthus)

General Description

Nākhūna **(Pterygium)**: a membranous, firm, vascular growth (usually red; sometimes whitish/yellowish) arising from *ṭabaqa multaḥima* (Conjunctiva), most often at the greater canthus (may rarely start at the lesser canthus), spreading over the ocular surface; with progression may encroach on qarniyya and obstruct the visual axis.

Classical Descriptions & Management

Al-Rāzī (Rhazes)

Classified Nākhūna into two forms:

1. Mild and thin type – causes minimal disturbance in vision; treated with *Shiyāf Akhḍa*r and *Bāslīqūn*.

2. Thick and heavy type – obstructs sight; treatment involves the use of kusht (caustic agent) followed by surgical excision with a hook (Ṣunnāra).

Thābit ibn Qurra

Dense hypertrophic mass from the nasal canthus, spreading across the conjunctiva.

Early/soft →treated with Warming & detergents (*nūshādar, qulqand, qulqandīs, bīkh-i sūsan; Shiyāf Qaysar*).

Advanced/indurated → When thick and indurated, excision was considered necessary.

Sarāfiyūn

"Nervous" hypertrophy from the nasal canthus → cornea; severe lesions may cover the pupil → blindness.

Large/indurated/chronic → surgical excision;

small/soft/recent → *adwiya ḥādda* (caustic/burning).

Muḥammad ibn Zakariyya Al-Rāzī

Membrane-like growth from the nasal canthus across the sclera *(Bayāḍ al-'Ayn)* towards the cornea;

- If it extends near the pupillary zone, the damage becomes serious.
- Mild and early form → *Shiyāf Akhḍar*.
- Thick and advanced form → *'Amal-i-Kusht*.

Abū Al-Qāsim Al-Zahrāwī (Albucasis)

Distinguished two forms of Ungula (Pterygium):

1. Nervous form – resembling a fine, tough membrane.

2. Non-nervous form – resembling a white coagulated exudate, which disintegrates when touched by cautery or hook.

Both varieties begin at the greater canthus and spread progressively until they cover the pupil, impairing both vision and ocular motility.

Etiology

Due to the accumulation of excessive morbid matter in the conjunctiva, extremes of *ḥarārat / burūdat* predispose and aggravate.

Types of Pterygium with Management

1) First Type

Thin membranous from one side of the conjunctiva (*Ṭabaqa Multaḥima*). (distinguish from corneal opacity, which encircles).

Management: Gentle suction if soft; if adherent → Surma (avoid instruments). If slightly elevated → careful excision without injuring *ṭabaqa multaḥima* (to avoid corneal ulcer/vision loss).

2) Second Type

Arises from the canthal margins *(watad)* and extends toward the cornea, thickens, and darkens; it halts at *Iklīl.*

Management: Responds to *Jali* (detergent) & *Muḥarrik* (stimulant) drugs.

3) **Third Type**

This type completely spreads over the corneal surface, covering the pupillary area and leading to significant visual impairment, often progressing to complete blindness.

Careful examination is required:

- If fine hair-like vascular streaks are seen within the lesion, medical treatment is possible.
- If these vascular signs are absent, it is referred to as *Ẓafara 'Aẓīma* (major pterygium), which is extremely firm like a nail and does not respond to medical therapy.

Surgical Management

Indications: When *Nākhūna* rises above the conjunctival surface *(Ṭabaqa Multaḥima),* or thick/firm with optical involvement; requires surgical excision with *Ṣunnāra.*

Technique :

1. **Elevation** — two *Ṣunnāra* placed beneath *Nākhūna* tips toward the canthus lift gently to test adhesions.
2. **Excision** — advance hook under lesion and peel (like animal skin); long, semi-circular, backwards-curved instrument of moderate sharpness; The excision is carried out up to the fleshy masses.

Immediate care — chew Cumin *(Zira),* apply juice, bandage; at midnight remove bandage, cleanse, repeat with cumin + salt; next day apply *Rūshnā'ī* and *Bāslīqūn.*

Classical Surgical Management

Ibn Zakariyā Al-Razi

Al-Razi describes two forms of Ẓafara:

- One is loosely adherent *(Mu'allaq),* which can be suspended and easily removed.
- The other is firmly united *(Muttahid),* requiring careful dissection.

Method :

suspend *Ẓafara* with a slightly curved, sharp needle, pass another threaded oblique-eyed needle to lift; if non-adherent, it separates; if adherent, dissect with *Mishrat* (moderately sharp); *Ṣunnāra* may elevate for limited scissor excision; *Āla Farj-Numa* (smooth, concave, comb-like ridges) to undermine.

Post-op:

saline + Cumins; *Safedi Bayza* + bandage; next day open, encourage ocular movements; repeat saline/standard therapy; if waram ḥārr → soothing meds.

Al-Majūsī(Haly Abbas)

Supine; soft pigeon feather slipped beneath lesion to separate; scrape reddish part with small knife; or pass fine sharp needle canthal-to-limbus to elevate/dissect; slender stylus fixes margin; remaining tissue lifted and scissored; avoid complete excision to prevent *Dam'a* (epiphora).

Post-op:

salt + cumin water, then *Zardi Bayza* + *Ravghan Gul* on bandage; next day assess; if heat/inflammation → *Shiyaf Abyaḍ* and treat as Conjunctivitis.

Abū Al-Qāsim Al-Zahrāwī (Albucasis)

Elevation: hook lifts Ungula; curved needle with thread/hair secures; traction for exposure.

Dissection: near *Ḥadaqa* with gentle sawing; excise residual at canthus but preserve *Laḥma Ma'aq* to prevent epiphora.

Alternatives: complete hook/thread extraction; blunt scraping, avoid corneal injury.

Post-op:

Instant powdered salt/verdigris collyrium; bandage 1 day; daily to heal.

Management of Non-Nervous Ungula *(Ghayr 'Aṣabi)*

- When the lesion cannot be lifted with a hook or pierced with a needle, it is treated medically in most cases.
- If surgery is attempted, a smooth, blunt scalpel is used to scrape the lesion gradually. If the tissue crumbles, red or verdigris collyria are applied, and the process is repeated until healing is achieved.
- If an abscess develops, surgical intervention is halted until the abscess resolves.

Diseases of the Cornea

Sabal (Jālā)

(Corneal Pannus, Vascular Keratitis)

Definition and Clinical Features

Sabal (Jālā) is a thin, membranous corneal opacity from engorged/ruptured ocular vessels. Symptoms: ocular redness, indurated lids, tearing, itching, photic discomfort; patients may sneeze or have nasal itching in sunlight; vision appears smoky. Considered hereditary by some; others note contagion.

Description by Abū Al-Qāsim Al-Zahrāwī

A network of abnormal vessels over the cornea that impairs vision and weakens the eye correlates with Corneal Pannus / Vascular Keratitis.

Pathogenesis According to Al-Rāzī

Results from *Dam Ghalīẓ* (thick, viscous blood) congesting ocular vessels → *Ḥumra* (redness), *Sailān* (lacrimation), *Ḥikka* (itching); analogised to *Dawālī* (varices) due to vascular engorgement.

Etiopathology

An *imtilā'ī* state (vascular engorgement) from thick blood in ocular veins → Waram (inflammation) with congestion, redness, pruritus.

Systemic Correlation

Intense ocular vascular engorgement may make objects appear red, suggesting *Imtilā' Dimāgh* (cerebral congestion/meningeal involvement) or *Waram Ḥārr* (acute inflammation).

Epidemiology

More frequent in hot, humid climates; noted as both contagious and hereditary — consistent with infectious keratitis (e.g., trachoma pannus) and genetic predisposition to corneal neovascularisation.

Types and Clinical Features of Corneal Pannus *(Sabal)*

1) Intracranial Vascular Origin

Cloud-like red streaks on the cornea; severe itching, sneezing, profuse tearing, lash disturbance, deep ocular pulsation.

2) Extracranial Vascular Origin

Burning lids, cheek redness, temporal throbbing; congested conjunctival–corneal vessels like clouds spreading over cornea → *Sabal* (Pannus).

3) Thin, Non-Chronic *(Sabal Raqīq Ghayr Muzmin)*

Fine, web-like membrane over Sawād al-ʿAyn with delicate red vessels; little visual impact.

Management: *Shiyāf Aḥmar, Shiyāf Akhḍar, Bāsalīqūn.*

4) Thick, Chronic *(Sabal Ghalīẓ Muzmin)*

Marked neovascular membrane, vision-affecting.

Management: *Luqṭah* (surgical lifting) with *Ṣanābīr* (hooks) or thread, then scissors excision;

post-op, Cumin water and *Dharūr Aṣfar* (yellow dusting powder).[8]

General Clinical Signs

Membranous corneal opacity, smoky/soot-like discolouration, prominent red streaks, photophobia with difficulty in sunlight/lamplight.

Surgical Management of Sabal (Corneal Pannus / Vascular Keratitis)

General Principles of Surgical Treatment

As Sabal *(Jālā)* arises from vascular engorgement of the ocular and cranial vessels, phlebotomy *(Faṣd)* of related veins is considered an essential preliminary step to relieve congestion.

Before surgery, a light diet *(ghidhā' khafīf)* and a preparatory regimen are prescribed.

Operative Technique According to Classical Surgeons

Positioning and Preparation

- The patient is placed supine, with the head slightly tilted. The surgeon opens and fixes the eyelids using *Miftāḥ al-ʿAyn* (eye speculum) for exposure.

Elevation and Fixation of the Membrane

- The pannus membrane *(Jālā)* is gently lifted with three fine hooks *(Ṣunnāra)*—
- one at the inner canthus, one at the outer canthus, and one beneath the lid margin. This allows clear separation from the *ṭabaqa multaḥima* (conjunctiva).

Excision of the Membrane

- A probe *(Al-Misbār)* is inserted beneath the pannus (as in *Nak̲ūnah / Pterygium* surgery). The upper half of the pannus is removed first, then the lower half.

The corneal surface is palpated with a smooth instrument—

- If smooth, removal is complete;
- If resistance is felt, residual vessels remain and should be excised.

Immediate Postoperative Care

- Apply chewed cumin and salt locally (antiseptic and anti-inflammatory). Dress with egg yolk mixed with *Ravghan-e-gul* (rose oil).
- Bandage the eyelid, instructing the patient to move the eyeball frequently to prevent adhesions between the cornea and eyelid.

Modified Technique According to Zakariyyā Al-Rāzī

Al-Rāzī opposed repeated suspension and piecemeal excision using bent needles, as it caused:

- Excessive bleeding,
- Inflammation (Waram), and
- Incomplete clearance of pannus.

Recommended Technique

- A thread (Khayṭ) is passed beneath the pannus using a curved needle *(Mibḍa' Munḥanī)*. The pannus is suspended and stabilised by the thread before a single, controlled excision is made.
- This ensures minimal bleeding, reduced inflammation, and complete removal in one step.

Surgical Technique According to Al-Zahrāwī Operative Steps

Elevation: Pannus and its abnormal vessels were gently lifted with fine hooks.

Excision: Vessels are cut precisely using scissors while maintaining corneal integrity.

Precautions:

Maintain a steady hand to prevent corneal injury. and perform slowly and meticulously under good light.

Postoperative Management

- Instil *Shiyāf Aḥmar or Shiyāf Akhḍar* to destroy remnants.
- If pannus is not fully removed in one sitting, then apply soothing plaster and allow inflammation to subside.
- Repeat the procedure after a few days until the corneal surface clears.

Midda Kāmina / Qalṭāyā

Hypopyon Ulcer

Definition

Hypopyon refers to a collection of pus in the anterior chamber of the eye, located behind the cornea.

When small, it may resemble *ṭarfa* (subconjunctival haemorrhage); when extensive,

It fills the corneal base. When associated with corneal ulceration and necrosis, it is termed *Qalṭāyā* or *Qalṭārā*.

Etiology (Asbāb)

- *Mādda* (morbid matter) descending from the brain accumulates behind the cornea, undergoes *ta'affun* (putrefaction), and forms pus.
- Trauma to the cornea producing a wound that closes externally, trapping pus within.
- Severe ophthalmia *(Āshūb al-'Ayn)* leading to inflammatory secretions and secondary abscess formation.

Surgical Management

Ibn Hubal Al-Baghdādī

- When medical therapy fails, make an incision at the corneal limbus *(Akhlīl)* or at the site used for cataract surgery *('Amal al-Qadḥ)* to drain the pus.
- After evacuation, the site is treated as an ordinary corneal ulcer *(Qarḥ al-Qarniyya)*.

Al-Majūsī (Haly Abbas)

- Incision made at *Akhlīl* using a fine scalpel *(Mibḍa' Laṭīf)*, avoiding deep penetration into the stroma.
- After pus evacuation, irrigate and treat as a corneal ulcer. Breast milk of a newly delivered mother may be instilled, followed by

dressing and bandaging.

Abū Al-Qāsim Al-Zahrāwī

Preoperative Assessment

Patient seated upright; gentle head shaking to differentiate:

Mobile pus → Hypopyon.

Fixed opacity → Cataract.

Operative Procedure

If pus remains immobile, make a small incision above the corneal tunic at the junction of the cornea and conjunctiva to allow drainage.

Postoperative Care

- Instil hot honeyed water or decoction of fenugreek with honey.
- Continue standard corneal ulcer therapy until healing is complete.

Diseases of the Iris

(Amrāḍ Ṭabaqa 'Inabiyya)

Morsarj

(Iridoptosis / Prolapse of the Iris)

Definition

The term *Morsarj* derives from *Mūrsarah*, meaning "the head of an ant", describing the prolapsed iris bulging through a corneal wound to a similar size.

Etiology

- Traumatic rupture of the cornea *(jarāḥat-e-qarīniyya)*
- Non-healing corneal ulcer or perforation
- Corneal melting due to suppurative processes — allowing part of the iris *('Inabiyya)* to protrude outward.

Classical Types of Iris Prolapse

1. ***Morsarj / Namalī*** – Iris protrusion the size of an ant's head.
2. ***Ra's al-Dhubābī (Dhubābī)*** – The size of a fly's head.
3. ***'Inabiyya / 'Inabī*** – Resembling a grape.
4. ***Tuffāḥī*** – Large, apple-sized protrusion.
5. ***Mismārī / Falakī*** – Chronic type where the prolapsed iris adheres to surrounding corneal tissue.

Surgical Management of Iris Prolapse *(Morsarj)*

Surgical Technique by Ibn Hubal Al-Baghdādī

- Old or chronic cases are incurable *(lā 'Ilāj);* surgery is performed only for cosmetic correction, not for restoring vision.

Operative Technique:

- A needle threaded with silk is passed beneath the prolapsed iris *(Morsarj),* and the thread is drawn to the opposite side. And the lifted segment is excised with scissors *(Al-Miqaṣṣ)* or a scalpel *(Qumādīn).*

Postoperatively, compresses of *Shādanj Maghsūl* or rose preparations *(Wardī)* are applied, followed by egg yolk dressing *(Safīdī Bayza).*

Alternative Method:

- Two threads are passed under the prolapse — one tied upward (toward the upper lid) and one downward. Gradual traction causes shrinkage until the prolapsed portion detaches naturally.
- Styptics like *Shādanj* and *Gil Makhtūm* control bleeding.

Surgical Technique of ʿAlī ibn al-ʿAbbās Al-Majūsī

The goal is cosmetic improvement rather than visual restoration.

Surgical Steps:

- **Needle Placement:** Insert a fine needle at the root of the prolapse under the upper eyelid; insert a second needle near the inner canthus.

- **Thread Application:** Pass a thread through both puncture sites, then divide the loop and tie one part upward, the other downward, securing the prolapse.

- **Excision:** The prolapsed portion gradually separates under gentle traction.

Postoperative Measures:

- Instil cumin and salt juice for cleansing. Apply gauze soaked in egg yolk and Ravghan-e-Gul (rose oil) and bandage firmly.
- On the next day, remove dressing and instil *Shiyāf Abyaḍ* till healing completes.

Care and Follow-up:

Regular lubricating therapy prevents adhesion of eyelids to the cornea and promotes gradual shrinkage of the prolapsed iris, ensuring a satisfactory cosmetic outcome.

Diseases of the Lens

(Amrāḍ al-Ruṭūbat al-Jalīdiyya)

Nuzūl al-Mā' (Cataract)

Definition

Nuzūl al-Mā' (Cataract) is an ocular disorder in which a dense or turbid humour obstructs the passage of light through the pupil and lens *(Ruṭūbat Jalīdiyya),* resulting in progressive visual impairment.

This occurs when a viscid humour accumulates between the iris *(Ṭabaqa 'Inabiyya)* and corneal membrane *(Ḥijāb Qarnī)* or within the pupillary axis, thereby blocking visual rays.

Definition: According to Al-Ṭabarī

Al-Ṭabarī explains *Nuzūl al-Mā'* as:

"An excess in the quantity (*Kammiyya*) and quality (*Kayfiyya*) of the aqueous humour (*Ruṭūbat Bayḍiyya*), obstructing the pupillary aperture (*Ḥadaqa*)."

Pathogenesis and Mechanism

1. Obstruction of Light Transmission

- A thickened humour or opacity blocks light passing through the iris and lens, leading to visual loss.

2. Localisation of Opacity

The opacity usually lies:

- Between the iris and cornea, most commonly,
- Behind the pupil, or
- Within the pupillary opening — obstructing the *Ruṭūbat Jalīdiyya* from transmitting light.

- Evidence from couching (*'Amal al-Qaḍḥ*) shows that after displacement of the opacity, the pupil regains its normal size, confirming the cataract's anterior location.

3. Visual Effects

Depending on the opacity's density and position, vision may be:

- Completely lost,
- Partially obstructed (half or one-third image), or
- Doubled (diplopia).

Etiology *(Asbāb)*

A. External Causes *(Asbāb Khārijiyya)*

- Trauma or head injury causing humoral accumulation between *Ghishā' 'Ankabūtiyya* (coverings of lens) and *Ṭabaqa 'Inabiyya* (Iris).
- Descent of matter from the ventricles of the brain *(Buṭūn al-Dimāgh)* into the optic nerve *('Aṣb Mujawwaf)*.
- If opacity forms within the nerve itself, Qaḍḥ (couching) is ineffective.

B. Internal Causes *(Asbāb Dākhiliyya)*

- Accumulation of Humours (Ruṭūbāt) – Dense vapours (*Bukhārāt Ghalīẓa*) ascend from the stomach or body to the eyes, depositing thick fluids.
- Weakness of Innate Heat *(Ḥarārat Gharīziyya)* – Causes stagnation and incomplete transformation (*Istiḥāla*).
- Headache (Ṣudā') / Shaqīqah – Alters humours and predisposes to opacity.
- Faulty Regimen *(Sū' Tadbīr)* – Cold exposure, poor diet, or exhaustion aggravate humoral imbalance.

Views of Classical Physicians

View of Jālīnūs (Galen)

Cataract results from thickening of the aqueous humour *(Ruṭūbat*

Bayḍiyya) due to processes resembling fermentation *(Takarruj).*

Causes include:

- Moist temperament of the brain or stomach,
- Excessive rising vapours,
- Trauma to the head or eye,
- Weak visual spirit (*Rūḥ Bāṣir*) — particularly in the elderly.

He noted it is more common in dark-eyed individuals with a moist temperament.

View of Zakariyyā Al-Rāzī

In old age, *Nazūl al-Mā'* develops due to weak innate heat and incomplete resolution of vapours.

Predisposing factors include:

- Exposure to cold winds,
- Severe vomiting or trauma,
- Headache (*Ṣudā'*), and
- Chronic illness.

View of Al-Ṭabarī and Al-Rāzī

Both agree that *Nuzūl al-Mā'* originates from the derangement of aqueous humour *(Ruṭūbat Bayḍiyya)* and deposition of thick vapours between the iris and corneal layers, obstructing the path of visual spirit *(Rūḥ Bāṣir).*

Types of Cataract

Classification by Al-Rāzī

1. Based on colour and transparency:

1. Dark bluish and transparent (*Zarqi wa Ṣāfi*)
2. Glass-like (*Zujājī*)
3. White, snowball-like (*Baradī*)
4. Sky-colored (*Āsmānī*)

5. Green (*Akhḍar*)
6. Bluish-tinged (*Mā'il bi'l-Zarq*)[4]

2. Stable and Unstable Cataract

(a) Stable Cataract – *Mustahkam:*

- Complete blindness; the pupil appears altered.

(b) Unstable Cataract – *Ghayr Mustahkam:*

- Partial visual disturbance with floating specks like dust or mosquitoes.
- Often related to gastric disorders. However, when the condition is limited to one eye and persists, the stomach is not the cause. If it affects both eyes, sometimes worsening or easing with gastric conditions, its etiology may be related to the stomach.

Clinical Features of Cataract

Early Symptoms

According to *Kitāb al-Mukhtārāt fī al-Ṭibb*, in the initial stage of *Nazūl al-Mā'*, the patient perceives illusory visual forms like cloth, hair, clouds, sparks, or lightning before the eyes. These persist and gradually lead to clouded vision *(kudūrat al-baṣar),* usually in one eye.

Signs of Advancement

As described in *al-Ḥāwī*, when the fluid (*Mā'*) condenses and matures, the patient sees small flies or hair-like lines moving before the eyes. With progression, vision diminishes completely.

Cataracts appear in various colours — *Hawā'ī* (air-like), *Zujājī* (glass-like), *Abyaḍ* (white), *Akhḍar* (green), *Āsmānī* (sky-colored), and *Mā'i bi'l-Nīlgunī* (bluish) — the latter being dense and resistant to *Qaḍḥ* (couching).

Illusory Visual Phenomena

According to Al-Rāzī, illusory images may arise from three origins:

1. **Ocular (*Nuzūl al-Mā'*)** – unilateral, persistent, followed by pupillary opacity *(Kudūrat al-Ḥadaqa),* unaffected by digestion.
2. **Gastrointestinal (*Mushārakat al-Mi'da*)** – bilateral, fluctuate with digestion, disappear after vomiting or correctives.
3. **Cerebral (*Mushārakat al-Dimāgh*)** – continuous, associated with fever *(Ḥummayāt)* or *Waram al-Dimāgh*, unaffected by gastric changes.

Comparative Diagnosis:

- Bilateral & digestive variation → Gastrointestinal origin
- Unilateral & persistent → Cataract *(Nazūl al-Mā')*
- Continuous with febrile/neural signs → Cerebral origin.

Surgical Management of Cataract *(Nazūl al-Mā')*

Indications for Surgery

- Surgical intervention (*'Amal al-Qadḥ* – couching) is indicated when medical management fails, and the cataract progresses, obstructing light and impairing vision.
- Operation should only be undertaken when the cataract is fully matured (*Nuzūl al-Mā' Mustaḥkam*) and of moderate consistency.
- Premature surgery *(Nuzūl al-Mā' Ghayr Mustaḥkam)* is contraindicated as it may lead to recurrence or loss of vision.
- Operable cataracts are those resembling pearl-like *(Lūluwī),* air-like *(Hawā'ī),* or lime-colored *(Qalā'ī)* opacity, while excessively dense or thin opacities are unsuitable for surgery.

Pre-operative Preparation

- Systemic Purification *(Tanqiya' al-Badan)* – elimination of morbid humours to ensure body readiness.
- Cranial Purification *(Tanqiya' al-Ra's)* – local evacuation from the head to prevent complications.
- Surgery should be postponed if systemic fullness (Imtilā'), morbid humours *(Akhlāṭ Radīya),* or headache *(Ṣudā')* are present.
- These measures minimize post-operative inflammation (Waram)

and enhance recovery.

Determination of Operable and Inoperable Cataracts according to Ibn Zuhr, Al-Rāzī, Sarāfiyūn, Ibn Hubal, Al-Majūsī

Nature and Classification

- Cataract *(Nazūl al-Māʾ)* occurs due to opacity (*Māʾ*) between the iris (*Ṭabaqa ʿInabiyya*) and the lens (*Ruṭūbat Jalīdīya*).
- Operable cataracts (*Qābil al-Qadḥ*) are clear, soft, moderately solidified (Muʿtadil al-Jumūd), allowing light perception.
- Inoperable cataracts (Nā-Qābil al-Qadḥ) are black, green, chalk-like (Jaṣṣī), or excessively fluid (Raqīq).

Clinical Tests for Operable Cataracts

1. Light Perception Test *(Imtiḥān bi'l-Ḍawʾ)*

If the patient faces sunlight or a lamp and brightness is perceived, the cataract is operable.

2. Pupillary Response Test *(Imtiḥān bi'l-Thaqb)*

Thumb pressure and release over the eyelid; if the pupil dilates and returns, cataract is operable *(Qābil al-Qadḥ)*. Absence of response, inoperable *(Nā-Qābil al-Qadḥ)*.

3. Digital Pressure & Massage Test

Gentle rubbing of the eyelid; if opacity shifts, cataract is immature *(Ghayr Mustaḥkam)*. Fixed opacity indicates maturity *(Istihkām)* and operability.

4. Sneezing Test *(Imtiḥān bi'l-ʿAṭs)*

Sneezing-induced movement or light streak *(Shuʿāʿ Mustaṭīl)* signifies a thin and mobile cataract → operable.

5. Bread-and-Breath Test (Functional Stress Test)

Warm bread placed on eye; if opacity moves or clears → operable; if fixed → inoperable.

Colour and Consistency as Prognostic Indicators

Al-Rāzī, Ibn Hubal, Al-Ṭabarī

Operable: *Ḥadīdī* (iron-gray), *Asrabī* (silvery), *Lūlawī* (pearl-like), or glassy-white opacities—indicate moderate solidity and translucence.

Inoperable: *Jaṣṣī* (chalk-like), *Bardī* (snow-white), *Asmānjūmī* (bluish), or *Muntashir* (diffuse watery) forms—either too hard or fluid.

Colour correlation: Favourable prognosis with clear, bluish-white cataracts; poor with black, green, or opaque forms.

General Principles and Contraindications

Ibn Zuhr, Al-Rāzī, Al-Ṭabarī

- Surgery is contraindicated in systemic disorders, cephalgia (Ṣudāʿ), or if the cataract is immature or excessively hard/soft.
- Operable cataracts are white, pearl-like, transparent, moderately consistent, allowing partial light passage.
- Post-operative care includes rest, supine position, and avoidance of exertion, anger, intercourse, and alcohol.

ʻAmal Qadḥ (Couching Operation for Cataract)

Methods of *ʿAmal al-Qadḥ* according to Al-Rāzī, Al-Majūsī, Al-Zahrāwī, Al-Ṭabarī, and Ibn Hub Al-Baghdādī.

Indication & Principle

When medical therapy fails, and *Nuzūl al-Mā'* (cataract) obstructs vision, proceed to ʿAmal Qadḥ (couching) to displace the crystalline lens from the pupillary axis and restore light passage.

Pre-operative Preparation

- **Positioning & Setup:** Patient seated in front of surgeon; healthy eye covered, assistant stabilizes head. Partial shade, which receives sunlight, improves visualisation. Fasting prevents vomiting/hiccup.
- **Purification/Evacuation:** Systemic *Istifrāgh/Tanqiya' al-Badan*

and *Tanqiya' al-Ra's* to reduce inflammation (Waram) risk.

- **Contra-prepare:** Delay if Imtilāʾ, Akhlāṭ Radīyah, or Ṣudāʿ present.

Fixation & Gaze

- Surgeon stabilises globe with left thumb–index over lids; surgeon seated slightly higher.
- Healthy eye occluded; gaze directed to canthus major / *zāwiya ʿuẓmā,* improving access and stability.

Entry Site, Depth & Needle Handling

- **Instrument:** *Ālā al-Qadḥ/ Miqdaḥ* (couching needle).
- **Entry:** Near limbus *(Iklīl al-ʿAyn),* close to lesser canthus; some describe near posterior conjunctival margin (Al-Ṭabarī).
- **Depth control:** Do not exceed "half barley breadth" (~1 mm) initially; overall penetration equals distance from pupil to iris edge (Al-Zahrāwī).
- **Angle:** Slightly toward inner canthus / zāwiya ṣughrā to avoid *ṭabaqa 'inabiyya* (iris) and *ṭabaqa qarnīyya* (cornea).
- **Stability trick:** Use the blunt end to indent the entry point (pain tolerance + anti-slip).
- **Adjunct:** If the sclera is rigid, make a small conjunctival perforation with al-Barid to admit the needle (Al-Zahrāwī).

Displacement of the Cataractous Lens (Core Manoeuvre)

- Advance into free intraocular space; visually confirm whitish opacity behind cornea.
- Engage Nuzūl al-Mā' and depress inferiorly away from the pupillary axis; hold briefly to prevent re-ascent.
- If lens re-ascends, repeat depression without removing the needle; manipulate across quadrants for dense/adherent opacities; use multiple up–down strokes for *lazūjat/ ghilaẓat/ raqiqat.*
- Surgeon confirms subjective return of vision during the act (Al-Ṭabarī).

Intra-operative Precautions & Complications

- Avoid excessive force/deviation to prevent damage to *ṭabaqa 'inabiyya, ṭabaqa qarnīyya or ṭabaqa ʿankabūtīya.*
- If blood appears: pause, relieve pressure; minimal bleeding is usually benign. Small ocular fluid discharge may be favourable (Al-Ṭabarī).
- If pain on entry, a small blunt lancet nick may reduce discomfort and facilitate passage.

Withdrawal & Immediate Adjuncts

- Withdraw the needle slowly with gentle rotation.
- Topicals: powdered *milḥ* for hemostasis; *Zardi al-Bayḍ* + *Ravghan Gul* (egg yolk + rose oil) or egg white dressings; saline/rock-salt wash; cumin –based applications noted by Al-Majūsī /Al-Zahrāwī.

Post-operative Regimen & Follow-up

- **Bandaging:** Both eyes bandaged; patient supine in a dark room. Avoid sneezing, coughing, exertion, anger, sexual activity, and alcohol.
- **Diet**: *Ghidha Latīf, Māʾ al-Shaʿīr* for hydration/cooling; avoid *Muwallid Riyāḥ* and *Thaqīl Ghidhāʾ*.
- **Mobilisation:** Brief rapid eyeball movements beneath closed lids to prevent corneo-conjunctival adhesions (Al-Mukhtārāt).
- **Timeline:** Bandage loosen Day-3 (Al-Zahrāwī) and removed Day-7 if no Waram; delay vision testing early to prevent re-ascent (Al-Rāzī).
- **Recurrence management:** If re-ascent during healing, re-enter via the same tract—not a new puncture (Al-Rāzī).

Surgeries of the Ear, Nose, and Throat

Diseases of the Ear *(Amrāḍ-i-Udhun)*

Sudda al-Udhun/ Udhun Ghayr Mathqūb

(Ear Obstruction / Atresia of External Auditory Canal)

Etiology ***(Asbāb)***

Obstruction of the ear *(Sudda al-Udhun)* may occur due to:

- Growth of *al-Laḥm al-Zā'id* (fleshy tissue) within the ear canal.
- Closure of the auditory passage after Iltihām-i-Qarḥa (ulcer healing) or trauma.
- Accumulation of cerumen (earwax) causing impaction.
- *Udhun Ghayr Mathqūb* (congenital aural atresia) — absence of ear opening since birth.

Classification

- ***Mahsūs*** **(Perceptible Obstruction):** Visible and detectable upon examination.
- ***Ghayr Mahsūs / Makhfī*** **(Hidden Obstruction):** Concealed within the canal, requiring careful probing for detection.

Surgical Management According to Al-Majūsī, Al-Zahrāwī, and Ibn al Quff

1. Obstruction Due to Fleshy Growth ***(al-Laḥm al-Zā'id)***

Both Al-Zahrāwī and Al-Majūsī describe excision of abnormal tissue obstructing the auditory meatus.

- The fleshy mass is gently grasped with a *Ṣunnāra* (hook) and excised carefully to restore patency.
- Following removal, *Dharūr Aṣfar* (yellow astringent powder) is applied to control bleeding and assist healing.

2. Obstruction Due to Ulcer Healing or Scarring

- When the auditory passage closes due to scar formation, it is reopened *with Al-Mibḍa'* (scalpel). After incision, Dharūr Aṣfar is sprinkled locally for drying and wound stabilisation.
- In postoperative care, a small medicated plug coated with *Marham Misrī* (Egyptian ointment) is inserted to maintain canal patency during healing.

3. Deep-Seated Ear Obstruction *(Sudda Dākhilī)*

- When the blockage lies deeper within the Udhun Dākhilī (inner auditory canal), a smooth, slightly heated probe *(Al-Mirwād)* is introduced carefully to create a small perforation without injuring the *'Aṣab al-Udhun* (auditory nerve).
- A soft plug coated with *Marham Misrī* may be kept for a few days to ensure healing and continuous opening.

4. Superficial Ear Obstruction *(Sudda Ẓāhirī)*

- In superficial obstruction visible near the opening, a fine, double-edged scalpel is used to make a minimal incision under good illumination (sunlight preferred).
- The incision should be smooth and shallow, avoiding trauma to surrounding tissues.

5. Obstruction Due to Cerumen Impaction (Earwax Blockage)

- Excess cerumen is gently removed using a scoop. After evacuation, *Ravghan Badam Talkh* (Bitter Almond Oil) or *Ravghan Gul* (Rose Oil) is instilled to soften residues and maintain the moisture of the canal.

6. Congenital Imperforate Ear /Congenital Aural Atresia (*Udhun Ghayr Mathqūb Khilqī*)

- In *Udhun Ghayr Mathqūb Khīlqī*, the absence of an external opening since birth is corrected surgically.

- A precise incision is made at the expected site of the auditory canal using *Al-Mibḍa* (scalpel).
- A medicated wick soaked in *Ravghan Gul* (rose oil) and dusted with *Dharūr Aṣfar* is inserted to maintain patency during healing. The wick is periodically changed until complete epithelialization occurs.

Surgical Principles Emphasised by Classical Unani Surgeons

- Excision of *al-Laḥm al-Zā'id* (fleshy masses) and reopening of the canal when scarred. Use of *Marham Misrī* and *Dharūr Aṣfar* for postoperative healing and infection prevention.
- Probing (Al-Mirwād) to maintain patency and prevent closure. Caution to protect the *'Aṣab al-Udhun* (auditory nerve) during all procedures.

Diseases of the Nose

Hashm al-Anf / Kasr al-Anf

(Nasal Fracture)

Etiology

Hashm al-Anf / Kasr al-Anf (fracture of the nose) occurs primarily due to trauma, such as collision, fall, or direct impact on the nasal region. It may also develop secondary to ḥarārat (excessive heat) and fasād-e-akhlāṭ (morbid humours), particularly in the early stages of *Judhām* (leprosy).

In such cases, *Istirkhā'* (relaxation) of the nasal structures or fracture of the *Ghuḍrūf* (cartilage) providing nasal support may occur.

Management of Nasal Fracture *(Kasr al-Anf)*

Initial Measures

- Faṣd (venesection) of the *Qifāl* vein should be performed to reduce local congestion. The patient should follow dietary restrictions, avoiding heavy and irritant foods to prevent inflammation.

Mechanical Reduction of the Fracture

- Insert an instrument called *Minshal* (similar to *Minqash* / forceps) into the nasal passage. The device is expanded by compression and release, separating the collapsed nostrils.
- The nose is then manually straightened by applying gentle pressure with both hands until normal alignment is restored.

Correction of Severe Deformity

- In cases of marked deformity, splint-like sticks are inserted into the nostrils to support the collapsed portion. The ends are fixed externally with sirish (glue) or starch paste to maintain alignment.

- Packing should be changed every third day to prevent *ta'affun* (putrefaction).

Management of Mild Fractures

- In minor nasal fractures, simply lift the depressed nasal portion, insert *Minshal,* and apply the medicated dressing described earlier.
- Perform Faṣd of both Qifāl veins and ensure a light diet and careful handling during recovery to promote proper bone setting.

Special Consideration — Separation of Cartilage *(Ghuḍrūf)*

- When the *Ghuḍrūf* (nasal cartilage) separates from the *'aẓm* (nasal bone), healing becomes difficult.
- The nose should be lifted upward toward the forehead, and Minshal or splints inserted to maintain structure.
- Medicated dressing is applied transversely across the nasal bridge to preserve stability, especially if the cartilage remains attached.

Bawāsīr al-Anf

(Nasal Polyps)

In Unani medicine, *Bawāsīr al-Anf* (Nasal Polyps) are also termed *Marḍ Kathīr al-Arjul, Bish Pāyah, or Basfayij.*

Jālīnūs compared the growth to a fish with multiple fins, describing its soft texture and branching reddish vessels similar to the appendages of the fish *arbiyan*.

Pathogenesis

Sometimes the disease arises without visible polypoid masses, due to narrowing of the nasal passage and rigidity of vessels, producing pain and congestion. Unani physicians describe this vascular engorgement and obstruction as *Bawāsīr al-Anf,* analogous to hemorrhoidal swelling elsewhere in the body.

Clinical Features

The swelling usually appears in both nasal cavities, causing thickening of the nasal septum. Its surface shows greenish vascular streaks internally and externally. In some cases, ulceration leads to a fistula *(Nasūr)* formation, whereas others remain non-ulcerated.

Due to vascular tension and congestion, patients may experience epistaxis (*Dam al-Bawāsīr*). Recurrent bleeding, particularly in hot climates, causes physical weakness and discolouration of the complexion.

Types of Nasal Growths in Unani Literature

1. Cancerous Growths *(Saraṭān)*

In some patients, the swelling becomes hard and resembles *waram-e-damawī* (vascular inflammation). Greenish vessels may appear over the surface, with pressure and tightness (*Tamaddud*) around the orbit and frontal region. These signs indicate *Saraṭān* (cancer).

Surgical excision with iron instruments is contraindicated, as it may lead to severe haemorrhage or meningeal inflammation with fatal outcome.

Management of *Saraṭān*

Treatment focuses on general evacuation and head purgation, using agents such as *Sibr* (Aloe vera), *Mastagī* (Mastic), and preparations like *Ayarij* or *Ḥabb-al-Qoqā,* if the patient's temperament allows.

2. Non-Cancerous Growths *(Marḍ Kathīr al-Arjul)*

When the swelling is soft, non-malignant, and vascular, it is termed Kathīr al-Arjul. It may present as:

***Mutaqarriḥ* (ulcerated)** – managed according to standard Unani ulcer therapy.

***Ghayr Mutaqarriḥ* (non-ulcerated)** – treated by evacuation of the body using decoction of *Aftimūn* (Cuscuta epithymum) followed by head evacuation with *Ḥabb al-Iyarij*.

Surgical Considerations for Non-Cancerous Growths

Earlier, ancient unani surgeons recommended complete excision with iron instruments for non-malignant polyps. Some Later Physicians avoided this due to the risk of bleeding. However, later consensus supported surgical removal with caution to prevent vascular injury.

Differentiation between *Bawāsīr al-Anf* (Nasal Polyp) and *Saraṭān* (Cancer)

1. Clinical Differences

Bawāsīr al-Anf **(Nasal Polyp):**

- Presents with Warm pulsation *(Nabḍ Ḥārr),* softness, and a sense of heat in the palate *(Hiddat al-Ṭalū).*
- Often accompanied by discharge *(Sailān Mādda)* following catarrh or *Amrāḍ al-Ra's* (head disorders).

Saraṭān **(Cancer):**

- Shows persistent hardness *(ṣalābat),* dryness, and progressive enlargement.
- Initially, nasal passages remain clear, but nodular growths later expand and become destructive.

2. Diagnostic Examination

Palpation of Palate:

- Hard and fixed → suggests *Saraṭān.*
- Soft and pliable → indicates *Bawāsīr.*

Inspection and Probing:

- *Bawāsīr* produces moist discharge; growth is soft and compressible.
- *Saraṭān* remains dry, rigid, and enlarges steadily.

3. Anatomical Growth Pattern

- *Saraṭān* originates within the *tajwīf al-anf* (nasal cavity) and tends to extend toward the palate rather than spreading internally.
- Probing with an instrument helps assess hardness *(ṣalābat)* and rate of progression.

Surgical Management of Nasal Growths

Surgical Instruments

Classical Unani surgeons recommended highly refined and delicate instruments for nasal surgery:

- ***Mibḍa'* (scalpel)** — thin, one-sided, sharp edge with a blunt paper-like tip to avoid deep injury.
- ***Ṣunnāra / Mirwād* (hook/probe)** — to grasp and draw the fleshy growth outward.
- ***Ālā Kharita* (scraping instrument)** — for removing residual tissue.
- ***Al-Minshār al-Khaytī* (thread-saw)** — a fine linen thread used for deep or inaccessible growths.
- ***Mawchana* (forceps) and *Mahsh* (probe)** — to extract excised tissue.
- **Brass guiding spout (similar to *Misa'at*)** — used to direct surgical access.

Patient Preparation and Positioning

All surgeons — Al-Rāzī, Al-Zahrāwī, Ibn al-Quff, and Al-Majūsī- emphasised proper illumination and patient stabilisation:

- The patient is seated facing sunlight or strong light for visibility. The head is supported and tilted backwards by an assistant.
- The nasal margins are elevated for clear exposure. For the left nostril, the surgeon operates with the left hand; for the right, with

the right hand, while the assistant stabilises.

Surgical Technique According to Al-Rāzī, Al-Zahrāwī, Ibn Al-Quff, and Al-Majūsī

Step 1: Excision of the Growth

- The growth *(al-Laḥm al-Zā'id)* is grasped with a hook (Ṣunnāra / Mirwād) and gently pulled forward.
- The visible portion is excised using a fine *Mibḍa'* (scalpel) sharpened on one side.
- Residual tissues are removed by scraping with *Ālā Kharita* or similar delicate tools.

Step 2: Clearing of Residual Tissue and Irrigation

- The cavity is cleansed with water and vinegar *(Mā' Khall)* or wine *(Khamr)* to prevent infection.
- If remnants persist, the procedure is repeated until the nasal passage becomes clear and *sayalān al-ruṭūbat* (mucous flow) resumes freely.

Step 3: Use of Medicinal Powders and Dressings (Al-Rāzī's Method)

- After removal, a mixture of *Qalqatar, Māzū* (oak galls), and *Zanjār* (verdigris) is applied to control bleeding.
- A cotton plug dusted with the powder is inserted, ensuring airway patency via a small tubular passage.

Step 4: Use of the Thread-Saw *(Al-Minshār al-Khayṭī)*

For deep-seated or posterior growths inaccessible to knife or forceps:

A fine linen thread with tied knots is passed through the nasopharyngeal passage using a needle. Both ends are alternately pulled, sawing through the lesion gradually.

The operation is repeated after 2–3 days if remnants remain.

Step 5: Management of Bleeding and Healing

- *Nazf al-Dam* (haemorrhage) is controlled using astringent powders and Marham Rusul ointment.
- A cotton wick *(fatīla)* or tube coated with lead oxide *(Raṣāṣ)* is inserted to maintain patency. The dressing is changed every 2–3 days until complete healing occurs.

Management of Malignant Nasal Growths *(Saraṭān al-Anf)*

All classical authorities (Al-Zahrāwī, Ibn al-Quff, Al-Rāzī) warned against surgical excision of *Saraṭān* (malignant growths) because of:

- Severe haemorrhage,
- Meningeal inflammation, and
- Fatal progression.

If surgery is attempted, cauterisation *(Kayy)* must follow immediately to control bleeding and destroy diseased tissue.

For inoperable cases, *iṣlāḥ-i-ghidhā'*(dietary correction) and *tanqiya* (evacuation of morbid humours)—especially *mushil-e-sawdā* (black bile purgation)—are advised.

Postoperative Care and Prognostic Signs

- Irrigation with *Mā'Al-Khall* (vinegar-water) or *Khamr* (wine) after every dressing change.
- Clear nasal breathing and free mucous flow *(sayalān al-ruṭūbat)* into the throat indicate a successful outcome.
- Persistence of blockage suggests residual growth, necessitating repeat scraping or thread-saw application.

Observations by Zakariyā Al-Rāzī

Principle of Management

Zakariyā Al-Rāzī emphasised that if abnormal fleshy masses *(Al-Laḥm al-Zā'id)* are merely excised with a *Mibḍa'* (scalpel) without subsequent treatment, they often regrow rapidly.

Therefore, every excision must be followed by *takviya bil-adwiya ḥārra* (cauterisation with caustic drugs) or *takviya bil-nār* (fire cautery) to prevent recurrence.

Types of Growths and Their Treatment

1. **Soft and loose masses *(Laḥm Rikhwa, Bayḍā'):***

   Excise thoroughly with a sharp knife, ensuring complete removal.

2. **Putrefactive, foul-smelling growths *(Mu'affin):***

   Cauterise using *adwiya muḥarriqa* (caustic medicines).

3. **Resistant cases:**

   When topical agents fail, apply *mikwā* (fire cautery) using fine, delicate cauteries to minimise tissue damage.

Management of Deep-Seated Growths

- After cauterisation, instil vinegar *(Khall)* and water into the nasal cavity.
- Improvement in breathing indicates successful clearance.
- If obstruction persists, pass a knotted thread through the nostril into the palate using a bent leaden needle. Move the thread to and fro like a saw *(Āla Manash al-Khiyāṭī)* until the deep-seated mass is excised.
- Finally, insert a leaden tube, wrapped in cloth to maintain patency.
- Apply astringent powders *(Qurs Andarūn, Dawā' Qirṭās)* to induce *tajfīf* (dryness) and prevent recurrence.

'Amal Kḥarṭ

The Procedure of Kḥarṭ (Scraping / Thread Excision)

Indication

Occasionally, *Al-Laḥm al-Zā'id* (fleshy growths) or *Massa* (wart-like swellings) form in the nasal cavity, leading to Sudda (obstruction).

If the lesion is *Saraṭān* (malignant), surgical intervention with ālāt ḥadīdiya (metallic instruments) must be avoided.

When the swelling is benign, excision is performed by kḥarṭ (thread excision method), which is considered safer.

Technique of Kḥarṭ

- A fine thread is prepared, with a twisted horsehair attached to one end. The thread is passed through the nasal cavity and brought out from the palatal opening.
- The horsehair loop is positioned around the fleshy mass. Both ends are gently tightened until the growth is severed and detached.
- The nasal passage is irrigated with *Khall* (vinegar) and *Milḥ* (salt) to stop bleeding.
- A Marham (healing ointment) is then applied, composed of Khall, Gulnār (pomegranate flower), Kundar (frankincense), and Murdārsaṉg (litharge).

Cautionary Note

Raban al-Ṭabarī warns that use of *ālāt ḥadīdiya* (metallic instruments) for nasal excision is dangerous and may result in severe haemorrhage or fatal complications.

The thread excision method *(Kḥarṭ)* followed by medicated dressings is regarded as the safest and most effective approach.

Nasal Tip Warts (Verruca Vulgaris)

Clinical Description

- Small wart-like growths often appear on the tip of the nose, gradually enlarging and causing cosmetic deformity.
- Early excision is advised, followed by cauterisation *(Mikwā /*

Adwiya Muḥarriqa) to prevent recurrence.

Classification

1. **Cancerous-like *(Saraṭānī):***

   Hard, pale, insensitive → not excised, as surgery worsens the condition.

2. **Benign *(Waram Salīma):***

   Soft, non-pale → safe for excision.

Surgical Management

Benign warts:

- Perform *tanqiya* (evacuation), then excise the wart.
- Apply astringent *(qābiḍ)* and styptic *(ḥābis al-dam)* agents.

Malignant warts:

- Avoid surgery; no curative outcome expected.

Postoperative Care and Prognosis

- Apply astringent–styptic preparations for bleeding control and healing.
- Benign warts: good prognosis after excision and cautery.
- Cancerous lesions: poor prognosis; excision contraindicated.

Diseases of the Oral Cavity

Al-Laḥm Al-Zā'id fī Al-Shafa

(Lip Fibroma /Lip Nodules)

Clinical Description

Small, firm swellings may develop inside the lips, usually vetch-seed sized (sometimes smaller or larger).

Surgical Procedure

- The lip is everted to expose the lesion.
- Each swelling is incised longitudinally, and the growth is lifted with a hook *(Ṣunnāra)* and completely excised.

Hemostasis and Medication

- After excision, powdered vitriol *(Zāj)* is applied to stop bleeding.
- The patient rinses the mouth with a mixture of vinegar (*Khall*) and salt *(Milḥ)*.
- The wound is then dressed with styptic *(ḥābis al-dam)* preparations until healed.

Prognosis

Full recovery occurs when the entire abnormal tissue is excised and bleeding is effectively controlled.

Khiyāṭa al-Anf wa'l Shafa wa'l Udhun (Suturing of the Nose, Lip, and Ear)

Indications

Applicable for wounds of the nose, lip, or ear involving cartilage separation, causing visible gaps or deformity. Surgical correction is possible in selected, manageable cases.

Management of Fresh Wounds

If the wound is recent and bleeding, the edges should be immediately approximated with sutures. The wound is dressed and kept stable until healing occurs.

Management of Old or Malunited Wounds

When the wound edges have healed separately:

- Scrape both margins until fresh bleeding appears, and reapproximate the edges using sutures.
- Apply *Dam al-Akhwāin* (dragon's blood) and *Lubān* (frankincense) as topical healing agents.
- Cover with *duhn al-nakhl* (palm ointment) or another *munbit-i-laḥm* (regenerative ointment) and bandage for 2–3 days.

Postoperative Care

After bandage removal, reapply fresh medication. Sutures are left to fall off naturally.

Continue local application of healing ointments until complete recovery.

Ṭūl al-Asnān / Zā'ida al-Asnān

(Macrodontia and Supernumerary Teeth)

Elongated Teeth Due to Congestion *(Imtilāʾ al-Asnān)*

When teeth elongate abnormally due to *Imtilāʾ* (congestion), they interfere with speech and mastication.

Management:

- Grasp the affected tooth firmly.
- File it down gradually with a fine rasp.
- Hold the tooth tightly during rasping to minimise pain and movement. If pain arises, pause for a few days, then resume treatment.
- Avoid excessive filing and refrain from using the tooth until it regains strength.

Supernumerary Teeth (*Asnān Zāʾida* / Excessive Teeth)

Extra or oversized teeth *(Asnān Zāʾida)* may cause deformity or discomfort within the oral cavity.

Management:

- File the excessive tooth or molar *(Aḍrās)* gradually with a Sohan (file) until level with adjacent teeth. If any sharp projections persist near the gum, scrape them carefully with a suitable dental instrument.
- Remove roughness or cavities using *ālat al-kḥarṭ* (tooth scraper) for smoothness and hygiene.
- These measures restore uniform alignment, oral aesthetics, and prevent gum irritation.

Tashbīk al-Aḍrās al-Mutaḥarrika

(Dental Wiring / Dental Splinting)

Clinical Indication

Applied in cases of loosening of anterior teeth (incisors) after trauma, fall, or blow, where the patient has difficulty biting and risks tooth loss.

If astringent therapy *(Adwiya Qābiḍa)* fails to stabilise the teeth, mechanical fixation becomes necessary.

Material Selection

- **Gold wire:** preferred for durability and resistance to tarnish.
- **Silver wire:** acceptable alternative but prone to corrosion and discolouration.

Application Technique

- Select a wire of appropriate thickness according to the spacing between teeth.
- Fold and pass the wire between two firm teeth. Using free ends, weave *(tashbīk)* the wire around loose teeth and interlace it with adjacent firm teeth in a lattice pattern.
- Tighten gently near the roots to ensure stability and prevent slippage. Cut excess wire, twist securely, and tuck the ends between teeth to avoid irritation.

Post-Treatment Care

Keep teeth bound permanently or until they regain stability.

Replace the wire if loosened or broken. This technique maintains tooth alignment and function lifelong.

Qal' al-Asnān / Ikhrāj al-Aḍrās

(Tooth Extraction)

Indications and General Principles

Extraction *(Qal')* is indicated when the tooth becomes loose, decayed, painful, or obstructive to mastication.

Abū Al-Qāsim Al-Zahrāwī (Abulcasis) emphasised that extraction should be the last resort, only after all therapeutic measures fail, since no replacement equals a natural tooth. He warned that misidentification of the diseased tooth may lead to unnecessary removal of a healthy one.

Surgical Technique According to Al-Zahrāwī, Al-Majūsī, and Ibn Hubal

Preparation and Exposure

- The gum *(Litha)* around the root is incised and cleared of tissue using a scalpel *(Mibḍa')*.
- For decayed or hollow teeth, insert a cloth plug *(Fatīla)* to prevent fracture during extraction.

Extraction Technique

- Place the jaws of forceps *(kalbatīn)* firmly over the tooth.
- Rock gently from side to side to loosen the root, then apply a sudden upward pull to dislodge it. If extraction is difficult, use a lever-like instrument beneath the tooth to elevate it gradually.

Special Instructions

- Secure the patient's head to prevent movement and avoid leaving root fragments, which may cause severe pain or infection.
- Barbers and unskilled practitioners were strongly warned against forceful extraction that may fracture the jawbone.

Use of Medicaments to Facilitate Extraction (Pharmacological

Methods)

- Certain drugs and compounds were used to loosen the tooth naturally before extraction:
- Powder of *'Āqir Qarḥā*, soaked in vinegar *(Khall)* for forty days, applied after incising the gum.
- Paste of *Shibram milk* applied for three hours → causes painless loosening.
- Seeds of Anjara and Qinna placed near the root → facilitate tooth separation.
- Hot fomentation *(takmīd)* with *jāwaras* was used for pain relief before extraction.

Management of Abnormal Fleshy Growth *(Al-Laḥm al-Zā'id)*

If excess tissue develops around the root:

- At the root, remove with *Minqār* (beak-shaped instrument) and file smooth with rasp.
- Outside the root, excise with forceps *(Kalbatīn).*

Post-Extraction Care

- Fill the socket with lint *(quṭn)* if the tooth is decayed, preventing collapse of space.
- Apply *munbit-i-laḥm* (flesh-promoting medicines) to aid granulation.
- Rinse mouth with vinegar *(khall)* and water or wine *(khamr)* to cleanse.
- If bleeding persists, apply *zāj* (powdered vitriol); if uncontrolled, cauterisation *(kayy)* may be used.
- Cotton dipped in *ravghan gul* (rose oil) is applied for soothing and healing.

Al-Laḥm al-Zā'id fi'l Litha

Epulis (Superfluous Growth on the Gum)

Definition

Epulis refers to an abnormal fleshy overgrowth arising on the gum (Litha), often resulting in swelling or mass formation.

Surgical Removal Technique

- The growth is lifted with a hook *(Ṣunnāra)* or grasped with forceps *(Kalbatīn)*.
- It is excised completely from the base, allowing drainage of pus or blood if present.

Post-Excision Care

- The operated site is treated with crushed vitriol *(zāj)* or similar desiccant astringent *(mujaffif-qābiḍ)* agents to dry and disinfect the wound.

Prevention of Recurrence

- If regrowth occurs—a frequent finding—the lesion should be re-excised and followed by cauterisation *(kayy)* to prevent recurrence.

Qaṣr al-Lisān / Rabṭ al-Lisān

(Ankyloglossia/Tongue-tie)

Causes *(Asbāb)*

- Spasm of tongue muscles, restricting voluntary motion.
- Attachment of the frenulum at the tip of the tongue, preventing upward and outward movement.
- Scarring after an ulcer *(qarḥa')*, forming a fibrous band beneath the tongue.

Surgical Procedure

1. **If caused by spasm:**

- Administer antispasmodic medicines before attempting surgery.

2. **If caused by frenulum attachment:**

- Seat the patient and ask them to open their mouth.
- Lift the tongue upward, exposing the frenulum, and incise the frenulum transversely using a scalpel *(Mibḍa')*. Avoid deep cutting to prevent injury to blood vessels and persistent bleeding.

3. **If caused by scar formation:**

- Insert a hook (Ṣunnāra) beneath the fibrous band. Elevate it gently and perform a transverse incision to release the tongue.

Precautions

- Avoid deep incisions, as they may injure arteries and lead to excessive bleeding.

Post-operative Care

- Rinse the mouth first with vinegar *(khall)* for cleansing. Follow with rose water *(mā' al-ward)* to promote healing. Usually, no further medication is required after this care.

Nodular Lesions of the Tongue

Causes *(Asbāb)*

- **Congenital:** Development of thick fibrous or ligamentous bands *(ribāṭāt)* beneath the tongue.
- **Acquired:** Formation of fibrous nodules after ulcer healing (Indimāl al-Qurūḥ) leading to restriction and induration.

Surgical Procedure

If congenital (due to thick fibrous bands):

- Seat the patient upright and open the mouth. Lift the tongue upward and cut the fibrous band transversely using a scalpel (*Mibḍa'*) to release tension.

If acquired (due to scar formation):

- Introduce a probe or hook (*ṣunnāra*) beneath the fibrous nodule. Pull upward to elevate the band.
- Incise transversely to free the adhesion and restore mobility.

Precautions

- Avoid deep incisions, as they may injure arterial branches and lead to severe bleeding (*nazf al-dam*).
- Maintain gentle dissection to prevent structural damage.

Post-operative Care

- Rinse the mouth with vinegar and water *(mā' al-khall)* immediately after surgery.
- Follow with meat broth (*mā' al-laḥm*) to encourage healing and prevent contraction (*inqibāḍ*) or Ḥardening *(ṣalāba)* of the tongue.

Ḍifda' al-Lisān (Ranula)

(Sublingual Salivary Gland Mucocele)

Definition and Description

Ranula (*Ḍifda' al-Lisān*) is a swelling beneath the tongue resembling the body of a frog. It results from the enlargement of a sublingual gland that interferes with tongue movement.

The swelling develops due to the accumulation and stagnation of thick humours *(ruṭūbat ghalīẓa)* beneath the tongue. Because of continuous motion, the thin portion of the humour dissipates, leaving the thick residue, which forms the mass.

Surgical Management

Preoperative Preparation:

Begin with evacuation (*tanqiya*) of thick humours from the body.

Clinical Examination:

- Examine the swelling in sunlight after the patient opens the mouth.
- If black, hard, and insensible → regarded as cancer (*saraṭān*); surgery is contraindicated.
- If pale or fluid-filled → considered benign and operable.

Surgical Technique according to Al-Zahrāwī and Ibn al-Quff

- Suspend the swelling with a hook (*ṣunnāra*). Make a small transverse incision with a fine scalpel (Mibḍa'). Free and excise the entire swelling from its margins.
- If bleeding (*nazf al-dam*) occurs, apply powdered vitriol (zāj) until it stops. Once hemostasis is achieved, continue dissection until complete removal.

Post-Operative Care

Rinse the mouth with vinegar (*khall*) and rose oil *(ravghan gul)* or salt solution to cleanse and contract tissues. Continue local wound care until full healing is achieved.

Diseases of the Pharynx

Waram-i-Lahāt / Istirkhā' al-Lahāt wa Suqūṭ al-Lahāt

(Uvulitis and Uvuloptosis)

Etiology

- The uvula *(Lahāt),* also called 'Inabiyya', resembles a small grape.
- The condition occurs when phlegmatic secretions from the head descend to the throat and accumulate on the uvula, causing relaxation (*Istirkhā'*), swelling *(Waram),* and elongation *(Suqūṭ).*
- The enlarged uvula may obstruct breathing and speech.

Types of Uvulitis

1. ***Waram-i-Lahāt 'Amūdī* (Columella type):** Uvula becomes swollen, elongated, and pale-white due to inflammatory discharges.
2. ***Waram-i-Lahāt 'Inabī* (Uva type):** Swelling confined to the lower part, round and grape-like, which may obstruct the throat.[5]

General Treatment Approaches

- **Surgical Removal:** Excision of the elongated portion when swelling causes airway obstruction.
- **Cauterisation** ***(Kayy):*** After excision, apply caustic medicine through a mould for about an hour until the uvula blackens and sloughs off naturally after three days.
- **Precaution**: Avoid entry of cauterising material into the mouth or throat.

Surgical Principles According to Classical Unani Surgeons

Al-Majūsī (Haly Abbas)

Indications: When the uvula is elongated, pale, and thin-stalked with a rounded head resembling a grape, and medical treatment fails.

Contraindications:

- Dark or black uvula → risk of haemorrhage.
- Broad base and non-pedunculated → do not excise.

Method: Excise only the excess length, avoiding root removal to prevent suffocation, loss of voice, or chest complications.

Ibn al-Quff

Indications: White, elongated uvula with a firm base → excision permissible.

Contraindications: Blackish, insensible, or red, inflamed uvula → avoid surgery.

Purpose: Relief of dyspnea and obstruction.

Zakariyā Al-Rāzī (Rhazes)

Indications: Thin, greyish, elongated uvula → excision safe.

Contraindications: Acute red swelling or phlegmonous inflammation → excision causes haemorrhage and worsening.

Precautions:

- Perform only after evacuation *(Istifrāgh)* and reduction of swelling.
- Avoid operation during acute inflammation.

Operative Technique for Removal of the Uvula

Preoperative:

- Purify the head and body using *tanqiya* (purgatives).
- Seat the patient in sunlight, open the mouth wide, and depress the tongue.

Excision Method:

- Hold the uvula with *masik al-lahāt or qalib al-bawāsīr*.and Pull downward and excise only the excessive part.
- Avoid cutting near the root to prevent haemorrhage *(nazf al-dam)* and voice loss.

Cauterisation Method:

- Apply asafoetida, alum, or ammonium chloride at the base.
- Uvula blackens and falls off in 3–4 days.

Hemostasis:

- Apply powdered vitriol or alum if bleeding occurs.

Post-Operative Care

- Gargle with vinegar, rose water *(arq-e-gulāb),* or Sumāq decoction.
- Avoid strong odours and irritants until complete healing.

Complications of Uvula Surgery

- Voice damage or hoarseness.
- Coughing due to loss of uvular protective barrier.
- Sensitivity to dust or cold air, causing throat irritation.
- Inability to tolerate thirst.
- Severe haemorrhage if excessive excision is performed.

Al-Zahrāwī's Method in *Kitāb al-Taṣrīf*

- Operate only after inflammation subsides.
- Suitable Case: Pale, elongated uvula.

Technique:

- Seat the patient in sunlight, depress the tongue. Grasp the uvula with a hook, pull downward, and excise with the tonsilar instrument.

Precaution: Never remove beyond normal length to prevent speech and respiratory harm.

Postoperative Care: Continue medical dressings until recovery.

Waram-i-Lawzatayn / Qat' Waram-i-Lawzatayn

(Tonsillitis and Tonsilectomy)

Waram al-Lawzatayn **(Tonsilitis)**

At the root of the tongue lie two glands called *Sākib al-Lu'āb* (salivary excretory glands). Their inflammation *(Waram)* leads to pain and difficulty in *swallowing ('Usr al-Bal')*. In severe cases, respiratory distress may occur, resembling *Khunāq* (diphtheritic sore throat).

Clinical Description According to Al-Majusi

On both sides of the uvula are two fleshy masses — the tonsils (Lawzatayn). Prolonged inflammation causes pain, dysphagia, and dyspnea. The tonsils appear enlarged, erect, and pedunculated, and medical gargles prove ineffective.

Surgical Management (*Qat' Waram-i-Lawzatayn* / Tonsilectomy)

When chronic inflammation persists, causing obstruction of swallowing and breathing, and medical management fails, surgical intervention becomes necessary.

Indications and Contraindications of Tonsilectomy

Indications:

- Chronic, pale, pedunculated, rounded tonsils with persistent fever → surgical excision indicated.

Contraindications:

- Carcinomatous tonsils (*Saraṭān*): Black, hard, insensate masses → avoid surgery.

- Acutely inflamed tonsils: Red, painful, broad-based swellings → wait for maturation (*nuḍj*) and incision after abscess formation.

Surgical Observation by Abū Al-Qāsim Al-Zahrāwī

When buboes appear in the throat resembling external abscesses, and medicines fail:

- Hard, dark, insensate swellings: Do not operate.
- Red, thick-rooted swellings: Avoid surgery; allow to mature or rupture.
- Pale, rounded, pedunculated swellings: Suitable for surgical removal.

Operative Steps of *Qat' Waram-i-Lawzatayn* (Tonsilectomy)

Preoperative Consideration:

Ensure inflammation has subsided before surgery to avoid haemorrhage.

Patient Positioning:

- Seat the patient in sunlight or rest the head on the surgeon's lap for better control.

Exposure:

- Open the mouth; depress the tongue using a smooth *lisāniya* (tongue depressor) made of gold, silver, or brass.

Grasping the Tonsil:

- Insert a hook (*ṣunnāra*) and pull the tonsil forward gently without tearing the mucosa (*aghshiya*) or capsule (ṣifāq).

Excision:

- Excise the tonsil at its base using *Miqās* (curved scissors) or *Mībda'* (scalpel) — sharp on one side, blunt on the other. Remove one tonsil first, then the other.

- The dissection is carried out in a circular manner close to the root, removing one Tonsil first and then the other in the same manner.

Hemostasis:

- Place the patient prone to allow blood drainage.
- Gargle with vinegar and cold water, or use alum, coriander, or pomegranate peel decoction for a styptic effect.

Post-operative Care:

- Gargle with Syrup of Pomegranate *(Sharbat Anar)* or alum water until bleeding stops.

Al-Zahrāwī's Operative Technique

Preoperative:

Operate only after inflammation diminishes to prevent excessive bleeding.

Positioning:

Patient seated in sunlight, with head supported in the surgeon's lap.

Exposure of the Tonsil

The mouth is opened, and an assistant depresses the tongue using a slender spatula-like instrument (*Lisāniya*) made of bronze or silver. With the tongue depressed, the Tonsillar swellings (*waram lawzatayn*) become visible for direct inspection.

Grasping of the Tonsil

A hook (*Ṣunnāra*) is inserted into one Tonsil to draw it forward as far as possible. Extreme care must be taken to avoid pulling away any part of the mucosa (*aghshiya*) covering the Tonsil.

Excision of the Tonsil

The Tonsil is excised with curved scissors (*Miqas*), sharp and made of Indian iron or Damascene steel. In the absence of these, a scalpel (*Mibda'*), sharp on one side and blunt on the other, may be used.

Hemostasis and Care:

- Gargle with cold water, vinegar, or decoctions of *Māzū* and myrtle leaves (*Āas*).

Khunāq and Dhabaḥa

(Choking; acute inflammation of pharyngo-laryngeal muscles)

Definition

Linguistic Meaning: *Khunāq* means suffocation or strangulation. *Dhabaḥa* literally means throat-cutting or severe choking.

Medical Definition: In Unani medicine, *Khunāq* is defined as an inflammatory swelling (*Waram*) occurring in the throat structures: Tonsils (*Lawzatayn*), external muscles of pharynx and larynx, upper oesophageal muscles, or internal pharyngo-laryngeal muscles. This results in difficulty in swallowing and respiration.

Clinical Classification

1. ***Khunāq Muṭlaq*** (simple),
2. ***Dhabaḥa*** (severe),
3. ***Khunāq Kalbī*** (cynanche canina).

Cynanche (Gk): "dog's suffocation" (breathing like a suffocating dog). Historically used for severe throat diseases (tonsillitis, croup, diphtheria).Angina = "choking."

Subtype Descriptions

1) *Khunāq Muṭlaq*

- **Site:** *Lawzatayn* & external pharyngeal muscles near the mouth/tongue.
- **Sign:** Swelling visible on the mouth opening with the tongue protruded.[9]

2) *Dhabaḥa*

- **Site/Severity:** Severe form; muscles on both sides of the pharynx or upper oesophagal muscles.

- **Sign:** Red ring-like halo between throat and both ears.
- **Greek correlation:** Cynanche/croup.
- **Classical debate:** Some equate with *Khunāq*; others restrict to waram Lawzatayn or pharynx.

Ibn Hubal Al-Baghdādī:

- **Internal muscles** → *Sutunji* (dangerous, obstructs swallowing).
- **External muscles** → *Futunji.*
- **Features:** fever, dyspnea, reduced voice, throat pain, conjunctival congestion/red eyes; least dangerous when swelling is externally visible.

Hallmark signs: Hoarseness/aphonia, severe dysphagia, nasal regurgitation, drooling, congested/bulging eyes.

Dhabaḥī vs Khunāqī Waram **(functional difference):**

- ***Dhabaḥa*:** Swallowing harder than breathing; in extremes, both are impaired.
- ***Khunāq*:** Breathing harder than swallowing; marked in *Khunāq Kalbī* when upper esophageal sphincter obstructed (*Fam-e-al-Marī*).

3) *Khunāq Kalbī*

- **Meaning:** "Dog-like suffocation."
- **Site:** Internal pharyngeal & laryngeal muscles; more severe than *Dhabaḥa*.
- **Signs:** Tongue protrudes like a dog; inability to swallow even liquids (upper oesophageal sphincter blocked); mouth gapes.

Ibn Hubal: External → *Khunāq Muṭlaq*; internal → *Khunāq Kalbī*; nasal regurgitation common.

Khunāq Wabā'iyya (Epidemic Khunāq)

- Severe, contagious; false membrane over palate/pharynx/larynx; toxemia, weakness.
- Cause: *Corynebacterium diphtheriae*.

Onset & Variants (Al-Rāzī)

- **Sudden onset:** Lesion usually laryngeal.
- **Gradual onset:** Lesion in respiratory tract structures.
- **Laryngeal (painless):** Intralaryngeal swelling, muscle paralysis, and/or *yubūsat* → hoarse voice, narrowed airway.
- **Laryngeal (painful):** waram ḥārr inside the larynx.
- **Respiratory causes:** Thoracic muscle paralysis, chest narrowing, lung swelling, *khilṭ ghalīẓ* retention (hot/cold).

'Unuqī Khunāq **(Cervical):** Combined oesophagus *(al-marī)*, larynx, trachea; dysphagia>dyspnea if esophageal; reverse if airway.

Further Classical Types (Al-Rāzī)

1. **With swelling of *Lawzatayn & larynx*:** Restricted respiration proportional to swelling; vomiting; firm/dry organs; neck swelling, facial oedema, salivation, red eyes, tongue protrusion, small-thick pulse; unable to lie down.
2. **Without swelling of *Lawzatayn & larynx*:** Emaciated neck, restricted neck movement, sunken eyes, taut forehead skin; no visible internal/external throat swelling; neck itching; longitudinal redness = good sign (its sudden loss = grave).

Common Clinical Features

Dyspnea, dysphagia, exophthalmos, mouth held open, throat/posterior oral pain, neck/face swelling in some, palpable/visible throat swelling.[1]

Vertebral Cause (Differential)

Neck drawn inward, prominent occiput, tenderness; abnormal motion reveals vertebral displacement.

Surgical Management of *Khunāq*

Tracheostomy (*Qat' al-Qaṣaba al-Ri'a)*

According to Ibn Hubal al-Baghdadi, when *Khunāq (Khunāq)* becomes severe, and the patient's death seems imminent, and if the inflammation (*Waram*) has not yet reached the ligaments of the trachea (*Qaṣaba al-Ri'a*), then an opening should be made in the trachea and widened. After recovery, it should be sutured.

Operative Steps:

- The patient's head is secured. An incision is made near the *Labaḥ* (suprasternal notch), away from the thyroid gland. The scalpel is directed posteriorly. And the skin over the trachea is lifted and incised.
- The incision is held apart with two hooks, exposing the trachea. The trachea is opened just enough to allow air passage.
- Once the patient improves and natural breathing resumes, only the skin wound is sutured without injuring the tracheal cartilages. *Dharūr Aṣfar* (yellow astringent powder) is applied locally.

Qat'al-Ḥanjara (Laryngotomy)

It is mentioned that a physician named Antalis used a fearful but life-saving operation for *Khunāq*, performed only when certain death from suffocation was expected.

Operative Steps:

- The head is extended backwards. And the skin over the larynx and trachea is incised longitudinally.
- Two sutures are used above and below to separate the tissues until the trachea is exposed.
- The membrane between two tracheal rings is cut to allow air entry. Once breathing is restored, the wound is sutured. Mild cauterisation and local application of *Dharūr Aṣfar (styptic*

powder) are advised.

- If Tonsils (*Lawzatayn*) are enlarged, they are hooked, incised in an oval manner, and partially excised (about one-fourth), ensuring bleeding is controlled with positioning (head down), gargles of vinegar, and local application of *zaj* (alum) and *qalqatar*.

Described in *Kitab al-Hawi*:

- If laryngeal swelling is evident, it should be palpated digitally. If soft and fluctuant, an incision is made with a scalpel to drain. Any obstructing tissue should be excised.
- A tube is inserted into the trachea to facilitate breathing.

Diseases of the Larynx and Trachea

Waram al-Ḥanjara, Qīla al-Ḥanjara, Qat'al-Ḥanjara

(Laryngitis, Laryngocele and Laryngotomy)

Classical Description:

When acute hot inflammation (*waram ḥārr*) occurs in the mouth and pharynx, leading to obstruction of the esophageal and pharyngeal openings (*Fam al-Marī wa al-Ḥalq*)—but the trachea (*Qaṣaba al-Ri'a*) remains unaffected as in Khunāq—the patient experiences suffocation (*Ikhtināq*). In such cases, incision of the larynx (*qat'al-ḥanjara*) is advised as a life-saving measure to restore airway patency.

Laryngocele (*Qīla Al-Ḥanjara*)

A localised swelling or herniation (*qīla*) occurring in the region of the larynx (*ḥanjara*), often representing an abnormal outpouching of laryngeal tissue.

Clinical Features:

May cause airway obstruction and difficulty in phonation, depending on the size and site of the swelling.

Laryngotomy *(Qat'Al-Ḥanjara)*

Indication:

Performed in severe airway obstruction due to laryngeal inflammation or swelling, when suffocation *(Ikhtināq)* threatens life and other remedies fail.

Classical Operative Steps by Al-Majūsī (Haly Abbas, 930–994 CE)

- The patient is seated upright, with the head extended. An incision is made below the upper border of the larynx.
- Three or four small circular incisions are given, corresponding to the round shape of the trachea. The incisions are kept limited to the

membranes between cartilaginous rings of the trachea; larger incisions are avoided due to risk.

- The skin of the larynx is lifted upwards with a hook (*Mawchana*) before making the incision. Once the skin is opened, the cartilages and small vessels are visualised.
- The membrane between the cartilaginous rings of the trachea is carefully incised, ensuring no vessel or artery is injured.
- The wound is left open until the disease resolves and the risk of suffocation subsides.
- Afterwards, the skin wound is closed with sutures, but the sutures should not pass through the cartilages.

Laryngotomy / Tracheotomy According to Al-Zahrāwī (Albucasis, 936–1013 CE)

Indication:

Recommended when:

- Abscesses in the mouth, throat, or tonsils cause airway obstruction.
- Trachea remains unaffected.
- Severe suffocation threatens life.

Contraindication:

Avoided in quinsy (Peritonsilar Abscess / severe *khunāq*), as the disease often extends to the lungs, rendering the operation ineffective.

Operative Steps

- Select the site below the third or fourth tracheal ring. and make a small transverse incision between two rings, cutting only through the membrane, not the cartilage. This area is chosen because it lacks flesh and is free of major blood vessels.
- If the surgeon is hesitant, he may first stretch the skin of the throat

with a hook, then incise carefully down until the trachea is exposed, avoiding visible vessels.

- The trachea is confirmed to be opened when:
  - Phlegm escapes from the wound.
  - The patient loses their voice.
- The wound is then left open for several days until the risk of suffocation passes. Once improvement occurs (usually after three days), the wound lips are approximated and sutured at the skin level only (without involving cartilage).
- Topical medicaments that stimulate granulation are applied until complete healing.

Al-Zahrāwī's View

When a laryngeal or pharyngeal tumour causes near-fatal suffocation, and the patient consents, laryngotomy may be performed.

- The wound remains open for about three days, allowing respiration.
- Once danger subsides, it is sutured and treated until healing occurs.

Qaṭ' al-Qaṣaba al-Ri'a (Tracheostomy / Tracheotomy)

Historical Overview

Tracheostomy is one of the oldest known life-saving surgical procedures performed to relieve upper airway obstruction.

Ancient Civilisations:

Evidence from Ancient Egyptian tablets suggests the practice existed as early as 3600 BCE. Early literary references appear in the Rig Veda (2000–1000 BCE) and the Ebers Papyrus (1550 BCE).

Classical Antiquity:

In Homer's account (1000 BCE), Alexander the Great is said to have saved a soldier from suffocation by opening the trachea with his sword. Hippocrates (460–370 BCE) described the theoretical basis of tracheostomy but discouraged it due to fear of injuring the carotid arteries. Later, Asclepiades of Bithynia (100 BCE) and Antyllus of Rome (340 CE) were credited with performing the first successful operations. Paulus of Aegina (625–690 CE) provided the first detailed technical description.

Islamic Golden Age (750–1257 CE):

During this period, Unani physicians refined the technique and introduced safer surgical approaches and antiseptic aftercare, establishing tracheostomy as a viable life-saving measure in airway obstruction.

Abū Bakr Muḥammad ibn Zakariyyā Al-Rāzī (865–925 CE)

***Al-Ḥāwī* (Liber Continens)**

In Volume III of *Al-Ḥāwī*, Al-Rāzī discusses diseases of the larynx, trachea, and pharynx, including inflammations, ulcers, and suffocative disorders. He describes tracheostomy as a life-saving procedure indicated only when the patient's life is endangered by asphyxia.

Operative Method:

The head is elevated slightly. The skin between the larynx and windpipe is incised and retracted, followed by a second incision below the laryngeal ridge. Using two threads, the tissues are gently pulled upward and downward until the trachea *(Qaṣaba al-Ri'a)* becomes visible. A small opening is then made to allow air passage. Once the obstruction resolves, the incision is closed, leaving small drainage spaces to ensure proper healing.

Clinical Note:

Historical accounts suggest Al-Rāzī performed this operation himself—most notably on Wazīr Aḥmad ibn Ismā'īl, who suffered from diphtheritic obstruction.

'Alī ibn al-'Abbās Al-Majūsī (Haly Abbas, 930–994 CE)

In the thirty-eighth chapter of the surgical section, titled *"On the Treatment of Pharyngitis,"* Al-Majūsī discusses *Shaqq al-Ḥanjara* (tracheostomy) as a last-resort procedure in cases of asphyxia *(Ikhtināq)*.

Operative Technique:

The patient is seated upright, with the head slightly extended. The incision is made just below the ridge of the larynx, creating three or four small circular cuts limited to the membrane between cartilaginous rings—never through the cartilage itself. The skin is lifted with a hook (*Ṣunnāra*), and the tracheal membrane is carefully divided to avoid injury to vessels. The wound is kept open until respiration is restored, and once the danger passes, only the skin is sutured without involving cartilage.

Al-Majūsī's approach emphasised precision, minimal trauma, and hemostasis—principles that foreshadow modern tracheostomy practice.

Abū Al-Qāsim Al-Zahrāwī (Albucasis, 936–1013 CE)

In the forty-third chapter of his surgical compendium, Al-Zahrāwī interprets earlier Greco-Arabic accounts of tracheostomy (*Qat' al-Qaṣaba al-Ri'a*).

Interpretation:

When a pharyngeal abscess or *khunāq* causes severe obstruction and suffocation, an incision through the larynx (*ḥanjara*) may allow temporary breathing until the crisis resolves. The wound should remain open for about three days, after which it may be sutured for complete healing.

Personal Observation:

He narrates a case of a maid who had accidentally cut her throat, partially severing the trachea. On examination, air escaped through the wound, but no major vessel was injured. Al-Zahrāwī sutured the trachea carefully; the patient recovered fully, retaining her voice with only mild hoarseness. From this, he concluded that laryngeal incision, if properly executed, is safe and effective.

Abū ʿAlī Ibn Sīnā (Avicenna, 980–1037 CE)

***Al-Qānūn fī al-Ṭibb* (The Canon of Medicine)**

In *Book III, Part IX, Chapter VI,* under "Treatment of Croup and Angina," Ibn Sīnā gives a detailed description of tracheostomy.

Operative Method:

The head is retracted and stabilised; the skin over the trachea is incised and lifted with a *ṣunnāra* until the tracheal rings are exposed. The incision is made between two rings, and the wound is then closed at the skin level only.

Postoperative Care:

He advises the application of *Dharūr-e-Aṣfar* (Yellow Powder) to promote healing and prevent infection.

Ḥakīm Sayyid Ismā'īl Jurjānī (1042–1137 CE)

Dhakhīra Khwarizm Shāhī

In Book VI, Jurjānī presents tracheostomy *(Qat' al-Qaṣaba al-Ri'a)* as a final life-saving measure for pharyngitis and asphyxia when all medical options fail.

Procedure:

The head is extended backwards, and the skin over the larynx is lifted and separated with a Ṣunnāra. An incision is made between two laryngeal rings, carefully avoiding cartilage. When the trachea is entered, the patient becomes aphonic (loss of voice)—a key sign, according to Jurjānī, of a successful airway diversion. After the danger passes, the skin wound is sutured without involving the cartilage.

Jurjānī's identification of aphonia as a clinical indicator of success reflects his empirical precision and surgical insight.

Abū Marwān ʿAbd al-Malik Ibn Zuhr (Avenzoar, 1091–1162 CE)

Ibn Zuhr, during the Almohad Caliphate, composed *Kitāb al-Taysīr*, a landmark text known for experimental validation in surgery.

The earliest specific reference to *Qatʿal-Qaṣaba al-Ri'a* (tracheostomy) in Unani medicine is found in Ibn Zuhr's (Avenzoar's) *Kitāb al-Taysīr fi 'l Mudāwā wa 'l Tadbīr*.

According to Ibn Zuhr, this surgical procedure was essentially an innovation of Arab physicians. He emphasises that treatment of diseases of the trachea (*Amrad al-Qaṣaba al-Ri'a*) requires careful assessment of causative factors before initiating surgery.

In cases of severe *Dhabaḥa* (excessive suffocative condition), physicians recommended making an opening in the trachea equivalent to the size of a nostril.

However, Ibn Zuhr admits that this operation is complicated and therefore not commonly practised. Later, physicians rarely mentioned it.

Classical Reference (Ibn Zuhr's Account)

Ibn Zuhr refutes those who claim that Jālīnūs (Galen) never mentioned this procedure. He notes that Jālīnūs (Galen) indeed wrote that "often the peritoneum is cut, and the trachea is incised," and that earlier physicians used the term "*Qaṣaba*" exclusively for the trachea.

Ibn Zuhr narrates his personal experience:

- Initially, he attempted tracheal incision after separating the skin and membranes overlying the trachea. The incision, however, turned out larger than intended.
- Postoperatively, the wound was irrigated regularly with water and honey until healing was achieved. And the patient eventually recovered.

Experimental Tracheostomy on a Goat:

To verify earlier medical opinions, he performed *Qat'al-Qaṣaba al-Ri'a* experimentally:

- Made a small incision in the trachea, about the size of a lupine seed (Tirmisa).
- Irrigated the wound daily with water and honey until complete healing. The animal recovered and lived long, showing no adverse effects.
- For final healing, he applied powdered cypress nuts (Cupressus sempervirens).

Significance:

This experiment established the feasibility and safety of tracheostomy, proving that the wound could heal without complication. His integration of honey and cypress for wound care demonstrated early principles of antisepsis and tissue regeneration, earning him recognition as the Father of Experimental Surgery.

Goitre (Elephant of the Throat)

History of Endocrine Disorders in Classical Medicine

The roots of endocrinology can be traced to the Hippocratic doctrine of four humours *(Akhlāṭ Arba'a)*, where disease was believed to result from their imbalance (Dyscrasia). Within this framework, Unani physicians recognised various endocrine disorders and their systemic manifestations.

They described:

- Endocrine syndromes (e.g., amenorrhea with galactorrhoea in non-pregnant women),
- Castration and contraception techniques,
- Infertility, obesity, and diabetes mellitus *(Dhayābīṭus)*.

The Jālīnūs concept of temperament *(mizāj)* formed the cornerstone of Unani understanding. The thyroid gland was believed to secrete a moist, lubricating substance that softened the larynx *(Ḥanjara)* and its cartilages, ensuring smooth voice production.

Prominent Unani scholars made foundational contributions:

Zakariyyā Al-Rāzī (Rhazes, 865–925 CE) — described the anatomy and physiology of sex organs and methods of contraception.

ʿAlī ibn al-ʿAbbās Al-Majūsī (Haly Abbas, 930–994 CE) — detailed surgical approaches for goitre.

Abū Al-Qāsim Al-Zahrāwī (Albucasis, 936–1013 CE) — performed the removal of a large goitre under sedation.

Ibn Sīnā (Avicenna, 980–1037 CE) & Jurjānī (1042–1137 CE) — described the association between goitre and exophthalmos, centuries before modern recognition of Graves' Disease.

ʿAlī ibn al-ʿAbbās Al-Majūsī

***Kāmil al-Ṣanā'a al-Ṭibbiyya* (Liber Regius)**

Al-Majūsī provided one of the earliest surgical descriptions of goitre in medical history. He described:

- Making a longitudinal incision through the skin of the neck,
- Carefully dissecting and excising the goitrous swelling along with its adherent tissue.

This early attempt represents the first documented concept of thyroidectomy in Unani surgical practice, emphasising both anatomical awareness and surgical precision.

Abū Al-Qāsim Al-Zahrāwī (Albucasis, 936–1013 CE)

Al-Zahrāwī is widely regarded as the first surgeon to perform a successful thyroidectomy. He described a condition termed "Elephant of the Throat" (*Waram al-'Unuq*) — now identified as goitre — characterised by large neck swelling, often more common in women.

Surgical Method:

- **Sedation:** Induced using opium (Papaver somniferum).
- **Technique:** The swelling was excised through a longitudinal incision.
- **Hemostasis:** Controlled with simple ligatures and hot cautery (*kayy*).

His careful use of ligatures and cautery marked a major advancement in haemostatic technique and safe surgical excision of vascular neck swellings.

Classification and Description by Al-Zahrāwī

Description:

Goitre (Elephant of the Throat) is described as a large, soft or firm neck swelling, usually of the same colour as the surrounding skin, and more frequent in women.

Types of Goitre:

1. **Congenital Goitre**

- Present from birth.
- Considered untreatable in classical texts.

2. **Acquired Goitre**

   Subdivided into:

a. Sebaceous Cyst-like Goitre

Cystic in nature; non-vascular and not adherent to vital structures.

Surgical management:

- Confirm cystic consistency with a probe.
- If confirmed, incise and excise completely with capsule. If non-encapsulated, dissect all adherent tissue.

- Treat wound with topical styptic and healing agents.

b. Aneurysmal (Vascular) Goitre

- Resembles an arterial aneurysm; high risk of fatal bleeding.
- Surgical intervention contraindicated, except for very small swellings.

Ibn Sīnā and Ismā'īl Jurjānī

In *Al-Qānūn fī al-Ṭibb* and *Dhakhīra Khwarizm Shāhī*, both physicians observed the coexistence of goitre and exophthalmos—an association described eight centuries before Parry (1825), Graves (1835), and Basedow (1840).

Their observations revealed an understanding of systemic thyroid pathology and its effect on the eyes, metabolism, and temperament *(mizāj)*—a concept now recognised as Graves' Disease (exophthalmic goitre).

Surgeries for Breast Diseases

'Aẓm e Tathaddi

(Gynaecomastia)

Definition:

Gynaecomastia refers to the enlargement of the male breast, resembling that of females. In certain cases, the breasts become pendulous, producing a feminine appearance. This condition is often associated with obesity and results in cosmetic disfigurement.

Etiology:

According to classical Unani physicians, the cause of gynaecomastia is the abnormal accumulation of fatty tissue within the breast.

Surgical Management

Preoperative Preparation:

Before surgery, venesection *(faṣd)* is performed to purify the body, followed by the administration of purgatives *(mus'hilat)* to expel morbid humours.

Operative Technique:

- A crescent-shaped *(hilālī)* incision is made over the breast. The fatty tissue is excised completely.
- The wound is packed with suitable wound-healing agents and closed with sutures.
- In cases of pendulous or sagging breasts, two crescent-shaped incisions are made, the intervening skin and underlying fatty tissue are removed, and the wound is sutured. Healing agents such as *dhārūr aṣfar* (yellow styptic powder)

are applied to promote granulation and prevent infection.

Al-Majūsī (Haly Abbas, 930–994 CE):

If the enlarged male breast tends to sag, two crescent-shaped incisions should be made in such a way that one begins where the other ends. The skin between them is dissected, the fat removed, and the wound sutured. *Dharūr Aṣfar* or similar healing agents should be applied to facilitate granulation.

Al-Zahrāwī (Albucasis, 936–1013 CE)

In *Kitāb al-Taṣrīf*, Al-Zahrāwī described the surgical management of male breast enlargement (*tathaddi*) with both simple and advanced methods depending on severity.

1. Simple Gynaecomastia:

A semicircular incision is made over the breast, the fatty tissue is excised, and the wound is packed with cicatrising material before suturing and dressing.

2. Severe / Pendulous Gynaecomastia:

When the breast becomes pendulous and flabby due to large size, resembling female breasts, a more extensive procedure is required.

Two semicircular incisions are made on the upper side of the breast, with the ends of the two incisions joining together. The longer incision encircles the smaller one.

The skin between them and the underlying fat is excised, and the wound is closed. *Dharūr Aṣfar* (styptic powder) is applied to prevent infection and promote healing.

Surgeries of Gastrointestinal Diseases

Diseases of the Oesophagus

Khadr wa Istirkhā'-i-'ḍālāt-i-Marī

Definition:

Achalasia cardia is a disorder characterised by *Khadr* (paralysis) and *Istirkhā'* (relaxation) of the oesophageal muscles responsible for swallowing, resulting in difficulty in the passage of food into the stomach.

Etiology *(Asbāb):*

- **Neurological Impairment:** Loss of motor nerve function supplying the oesophageal muscles causes disturbance in movement and localised pain.
- **Cold Temperament *(Mizāj Bārid):*** Excessive cold weakens muscular activity, leading to *Khadr*. This *Burūda* may be constitutional (*bi'l-quwwa bārid*) or due to excessive intake of cold substances, particularly cold water.

Clinical Features:

- **Initial Stage:** Mild pain and difficulty in swallowing (*odynophagia*, *dysphagia*).
- **Progressive Stage:** Increasing severity of dysphagia with persistent swallowing difficulty.
- **Severe Stage:** Complete inability to swallow, leading to nutritional deficiency (*qillat taghdhiya*) and weakness (*Suqūt Quwwat*).
- In chronic cases, the condition may become resistant to medical treatment and may prove fatal.

Management:

Supportive and Nutritional Therapy:

Since swallowing is impaired, nutrition is maintained through alternative routes.

- **Orogastric Feeding *(Taghdhiya bil Al-Unbūba):*** A silver or firm copper tube is gently introduced into the oesophagus for feeding. Though it may initially induce nausea or vomiting, gradual adaptation occurs.
- **Diet (*Ghidhā' Laṭīf*):** Administer *Sawīq al-Sha'īr* (barley gruel), fresh milk, and *Ravghan Zaitūn* (olive oil), which provides nourishment and mitigates underlying cold temperament.

Prognosis:

Symptomatic improvement is observed in many cases; however, severe forms may lead to complications due to pharyngeal muscle weakness or associated disorders.

Surgeries of the Liver

Dubayla al-Kabid

(Liver Abscess)

Definition:

Liver abscess refers to the accumulation of pus (*Mādda Ṣadīd*) within the hepatic parenchyma, resulting from suppuration following hepatic inflammation (*Waram*).

Aetiology and Pathogenesis:

The term *Dubayla*, of Persian origin (from *Do Beela*, meaning "two sacs of pus"), denotes a thick morbid substance (*mādda fasida*) accumulating within hepatic vessels. The rupture of these vessels leads to pus formation between the hepatic covering (*ghishā'-i-'aḍlah*) and the peritoneal layer (*al-ṣifāq*).

When localised beneath these layers, it is termed *Dubayla-i-Kabid*.

If the abscess ruptures and pus is evacuated—especially through urinary discharge—the patient may recover due to expulsion of the *Mādda Fāsida* (morbid material).

Classical View on Hepatic Surgery:

Opinion of Abū'l-Ḥasan Aḥmad ibn Muḥammad Al-Ṭabarī:

On Surgical Evacuation:

- Al-Ṭabarī stated that pus collected deep within the hepatic parenchyma cannot be surgically drained, as incision (*shaqq al-kabid*) leads to fatal outcomes due to uncontrollable haemorrhage and hepatic failure.

On the Site of Dubayla Formation:

- He further noted that *Dubayla* formation occurs only near the hepatic surface (perihepatic area), where surgical access may be possible with reduced risk, while deep hepatic abscesses are rare or improbable.

Treatment:

General Principles:

The main therapeutic goal is the evacuation of pus either through:

- Surgical intervention, or
- Purgative therapy (*Mushilāt*) for internal cleansing (*Tanqiya'*).

Site-Based Management:

- **Convex (superior) surface abscess:** Evacuation is facilitated by promoting urination.
- **Concave (inferior) surface abscess:** Purgative medicines (*Adwiya Mushila*) are recommended to eliminate morbid matter through the intestines.

Ḥaṣāt al-Kabid

(Hepatic Stones /Cholelithiasis)

General Concept:

According to *Aṭibbā' al-Mutaqaddimīn* (Ancient Unani Physicians), all *A'ḍā' Mujawwafa* (cavitary organs) capable of retaining viscid humours (*Ruṭūbāt Ghalīẓa*) are prone to stone formation (*ḥaṣāt*). Examples include the kidney (*al-kulya*), urinary bladder (*mathānah*), intestines (*am'ā'*), and liver (*kabid*).

***Ḥaṣāt al-Kabid*:**

According to Abū'l-Ḥasan Aḥmad ibn Muḥammad Al-Ṭabarī, calculi may form within the hepatic tissue but cannot naturally pass out, as the hepatic ducts (*majārī al-kabid*) that connect with the intestines and kidneys are extremely narrow.

Clinical Manifestations:

- Signs and symptoms of hepatic dysfunction.
- Whitish urine (*Bawl Abyaḍ*), indicating the involvement of the liver and biliary system.

When these symptoms coexist, *Al-Ṭabarī* advises that the physician should strongly suspect *Ḥaṣāt al-Kabid* (hepatic stones).

Istisqā', *Ḥabn*

(Ascites / Dropsy)

Definition:

Ascites (*Istisqā'*) is a pathological condition characterised by the accumulation of watery or phlegmatic matter (*mādda balghamiyya*) within the abdominal cavity (*Baṭn*), resulting in abdominal distension and secondary swelling of surrounding tissues. In certain cases, the effused material is minimal, yet it produces thick, difficult-to-resolve flatus (*riyāḥ ghalīẓa*).

Etiology:

1. Primary Cause:

Weakness of hepatic digestion (*ḍu'f-i haḍm kabidī*) leading to defective transformation and excretion of fluids, resulting in accumulation of serous material within the peritoneal cavity.

2. Secondary Causes:

1. **Diseases of the Liver *(Amrāḍ-i Kabid):***

- *Waram* (swelling) — *Ḥārr* or *Bārid* in nature.
- *Sū'-i Mizāj* (altered temperament).
- *Sudda* (obstruction).
- Weakness from excessive evacuations (*Istifrāghāt*) such as diarrhoea, menorrhagia, or haemorrhoids.

2. **Chronic Debilitating Diseases:**

   - Prolonged illness, causing depletion of body fluids, predisposes to *Istisqā'*.

3. **Splenic Enlargement (*'Aẓm al-Ṭiḥāl*):**

   - The spleen draws materials from the liver, weakening its *quwwat-i mumayyiza* (discriminative faculty) and impeding production of healthy blood due to contrary temperament.

4. **Renal Disorders *(Amrāḍ-i Kulya)*:**

   - Inflammation, obstruction, or *Sū'-i Mizāj* of the kidneys impair absorption of watery fluids, leading to diluted blood unable to undergo proper *Haḍm 'Urūqī* (third digestion) and *Haḍm 'Uḍwī* (fourth digestion).

5. **Gynaecological Causes *(Amrāḍ-i Raḥim)*:**

   - Uterine inflammation, pain, or *Iḥtibās-i Ḥayḍ* (Amenorrhea).

6. **Respiratory Causes: (*Amrāḍ-i Tanaffus)***

   - Diseases such as asthma *(Ribw/Dama')* and dyspnoea (*Ḍīq al-Nafas*) can lead to transudation of serous fluid into the peritoneal cavity.

Pathophysiology Of Ascites

Not every patient with hepatic weakness develops ascites.

- In some individuals, ascites occurs even without hepatic failure.
- The general constitution of the patient is one of organ weakness (*ḍu'f al-a'ḍā'*).
- Within the liver, faculties are disordered and fail to act in harmony.
- The stomach orifice (*fam-i-mi'da*) is intrinsically cold in temperament.
- Liver dryness (*yubūsat*) is reduced, while moisture (*ruṭūbat*) is

increased.

- The heart (*qalb*) is unable to resist this excess of moisture.
- The vessels between the liver and intestines are markedly narrow.
- In this pathological milieu, the patient becomes susceptible to ascites.

Types of Ascites *(Istisqā' / Ḥabn)*

Unani physicians classified *Istisqā'* into three types based on the nature and location of accumulated matter:

1. ***Istisqā' Ziqqī:*** Accumulation of serous fluid in the peritoneal cavity.
2. ***Istisqā' Ṭablī:***Abdominal distension due to gaseous accumulation (*riyāḥ ghalīẓa*), producing a drum-like resonance.
3. ***Istisqā' Laḥmī:***Generalized edema involving flesh and musculature with fluid retention.

***Istisqā' Ziqqī* (Peritoneal Ascites)**

The term *Istisqā' Ziqqī* is derived from *Ziq* (a leather water bag), as the abdomen in this condition resembles a water-filled skin—collapsing when pressed and re-expanding when released.[7]

Pathogenesis *(Asbāb al-Ḥudūth):*

This condition arises primarily from renal insufficiency, not initial hepatic failure. When kidneys fail to absorb the watery fraction of blood (*mā'iyyat al-dam*), excess fluid passes from the vessels into the peritoneal cavity. The absorptive faculty (*quwwat jādhiba*) becomes weak, preventing proper transmission of fluid from the liver to the kidneys, with hepatic weakness *(ḍu'f-i kabid)* developing secondarily.

Ascites *(Istisqā' Ziqqī)* – Classical Description by Al-Ṭabarī

Anatomical Localisation and Clinical Progression:

According to Abū al-Ḥasan Al-Ṭabarī, in *Istisqā' Ziqqī*, fluid accumulates between the *ḥijāb* (diaphragm) and *ṣifāq* (peritoneum). As fluid increases, it exerts pressure on the diaphragm upward, leading to dyspnea *(ḍīq al-nafas)* and cough due to pulmonary compression.

Hippocrates considered such cases grave, with little hope of recovery.

Causative Factors *(Asbāb):*

1. Retention of serous fluid *(mā'iyyat)* in the abdominal cavity.
2. Leakage from mesenteric vessels carrying nutrients from the stomach to the liver.
3. Persistence of fetal vascular remnants (*'urūq nafilīyia*).
4. Renal disorders—inflammation or obstruction impairing excretion.
5. Hepatic dysfunction—failure of the *Quwwat Mumayyiza* (discriminative faculty) to separate fluid from blood.
6. Ureteric rupture or obstruction of urinary passages.

Classical Observations:

Ibn al-Quff:

Attributed ascitic accumulation to *sudda-i majrā al-kabid* (hepatic obstruction) and rupture of fetal vessels, causing intestinal "floating." In such cases, *'Amal-i Bazl* (paracentesis) was the only effective treatment.

Al-Ṭabarī:

Linked *Istisqā' Ziqqī* to *Barūdat-i Kabid* (cold temperament of the liver), weakening the *Quwwat Istiḥāla* (metabolic faculty). Contributing causes include cold humours *(Ruṭūbat Bārida),* excessive haemorrhage, and coldness of associated organs (kidneys, lungs, intestines).

Pathophysiology of *Istisqā' Ziqqī* (Peritoneal Ascites)

The disease involves dysfunction of *a'ḍā' ra'īsa* (vital organs) — liver, heart, brain, and testes.

Excessive *Sukhūnat* (heat) and defective digestion lead to weakness of hepatic faculties in the following sequence:

1. *Quwwat Māsika* (retentive faculty).
2. *Quwwat Hāḍima / Mughayyira* (digestive faculty).
3. *Quwwat Jādhiba* (absorptive faculty) and *Quwwat Dāfi'a* (expulsive faculty) if pathological change persists.

Unprocessed material (*Ghidhā' Khām*) enters intestinal vessels and diffuses into the peritoneal cavity (*ṣifāq*), causing abdominal distension and peritoneal swelling.

The fluid is viscid and yellowish due to immature humours.

Clinical Features *('Alāmāt):*

- Abdominal distension with tense, shiny skin.
- Positive fluid thrill and shifting dullness.
- Scrotal swelling in advanced cases.
- Generalised weakness and emaciation.

Prognosis and Management:

According to *Mutaqaddimīn Falasafa*, recovery is possible only if the *Jawhar-i-Kabid* (hepatic essence) remains intact. Once complete morbid changes (*Fasād-i-Kāmil*) occur, prognosis becomes poor.

Istisqā' Ziqqī originates from excessive hepatic heat *(sukhūnat)*—unlike other types, which arise from coldness (*burūda*).

Principles of Treatment:

- Employ cooling and hepatic-strengthening therapy to restore balance.
- Correct digestion and maintain a temperate diet; avoid hot or irritant foods.
- *'Amal-i-Bazl* (Paracentesis): If medical therapy fails, ascitic fluid

should be evacuated.

Five anatomical sites are described for puncture or cauterization:

1. *Mi'da* (stomach region)
2. *Kabid* (liver)
3. *Ṭiḥāl* (spleen)
4. *Qa'r al-Mi'da* (gastric fundus)
5. *Surra* (umbilicus)

Instruments used include metallic and wooden (oak) cauteries.

Surgical Management of *Istisqā' Ziqqī*

***'Amal-i Bazl /Bazl al-Mā'* (Paracentesis)**

Indication (Only in *Istisqā' Ziqqī*)

Paracentesis is performed exclusively for *istisqā' ziqqī* (peritoneal fluid), not for *istisqā' laḥmī* (interstitial) or *istisqā' ṭablī* (gaseous).

General Principles (Pre-op Assessment)

- Assess Quwwat (patient strength); operate only if robust.
- In weak patients, evacuation is avoided due to the risk of collapse/fatality.

Classical Surgical Technique According to Al-Zahrāwī, Al-Majusi and Early Unani Surgeons

Position & Preparation

- Patient upright/standing or squatting; assistant compresses abdomen from behind to shift fluid downwards.

Site Selection (Aetiology-based; as per classical texts)

- **Intestinal origin:** 3 finger-breadths below the umbilicus (midline/above pubis).

- **Hepatic origin (*Marḍ al-Kabid*):** on the left side of the umbilicus.
- **Splenic origin (*Marḍ al-Ṭiḥāl*):** on the right side of the umbilicus.

Avoid the side on which the patient prefers to lie.

Operative Steps

- Mark the site (palpate from Surra downward).
- Incise skin with *al-mibḍaʿ / mishraḥ;* gently retract skin.
- Pierce *ṣifāq* (peritoneum) to enter cavity.
- Insert silver/copper cannula or *Āla Mujawwaf;* drain slowly to patient tolerance—never complete evacuation in one sitting.
- Dress wound. Provide *ghidhāʾ muqawwī* (e.g., *māʾ al-laḥm*); use *muʿarriq* (sudorifics), *mudirr-i bawl* (diuretics) as needed.
- Staged drainage on day 2–4 with reassessment of pulse/Quwwat; always leave some residual fluid for gradual elimination (e.g., mild *adwiya mushila*).

Side-Guided *Bazl* by Organ Pain (per classical rule)

- Liver pain *(Kabid):* left of the umbilicus.
- Spleen pain *(Ṭiḥāl)*: right of the umbilicus.
- Both weak: midline.

Alternative Methods According to Classical Unani Surgeon

Abū al-Ḥasan Al-Ṭabarī (Umbilical Thread Technique)

- In strong patients (preserved hepatic vitality, no excessive urinary heat): fine opening at Surra (Umbilicus); insert a hair thread to permit slow leakage; reposition if flow stops.
- For thick fluid: use *Jawf al-Munajjal* (hollow iron).
- After ~40 hours, bandage; nourish; assess *qārūra* (urine) and pulse; repeat up to three stages if stable.

Ibn Hubal Al-Baghdādī

- Squatting position; compress flanks to pool fluid anterior to pubis.
- Sites: 3 cm below the umbilicus in intestinal diseases, left of the umbilicus in hepatic diseases, right in splenic diseases.
- Copper tube drainage gradually over 3–4 days; never one-time emptying; continue with pharmacologic therapy thereafter.

Contraindications & Cautions

- **Absolute/relative**: *Ḍuʿf Quwwat*; extremes of age; concurrent systemic illness *(Suʿāl Muzmin, Ishāl, Fasād al-Kabid)*.
- Do not evacuate all fluid at once—risk of sudden collapse (*inḥilāl arwāḥ ḥaywāniyya)* and death.

Post-Operative Course

- Daily reassessment of pulse/strength; staged drainage until clinically adequate.
- If residual lower-abdominal fluid persists and *Quwwat* is low: suture and continue *mudirr-i bawl* / *muʿarriq* and dietary strengthening.

Istisqāʾ Ṭablī (Tympanitic Ascites)

Definition

A relatively rare form of ascites marked by predominant gaseous distension rather than free fluid; more often linked with splenic enlargement *(ʿiẓm al-ṭiḥāl)* than primary hepatic disease. Failure of the liver to transform Kaylūs leads to excess *quwwat ḥārra* acting on it, generating pathological vapours diverted toward the spleen, producing splenomegaly.

Etiology:

1. ***Ḍuʿf Haḍm Miʿdī / Haḍm Awwal*** → excess *bukhārāt* around stomach/intestines;

2. ***Ḍu'f-i Ḥarārat Gharīziyya*** (weak innate heat);

3. ***Ghilẓat wa Qillat Nuḍj al-Mādda*** (thick/immature matter) → indigestible vapours;

4. ***Ghalaba'-i--Ḥarārat Gharība*** preceding innate heat → *Bukhārāt Radī'a;*

5. ***Ḍu'f al-Kabid wa al-Ṭiḥāl*** and related organs.

Pathophysiology *(Māhiyyat-i Maraḍī)*

Organs prone to retaining abnormal vapours develop thick humid vapours *(ruṭūbat bukhārīyya ghalīẓa)* in the stomach that only partially resolve and then spread to the intestines/viscera. Immature *kaylūs* reaching a weak hepatic heat produces poor-quality blood and *riyāḥ ghalīẓa* that infiltrate vessels and accumulate in the *ṣifāq* (peritoneum). The resultant nourishment is unsuitable for *a'ḍā'*, causing tympanitic distension—*Istisqā' Ṭablī.*

Pathogenesis: According to Ibn Zuhr (Avenzoar, 1091–1162 CE)

Incomplete *Istiḥāla of Kaylūs* in the liver leaves components improperly mixed; dysregulated *ḥarārat* (innate or extraneous) degrades matter into vapours that ascend to *marāq al-baṭn* (peritoneum), causing abdominal distension. With persistent defective transformation, subsequent foods are likewise affected; loss of *laṭāfat* sustains thick vapours and chronic tympanites.

Clinical Features *('Alāmāt)*

- Abdominal distension predominantly gaseous; umbilical protrusion.
- Tympanitic (drum-like) note on percussion; no fluid wave (unlike *Istisqā' Ziqqī*) and no dependent oedema (unlike *Istisqā' Laḥmī*).
- *Al-Jashā'* (frequent belching); advanced *ḍīq al-nafas* from fullness of *ālāt al-tanaffus / rī'a / ḥijāb;* resemblance to *Khunāq*.
- Return of putrefied nutriment via *māsāriqā* → *ishāl*; malnutrition,

suqūṭ al-quwwat, and possible death.

Subtypes of Tympanitic Ascites

1. **Classical Tympanitic Ascites:** Accumulation of *riyāḥ ghalīẓa* within the abdomen due to hepatic/splenic dysfunction and defective transformation of *Kaylūs*.

2. ***Ḥabn:*** Part of *ruṭūbat* undergoes *taḥlīl*, part remains unresolved; *Quwwat al-Kabid* and *Quwwat al-Haḍm* usually preserved, so *taghdhiya* continues, and general strength remains. Persistent unresolved moisture causes chronic distension; once resolution is achieved, prognosis is favourable.

Istisqā' Laḥmī

(Anasarca / Muscular or Fleshy Dropsy)

Pathological Description

Istisqā' Laḥmī is characterised by abnormal accumulation of moisture *(ruṭūbat)* within the flesh, muscles *('aḍalāt),* ligaments *(ribāṭāt),* membranes (*aghshiya*), and connective tissue, leading to generalised swelling. The body becomes pale and blood-deficient (*qillat al-dam*), and on incision, only a watery, snail-saliva-like fluid exudes. Ancient physicians described such bodies as "soaked like a corpse"—not lifeless, but deprived of vitality due to lack of blood.

Etymology

The term *Laḥmī* refers to its involvement of muscular tissue. Thin and thick moistures (*Ruṭūbat Raqīqa wa Ghalīẓa*) infiltrate flesh, ligaments, and nerves (*a'ṣāb*). The space between the peritoneum *(ṣifāq)* and its covering membrane—occupied by fluid in *istisqā' ziqqī*—is, in *istisqā' laḥmī*, filled with cold moisture (*ruṭūbat bārida*). Hippocrates (Buqraṭ) and Jālīnūs (Galen) compared the body to an object drenched in liquid (*Mablūl*).

Etiology *(Asbāb)*

Unlike *Istisqā᾽ Ziqqī* and *Ṭablī*, which arise from hepatic heat (*sukhūnat al-kabid*), *Istisqā᾽ Laḥmī* results from hepatic coldness *(burūdat al-kabid)* and systemic deficiency of innate heat (*ḥarārat gharīziyya*).

Predisposing Factors include:

- Suppression of hemorrhoidal or menstrual bleeding (*iḥtibās al-bawāsīr / al-ḥayḍ*).
- Excessive haemorrhage.
- Coldness of the lungs, kidneys, or intestines.
- Cold temperament of other vital organs.
- Constitutional deficiency of hepatic heat and disordered digestion with vapour production.

Views of Classical Physicians

Ibn Hubal Al-Baghdādī:

Attributed the disease to *ḍu'f al-kabid* (hepatic weakness) in transforming humours (*Akhlāṭ*). Causes include *sudda* (obstruction), *sū᾽ mizāj bārid*, or hepatic inflammation (*Waram*). Participation of the stomach, spleen, intestines, or mesentery *(masāriqā)* may contribute. In women, suppression of natural bleedings predisposes the condition. Incomplete digestion results in immature humours (*akhlāṭ naḍīja*) infiltrating tissues, producing generalised swelling (Waram).

Ibn Zuhr :

Linked *Istisqā᾽ Laḥmī* to failure of *quwwat hāḍima* (digestive faculty) and incomplete transformation (*istiḥāla*) of *Kaymūs* (chymous matter) into a healthy *dam*. The undigested material tends toward *balgham* (phlegm) formation, disrupting nutritional resemblance between the *jawhar al-kabid* and *jawhar al-a'ḍā'*, leading to diffuse tissue infiltration.

Pathological Nature *(Māhiyyat-i Maraḍī)*

The disease arises from poor dietary regulation, excessive moist or harmful foods, and chronic indigestion, resulting in hepatic coldness and deficient innate heat. Consequently, blood becomes cold and moist (*burūdat wa ruṭūbat*).

These moistures permeate vessels and tissues, saturating the entire musculature—hence the term *Laḥmī.*

Unlike *Istisqā' Ziqqī* (peritoneal) or *Ṭablī* (gaseous), *Laḥmī* involves fluid accumulation within tissues rather than between membranes (*ṣifāq wa ghishā'*).

Clinical Features

- Generalised swelling and puffiness of the body.
- Eyelid oedema, protruding eyes.
- Pitting oedema—indentation persists after pressure.
- No abdominal distension or fluid thrill, unlike *Istisqā' Ziqqī.*
- No tympanitic note, unlike *Istisqā' Ṭablī.*

Treatment

1. Restoration of the Liver Functions *(Iṣlāḥ al-Kabid):*

Therapy aims to restore hepatic strength by stimulating *ḥarārat gharīziyya* and improving transformation and assimilation, thereby reducing tissue moisture.

2. Venesection *(Faṣd):*

Used to:

- Evacuate excessive moisture from circulation.
- Generate internal heat (*tawlīd al-ḥarārat*) and restore hepatic temperament (*i'tidāl mizāj*).

Jarāḥāt e Baṭn

(Abdominal Injuries / Abdominal Trauma)

Surgical Considerations in Abdominal, Mesenteric, and Intestinal Injuries *(Jarāḥat al-Shikam, al-Marāq, wa al-Am'ā')*

Introduction

Classical physicians regarded injuries of the abdomen, mesentery *(marāq),* and intestines *(am'ā')* as life-threatening due to the involvement of vital organs and risk of fatal complications. Their surgical management emphasised the careful repositioning of prolapsed viscera, handling of the omentum *(al-tharb)*, and appropriate use of suturing *(khiyāṭa)* techniques.

Prolapse of Intestinal Loops

When intestinal loops protruded through an abdominal wound, surgeons prioritised gentle reintegration into the cavity while preventing torsion, maintaining circulation, and minimising trauma. Delayed repositioning was discouraged, as distension could prevent reinsertion.

Prolapse of the Omentum *(Al-Tharb)*

In cases where the omentum protruded, two main approaches were adopted:

Excision ***(Qaṭ')*** – if the part was devitalized or infected.

Ligation ***(Ribāṭ)*** – if viable tissue requires stabilisation or bleeding control.

The choice depended on tissue condition and the extent of prolapse.

Decision on Suturing *(Khiyāṭa)*

The necessity of suturing was carefully weighed:

Indicated in large wounds to approximate tissues, prevent evisceration, and secure the abdominal wall.

Avoided when there was a risk of trapping infection or where natural healing with dressings was sufficient. The suturing technique varied with wound size, involved structures (intestine or omentum), and the surgeon's judgment for optimal healing.

Anatomical Considerations

Rupture at the flanks *(khāṣira)* was considered less dangerous, while rupture at the midline *(wasṭ al-bahra)* was more serious due to easy intestinal prolapse.

Two longitudinal muscles extend from the thorax *(ṣadr)* to the pubic bone (*aẓm al-ʻāna);* rupture along this line often leads to bowel protrusion. In contrast, the lateral muscles of the flanks act as protective barriers.

Clinical Manifestations

A large rupture allows more bowel to prolapse but may permit easier repositioning.

A small rupture, if untreated promptly, causes bowel distension due to trapped air, hindering reinsertion.

Paradoxically, smaller mesenteric *(marāq)* injuries were often considered more dangerous than larger ones.

Jarāḥat al-Amʿā'(Injuries to the Intestines)

Jarāḥat al-Amʿā' al-Ghilāẓ wa al-Diqāq

(Injuries to the Small and Large Intestine)

Introduction

Classical physicians distinguished between injuries of the small intestine *(al-amʿā' al-diqāq)* and the large intestine (*al-amʿā' al-ghilāẓ*) based on their anatomical structure, vascularity, and physiological function. They noted that the site of injury significantly influenced prognosis and healing.

Healing Potential of the Large Intestine (*Al-Am'ā' al-Ghilāẓ*)

The large intestine was considered more resilient and easier to heal due to its muscular-like *(laḥmī)* texture and thicker wall. Medicinal preparations were believed to remain longer within it, enabling sustained therapeutic action.

Healing Challenges in the Small Intestine *(Al-Am'ā' al-Diqāq)*

- Injuries to the small intestine, especially the jejunum *(ṣā'im)*, were considered
- difficult to heal. The reasons cited include:
- High vascularity with numerous large vessels (*'urūq*).
- Thin, delicate wall prone to rupture.
- Physiological resemblance to nerves (*'aṣab*), making it highly sensitive.
- Exposure to pure bile (*mirra*), which is hot *(ḥārr)* in temperament and delays healing.

Relation to the Liver *(Kabid)*

All intestinal segments were considered closely associated with the liver, explaining why hepatic disturbances often manifested in intestinal disorders and delayed wound healing.

Clinical Implications

- Injury to the small intestine → poor prognosis and higher risk of complications.
- Injury to the large intestine → better prognosis and easier surgical repair.
- Lower intestinal parts → retain medications longer, enhancing treatment efficacy.

Classical Opinions *(Aqwāl-i-Aṭibbā')*

Al-Rāzī (Rhazes, 865–925 CE)

stated that larger ruptures of the *marāq* (mesentery) may be less dangerous than smaller ones.

Al-Zahrāwī (Albucasis, 936–1013 CE)

observed:

"If the injured bowel be the large intestine, it will heal more easily; if it be the small intestine, healing is difficult; and injury to the jejunum *(ṣā'im)* is rarely curable."

Jarāḥāt al-Mi'da

(Traumatic Lesions of the Stomach)

Lesions of the Lower Part of the Stomach *(Asfal al-Mi'da)*

Wounds involving the lower stomach often heal more favourably since medications reach and remain at this site long enough to exert their therapeutic effect. The presence of natural flesh *(laḥm ṭabī'ī)* further enhances recovery by retaining drugs for extended periods.

Lesions of the Upper Part of the Stomach *(A'lā al-Mi'da)*

In contrast, injuries near the cardiac orifice *(fūhāt-i-mi'da)* generally show poor healing. The upper part is highly sensitive and fails to retain medications, as they pass rapidly through this region. This heightened sensitivity aggravates the wound and limits the effect of treatment.

Opinion of Zakariyā Al-Rāzī

Al-Rāzī noted that if the lower stomach contains natural flesh, treatment is more reliable, as the organ can retain medications for several days. However, the upper orifice seldom recovers because of its extreme sensitivity and inability to hold therapeutic substances.

Surgical Principles in Unani Medicine

Classical surgeons emphasized repositioning *(radd)* of protruded intestines, suturing *(khiyāṭa)* when necessary, and topical application of medications. They advised the protection of vital organs (A'ḍā'

Ra'īsa) from secondary trauma.

In smaller wounds, expulsion of trapped air was essential, sometimes requiring enlargement of the opening *(tawsiʿat al-kharq)*. The omentum *(al-tharb)* was assessed for excision *(qaṭʿ)* or ligation *(ribāṭ)*. Early intervention was recommended to prevent gaseous distension. Injuries to the large intestine were managed confidently due to its Laḥmī nature and ability to retain drugs.

Positioning the Patient in Abdominal Injuries *(Jarāḥāt al-Baṭn)*

Principles of Positioning

Proper patient positioning was considered vital to prevent protrusion, fluid collection, and injury to vital organs (*aʿḍā' ra'īsa*):

- **Downward-facing wounds *(Asfal):*** Elevate the upper body.
- **Upward-facing wounds *(Aʿlā)*:** Elevate the lower body.
- **Combined wounds:** Reinsert all intestines *(amʿā')* together.
- **Left-sided wounds *(Jānib Aysar):*** Incline toward the right side (Jānib Ayman).
- **Right-sided wounds *(Jānib Ayman)*:** Incline toward the left side.

The objective was to maintain the injured side elevated to reduce complications.

Opinions of Abū Al-Qāsim Al-Zahrāwī

Al-Zahrāwī emphasised differential positioning according to the wound site:

- **Lower abdominal wounds:** Patient supine, legs elevated — to aid repositioning and reduce intra-abdominal pressure.
- **Upper abdominal wounds:** Head and chest elevated — to prevent regurgitation and protect organs like the stomach (*miʿda*) and liver (*kabid*).
- **Lateral wounds:** The injured side was kept higher to reduce

compression and ease reduction.

- **Small wounds:** Positioning may be adjusted for the surgeon's convenience.

He highlighted posture as a determinant of surgical success and emphasised preventing evisceration and fluid accumulation.

Management of Abdominal Wounds with Protrusion of Intestines and Omentum

Introduction

Penetrating abdominal wounds that rupture the peritoneum (*ṣifāq*) may lead to protrusion of the intestines (*amʿāʾ*) or omentum (*al-tharb*). Early and appropriate management is essential to prevent inflammation, distension, ischemia, or gangrene.

Common signs include swelling (*waram*) and distension (*infākh*) around the wound site. Al-Rāzī attributed these to the *coldness of entrapped air* (*burūda al-hawāʾ*).

Conservative Management

- Application of heated astringent wine (*khamr qābiḍ sakhīn*)—preferably dark-colored—over the wound to relieve *waram* and *infākh*.
- Hot fomentation using a warmed sponge or cloth to soften tissue and ease reduction.
- Warmed wine compresses were preferred over water for their greater heat retention and strengthening effect on the intestines.

Surgical Management

If swelling persists or reduction is impossible by conservative means:

- The wound may be enlarged *(tawsīʿ al-kharq)* with a fistula scalpel (*mishrat al-nāsūr*) to facilitate repositioning.
- Sharp double-edged instruments were avoided to prevent collateral

injury.

Reduction of Protruded Viscera

- Gentle repositioning (*radd al-amʿāʾ / radd al-al-tharb*) into the abdomen is recommended.
- If resistance occurs due to distension, limited controlled enlargement of the wound is preferred to forced reduction.

Management of Gangrenous Intestine/Omentum

- Delay in reduction may cause discolouration (green/black), indicating gangrene.

Procedure:

- Ligate affected vessels with fine silk.
- Excise necrotic portions only, and reposition viable structures into the cavity carefully.

Early reduction improves prognosis; delay leads to necrosis and sepsis.

Reduction of Protruded Intestine after Trauma According to Al-Zahrāwī

Nature of Abdominal Tears

Al-Zahrāwī classified abdominal wall ruptures (*shaqq al-baṭn*) as:

1. **Large *(Kabīr):*** Allow multiple intestinal loops to protrude; difficult to reduce.
2. **Small *(Ṣaghīr):*** Appears minor but more troublesome due to tight openings and early swelling.
3. **Medium *(Mutawassiṭ):*** Most manageable and favourable for reduction.

Causes of Difficulty in Reduction

- Narrow tearing (*Shaqq Ṣaghīr*) obstructing reinsertion.

- Distension (*Infākh al-Amʿāʾ*) caused by exposure to cold air (*burūda al-hawāʾ*).

Conservative Measures

Warmed fomentation with water or wine compresses relieves distension and facilitates reduction. Conservative treatment was preferred initially, being safer than immediate incision.

Surgical Intervention

When conservative therapy fails, careful enlargement *(tawsīʿ al-kharq)* using precise surgical tools was advised, avoiding tissue trauma.

Repositioning Technique

The intestines should be returned gently to their anatomical position, ensuring proper alignment to prevent postoperative complications and promote healing.

Methods of Suturing *(Khiyāṭa)* in Abdominal Wounds

Selection of Suture Material

The suture thread (*khayṭ*) should possess *moderate consistency*—neither excessively hard nor too soft.

- If too hard → may lacerate the *ṣifāq* (peritoneum).
- If too soft or weak → may rupture prematurely, causing wound dehiscence.

Technique of Stitching *(Ṭarīqa-i-Khiyāṭa)*

a. Needle Placement

- The needle should pierce the tissue at an appropriate distance from the wound edge.
- Too close → tearing and *infiṣāl al-khayṭ* (suture separation).
- Too far → improper approximation and gaping of the wound.

b. Depth of Needle Bite

- The bite should be balanced—neither too deep into the muscle nor too superficial in the skin.
- Proper depth ensures accurate coaptation and promotes healing.

c. Knotting ***(ʿAqad)***

- Each suture should be tied externally over the muscular layer.
- Knots must be firm yet gentle to prevent ischemia.
- Successive stitches are placed close together in sequence until closure is complete.

Post-Suturing Care

- After suturing, *Dharūr Aṣfar* (yellow astringent powder) is applied to check bleeding and prevent suppuration.
- The wound is dressed and bandaged until mild tension and contraction appear. Subsequently, *Marham Bāsalīqūn* is used to aid cicatrization, after which sutures are removed.

Dietary Regulation ***(Tadbīr al-Ghidhā)***

Diet plays a vital role in recovery. Foods producing flatulence should be avoided as they may cause abdominal tension, disrupt sutures, and delay healing.

Principles Highlighted by Zakariyyā Al-Rāzī

Al-Rāzī emphasised *balance* in all aspects of suturing:

- The distance between stitches should be neither too wide nor too close.
    - Wide → incomplete wound closure.
    - Narrow → tissue strangulation and poor healing.
- Sutures in tendinous tissue *(Watr)* require stronger tension to prevent rupture.
- The depth must always be moderate to ensure firm union without

tissue necrosis.

Suturing Techniques in Abdominal, Omental, and Intestinal Wounds *(Khiyāṭa fīl Jarāḥāt al-Baṭn wa al-Am'ā' wa al-Tharb)*

Purpose of Abdominal Suturing

The primary objective of abdominal suturing is the approximation of the peritoneum *(ṣifāq)* with the muscular layer *(marāq)*. This is technically challenging due to the delicate and nervous nature (*'aṣabī ṭabī'at*) of the muscular wall.

Technique of Approximating the *Ṣifāq* with *Marāq*

- **Initial Needle Insertion:** The needle is introduced from outside inward through the skin and into the *marāq*—while sparing the *ṣifāq* edge.
- **Alternating Sutures:** It is then passed from inside outward through the opposite *marāq*, again avoiding direct passage through the *ṣifāq*. This alternating pattern continues until complete closure.
- **Reinforcement:** This method provides a stronger approximation, as the *Ṣifāq* remains tightly drawn behind the *Marāq*, ensuring deeper layer integrity.

Complications of Faulty Suturing

Al-Rāzī cautioned that improper union of the *Ṣifāq* and *Marāq* may lead to postoperative herniation. During exertion or distension, the intestines could protrude beyond the peritoneum, causing pain and impaired function.

Special Technique by Ibn Hubal Al-Baghdādī

Ibn Hubal introduced a refined alternating suture method:

- The needle is inserted into the outer *marāq* margin and brought out without piercing its adjacent *ṣifāq*, then it enters the opposite *ṣifāq* margin from inside outward.
- The process is alternated repeatedly, joining *ṣifāq* and *marāq* in an

interlaced pattern for stronger closure.

Suturing in Case of Peritoneal Rupture *(Inshiqāq-i-Ṣifāq)*

When both *Ṣifāq* and *Marāq* are torn, they must be sutured together. Because *Marāq* is *ʿAṣabī* (nervous), failure to achieve firm union delays healing. Proper approximation ensures structural and functional restoration.

Post-Suturing Care

- **Medicinal Application:** Use of *Inbāt-i-Laḥm Adwiya* (wound-healing remedies).
- **Bandaging:** Application of soft wool soaked in *ravghan zaytūn* (olive oil) over the abdomen and groin.
- **For Intestinal Injuries:** Use of an astringent enema (*ḥuqna*) with concentrated black wine (*sharāb aswad qābiḍ*) when the rupture extends to the intestinal cavity (*tajwīf al-amʿā'*).

Suturing According to Abū Al-Qāsim Al-Zahrāwī

Al-Zahrāwī described four techniques—two general and two specialised—for *Khiyāṭat al-Baṭn* (abdominal suturing).

1. First Technique of Abdominal Suturing

- **Needle Choice:** Select needles of moderate thickness according to incision size.
- **Needle Insertion:** Introduce the needle initially unthreaded from inside outward through both cutaneous and peritoneal edges, securing a four-layer closure.
- **Securing the Suture:** The double thread is wrapped around the needle and tightened from both ends, aligning wound margins.
- **Spacing:** Keep intervals equal to one finger's breadth.
- **Precautions:** Avoid placing stitches too close (causing tearing) or too far (causing poor union).

- **Final Adjustment:** Cut projecting ends to prevent irritation.

2. Second Technique of Abdominal Suturing

- **Needle and Thread:** Use a moderately thick, twisted thread.
- **Insertion:** The needle passes through all four wound margins—two cutaneous and two peritoneal—and returns to its origin, producing a looped, interlocking stitch resembling a knitted pattern.
- **Spacing:** Leave approximately one small finger's breadth between stitches to maintain uniform tension.

Suturing Techniques According to Jālīnūs (Galen)

1. First Special Technique

Jālīnūs (Galen) described an alternating interlaced suture resembling the furrier's skin-stitching technique:

- The needle is inserted from outside inward through *jild* (skin) and *ʿaḍal al-baṭn* (abdominal muscle), leaving *ṣifāq* intact.
- Then from inside outward through the opposite *ṣifāq*.
- The process alternates to achieve a strong, flexible closure with minimal tension on the peritoneum.

2. Second Special Technique

This advanced method aligns each layer with its counterpart:

- The needle first enters through the outer abdominal wall without piercing *ṣifāq*.
- Then it joins both *ṣifāq* margins (*Ghilāf al-Bāṭin ilā Ghilāf al-Bāṭin*).
- Finally, it passes outward through the cutaneous edges.
- This layer-by-layer approximation restores the physiological continuity of the abdominal wall and was considered superior to

simple sutures.[5]

Jurūḥ-i-Am'ā'

(Traumatic Injuries of the Intestine)

Introduction

Abū Al-Qāsim Al-Zahrāwī, in *al-Taṣrīf*, elaborated on the surgical management of intestinal wounds (*Jurūḥ-i-Am'ā'*), describing both spontaneous healing and operative intervention. He recognised the complexity and high mortality associated with such injuries, particularly in the small intestine (*am'ā' ṣaghīr*).

Natural Healing (*Indimāl-i-Jarāḥat bi-Ṭabī'at*)

Small intestinal perforations were occasionally observed to heal spontaneously, though such natural recovery was rare and unpredictable. Al-Zahrāwī considered this outcome an exception rather than a rule.

Traditional Method of Ant Suturing (*Kharṭ bil-Naml*)

Selection and Technique

- Large-headed ants were selected for their strong mandibles.
- The edges of the intestinal wound were manually approximated, and each ant was applied so that its jaws clamped both margins together. After firm clamping, the ant's body was cut off, leaving the head attached as a biological clip.

Sequential Closure and Reintegration

Several ants were applied along the wound, depending on its length. After achieving closure, the repaired intestine (*am'ā'*) was carefully repositioned into the abdominal cavity, and the abdominal wall sutured.

Outcome

The ant heads functioned as natural clamps until healing occurred.

Al-Zahrāwī noted that this procedure caused no significant pain or adverse effect.

Use of Animal Gut Sutures *(Al-Khiyāṭa bil-Amʿāʾ al-Ḥaywān)*

Preparation and Application

The animal gut was cleaned, softened, and attached to a fine twisted linen thread, which was threaded through a surgical needle (*Ibra*). The suture was then passed through the wound margins of the intestine to secure coaptation.

Procedure and Reintegration

After completion, the sutured intestinal loop was replaced within the abdominal cavity to heal naturally.

Prognosis

Although innovative, Al-Zahrāwī admitted that both the ant suturing and animal gut suturing methods carried only a remote hope of recovery, with limited success in practice.

Limitations of Surgical Repair

Al-Zahrāwī regarded large perforations, particularly of the small intestine (*amʿāʾ ṣaghīr*), as incurable. The absence of dependable methods for extensive intestinal repair reflected the surgical limitations of the time, despite remarkable ingenuity in technique.

Khurūj al-Tharb (Protrusion of the Omentum)

Classical Unani View

When the Omentum (*Al-Tharb*) protrudes through an abdominal wound, it rapidly undergoes *taʿaffun* (putrefaction) due to air exposure, even if externalised for a short duration. Unlike the intestines or liver, the omentum seldom regains vitality after protrusion and becomes hard and corrupt.

Surgical Principle:

The protruded segment should never be reinserted once exposed. Only the internal healthy portion is preserved, and the external putrefied segment must be excised early.

Ibn Hubal Al-Baghdādī's View

Clinical Presentation:

Protrusion of *am'ā'* or *al-tharb* is frequently accompanied by swelling (*Waram*), especially in cold environments, making reinsertion difficult.

Therapeutic Measures:

- Foment the wound with Warm wine *(khamr ḥārr)* to reduce swelling.
- Place the patient in a *hammām* (bath) or suspended posture with an arched back and contracted abdomen to facilitate reduction.

Surgical Technique:

- If *Al-Tharb* remains viable (not green or black), gently reposition it.
- If the opening is narrow, perform *tawsī' al-kharq* (controlled enlargement).
- If gangrenous, ligate the vessels with a fine thread, excise the necrotic portion, and dust *dharūr mudammil* (wound-healing powder) over the site.

Ibn Zuhr's View

Clinical Observation:

Penetrating abdominal wounds by sharp instruments may cause *khurūj-al-tharb*.

Surgical Management:

- Wash gently with lukewarm water if contaminated.
- Reinsert if the omentum is viable and intact.
- Excise necrosed or blackened portions.
- Suture the abdominal wound with silk thread and apply *adwiya mundamilal* (healing agents).
- Advise a light, easily digestible diet to prevent morbid accumulation.

Zakariyyā Al-Rāzī's View

Clinical Observation:

If the omentum appears cold (*barūdat*) but not discoloured, it may be safely repositioned. However, if green or black, it indicates gangrene.

Surgical Management:

- Ligate above the necrotic area to prevent haemorrhage, leaving the tied portion outside for natural sloughing.
- Excise necrosed tissue after ligation.
- Since *Al-Tharb* lacks nerves and has small vessels, excision causes minimal pain, but total removal weakens digestion and reduces natural Warmth (*Sukhūnat*), especially in debilitated patients.

Abū Al-Qāsim Al-Zahrāwī's View

Clinical Observation:

If the omentum is freshly protruded, it should be reduced like intestines. Once it turns green or black, reinsertion is contraindicated.

Surgical Management:

- Apply a ligature above the discoloured segment.
- Excise the gangrenous portion below the ligature to prevent bleeding and infection.

Surgeries of Anorectal Diseases

Bawāsīr (Haemorrhoids)

Clinical Challenges of Anal Diseases

Diseases of the anal region are difficult to cure due to several anatomical and physiological factors:

- The anus is a mobile organ, continuously in motion.
- It is the outlet for faeces and morbid humours, leading to recurrent contamination.
- Its inverted structure complicates surgical and local management.
- Rich nerve supply makes it highly sensitive, causing intense pain.

Hence, a complete cure of anorectal diseases is rarely achieved. Among these, *Bawāsīr* (haemorrhoids) is the most common and significant disorder.

Definition of Haemorrhoid;

- Hippocrates has defined *Bawāsīr* as varicosity and swelling of anal and rectal veins, similar to the varicosity of lower limb veins.
- Ibn al-Quff Masīḥī opined that excessive growth of flesh around or inside the anus is *Bawāsīr*.
- Mohammad Tabri defined piles as congestion of morbid viscid *Sawdāwī* blood in anal veins.
- Al-Majūsī defined it as an excess growth at the mouth of vessels present in the anus.
- Al-Razi has mentioned that piles are reddish black, bleeding per rectum due to the opening of the anal blood vessels.
- Avicenna and Sayyid Ismā'īl Jurjānī have not defined haemorrhoids but have given an illustrative description of their physical types.
- According to Azam Khan, *Bawāsīr* is a vascular dilatation at the mouth of haemorrhoidal veins filled with morbid *Khilṭ-i sawdā* (bilious melanchole).
- Ibn Hubal Baghdādī said that the formation of a haemorrhoidal

lesion is due to the precipitation of blood at the mouth of anal veins.

- Akbar Arzani has defined haemorrhoids as development of polyps at anal verge that may or may not present with per rectal bleed.[16,17]
- According to Samarqandi, haemorrhoid is a fleshy or callus like growth at mouth of anal vein due to accumulation thick *Sawdāwī* blood.
- Thus, it is clear that a haemorrhoidal lesion is a vascular dilatation in haemorrhoidal veins due to accumulation of bilious melanchole.

Pathogenesis of *Bawāsīr* (Hemorrhoids) in Unani Medicine

In Unani medicine, *Bawāsīr* results from the accumulation of morbid humors (*mādda fāsida*)—particularly of melancholic origin (*sawdāwī mādda*)—causing venous congestion and swelling in the anal vessels. This abnormal humoral accumulation leads to vascular dilatation, inflammation, and sometimes haemorrhage in the anal region.

Ibn Sīnā's View

Primary Cause:

- Chiefly due to *Sawdāwī Mādda* or *Sawdāwī Dam* (melancholic blood).
- Rarely associated with *Balgham* (phlegmatic humour).

Types of Haemorrhoids:

1. ***Flatulent Type*** – caused by *Balgham*, forming air-filled swellings.
2. ***Sūlūlī Type*** – nearer to *Sawdā'* (black bile).
3. ***Tūtī Type*** – related to *Sawdāwī Dam*.
4. ***'Inabī Type*** – mixed form of both *Sawdā'* and *Sawdāwī Dam*.

Ibn Lūqā's View

- Excessive use of castor oil predisposes to Bawāsīr.
- Common in humid climates and among those consuming milk, curd, dry fruits, and dry fish.
- Individuals with *Sawdāwī Mizāj* (melancholic temperament) or

Sawdāwī disorders are more susceptible.

Ibn Hubal Baghdādī's View

- Viscid humours (*Akhlāṭ Lazija*) accumulate in the liver, which then diverts them to the anal veins.
- Their precipitation and stagnation cause dilatation and engorgement of venous walls.
- Haemorrhage occurs when morbid blood *(dam fāsid)* obstructs or ruptures vessels.

Jurjānī's View

- The root cause is *Sawdāwī Dam* (melancholic blood).
- Two primary mechanisms:

1. Burning or corrosion of blood by hot and acrid substances, producing morbid *Sawdāwī* blood.
2. Excessive consumption of melancholic-producing foods, resulting in thick, dark blood.

Predisposing factors: chronic illness, prolonged sitting or walking, excess castor oil, and dry foods.

View of Chandpūrī

The most common cause of *Bawāsīr* is:

- *Mādda Sawdā'* (black bile material), or
- *Sawdāwī* blood (melancholic blood).

Rarely, it may arise from *mādda balghamī* (phlegmatic matter).

Classification

bawāsīr has been classified in three ways:

1. According to shape
2. According to the site
3. According to the presence or absence of bleeding

According to Shape

1. ***Sūlūlī:*** polyps in the shape of *'Adasiyya* (lentil) or *Himsiyya* (gram)
2. ***'Inabiyya:*** shape of the polyp resembles grapes
3. ***Tūtī:*** polyp resembles the shape of a mulberry
4. ***Naffākhī:*** polyps resemble the shape of a small bubble
5. ***Nakhlī:*** Vessels of the polyps are spread like the branches and roots of a date tree
6. ***Tīnī:*** Shape of the polyps is flat and round, similar to that of *Injir* (fig)
7. ***Tamrī:*** Shape of the polyps is similar to the shape of a date, i.e., long and oval.

According to the Site

These are of three types:

1. ***Dākhilī Bawāsīr* (internal piles):** hemorrhoidal lesions are deep-seated with bleeding and slight pain.

2. ***Khārijī Bawāsīr* (external piles):** hemorrhoidal lesions are located outside the anal verge and can be seen externally. It is very painful but with scanty bleeding. It may be *Sūlūlī, 'Inabi* or *Tūtī.*

3. ***Mukhtalit Bawāsīr* (intro-external piles):** it is a mixture of the above two types of *Bawāsīr* marked with severe pain and profuse rectal bleed.

According to Bleeding

There are two types:

1. ***Bawāsīr Dāmiya* (bleeding piles):** there is bleeding and yellowish watery discharge from the anus.

2. ***Bawāsīr 'Amyā'* or *Bawāsīr Aṣamm:*** there is no bleeding. Only yellowish watery discharge is seen coming out of the anus.

Clinical Features of *Bawāsīr* in Unani Medicine

According to Unani literature, the common symptoms of *Bawāsīr* include:

- Burning sensation *(Iḥtirāq)* in the anal region.
- Pain, irritation, and heaviness around the anus.
- Rectal swelling due to venous engorgement and congestion.
- Constipation with straining during defecation.
- Presence of blood streaks on stool or mixed with faeces.
- Weakness and, in severe cases, syncope *(Ghashī)* due to blood loss.

Anṭākī's Description

According to Dā'ūd al-Anṭākī, systemic manifestations may accompany local symptoms, such as:

- Scales on lips.
- Eyelid oedema.
- Headache, vertigo, and general weakness.
- Loss of appetite and sū' al-haḍm (indigestion).
- Restlessness and irritability.

Interpretation of Anṭākī's View

Anṭākī's systemic findings reflect advanced haemorrhoids with chronic or profuse rectal bleeding. These symptoms indicate anaemia, nutritional depletion, and hypovolemia, presenting as fatigue, pallor, and neurological signs like vertigo and weakness.

Therapeutic Significance of Hemorrhoidal Bleeding

Hippocratic Recommendation

- Hippocrates advised excision of at least one haemorrhoid when multiple are present.
- Purpose: to allow continuous evacuation of morbid blood (*Dam Fāsid*), preventing its return to circulation.
- Philosophy: Evacuation is better than retention, as retained morbid blood predisposes to systemic diseases.

Clinical Observation in Habitual Cases

In habitual *Bawāsīr*, cessation of bleeding causes:

- Pain in the back, knees, and ankles.

- Heaviness in body and head.
- Loss of appetite.

When bleeding resumes:

- Heaviness subsides.
- Appetite and vitality return.
- Patient experiences general well-being.

Effects of Excessive or Retained Blood

Excessive bleeding → weakness, emaciation, and dysfunction of vital organs.

Retained morbid blood → coagulation in liver, causing *sudda* (obstruction), waram (inflammation), and may lead to *ishāl* (diarrhoea) or *istisqā'* (ascites).

If diverted elsewhere:

To heart → palpitation, anxiety.

To brain → *Mālankhūliyā* (melancholia), *Junūn* (insanity).

To body → boils, ulcers, *bahaq aswad* (pityriasis nigra), pruritus, and systemic decline.

Protective Role of Hemorrhoidal Bleeding According to Ibn Hubal

Regular bleeding prevents diseases linked to *Sawdā'* (black bile) predominance, such as *Junūn, Mālankhūliyā, Ṣar' Sawdāwī, Bahaq, Judhām, Sarṭān, Dhāt al-Janb, Dhāt al-Ri'a,* liver disorders, and *Istisqā'*.

Hence, evacuation of *Dam Fāsid* acts as a protective mechanism, while retention leads to severe complications.

Surgical Management of Haemorrhoids

Principles of Excision in Haemorrhoids *(Bawāsīr)* According to Classical Unani Surgeons

Conditions Where Excision Should Be Avoided

(a) In Case of *Tūtha* (Polypoid Haemorrhoids)

- Black or purplish, Hard, mulberry-like (*Shahṭūt-shaped*) swellings near arterial margins.
- Contain multiple vessels—cutting may cause severe haemorrhage.
- Cauterisation may induce swelling of the genitalia, navel, and abdomen, leading to fatality.

(b) Watery / Non-Bleeding Lesions

- Round swellings discharging fluid but not blood. If irritation is mild, avoid surgical or iron instruments.

(c) Single Haemorrhoid with Profuse Bleeding

- When one swelling discharges a large amount of blood, do not excise.
- Excision may disturb humoral equilibrium and provoke systemic disorders.

(d) When Blood is Black, Thick, and Foul-Smelling

- Such haemorrhoids should bleed naturally until morbid blood (*dam fāsid*) is expelled.
- Premature excision may weaken the liver and cause ascites (*istisqā'*).

(e) Protected or Painless Haemorrhoids

- If non-painful and stable, excision is contraindicated. May result in *Nawāsīr* (fistula) or *Shiqāq* (anal fissure).

Conditions Where Excision is Permissible

- In cases of multiple swellings (two or three), excise the largest or most bleeding one.

- If haemorrhoids cause severe and unbearable pain, excision may be done with medicinal or surgical means.

- Only pendulous (externally hanging) haemorrhoids should be removed, as they serve no physiological benefit.

Classical Surgical Management of Different Types of Hemorrhoidal Masses

1. *Tīnī* Type Haemorrhoids

- Managed by surgical excision *(qaṭ')*. No need for corrosive agents (*dawā'' ḥādd*).

2. *Tūlī* Type Haemorrhoids

- Excision not required. Managed with hot poultices *(ḍimādāt ḥārrra)* to promote resolution.

3. *Tūtī* Type Haemorrhoids

- Surgical excision contraindicated due to vascular involvement.
- Cauterization discouraged, as it may deform the anal orifice.
- Conservative management is preferred.

4. Recurrent or Greenish Swellings

- Managed by application of *dawā' ḥādd* (corrosive agents) to destroy the root. Followed by healing ointments for tissue repair.

5. External Haemorrhoids

- If excision is contraindicated, use *dawā' ḥādd* to remove from the base.

Surgical Procedures for Bawāsīr as Described by Ibn al-Quff

Masīḥī in *Kitāb al-'Umda fi'l Jarāḥa* has described three types of surgical procedures for *Bawāsīr* :

1. *Khazam* (Transfixation of Pile Mass)

Technique:

- A needle armed with silk thread is passed into the root of the hemorrhoidal polyp. And the mass is tied tightly at its base, sometimes in multiple loops.
- After a few days, the pile mass shrivels and sheds off naturally.

2. *Shad* (Gradual Ligation of Pile Mass)

Technique:

- The root of the hemorrhoidal mass is tied with a ligature. After 24 hours, the knot is untied and then re-applied more tightly.
- This process is repeated daily until the hemorrhoidal mass falls off.

3. *Qaṭ‘* (Hemorrhoidectomy)

Technique:

- The hemorrhoidal polyp is held with a rough cloth to secure a grip. And the mass is then slowly pulled out and excised with scissors.
- Afterwards, dusting powder (*Dawā' Qābiḍa*) is sprinkled over the excised site to promote healing and prevent infection.

Raban Al-Ṭabarī's Description

Raban Al-Ṭabarī recommended different surgical approaches based on the type of haemorrhoids *(bawāsīr):*

Projected piles – may be excised, but not all at once, following Hippocratic principles.

Methods of Excision:

Application of corrosive agents (*dawā'' ḥādd*) such as *Ravghan-i-Jālīnūs* or *Deg-bar-Deg.*

Hot iron cautery when indicated.

Precaution: Cauterisation demands high surgical skill; excessive or improper cautery may result in anal deformity and complications.

Post-Operative Care in Classical Literature

After excision, cautery, or use of *dawā'' ḥādd,* the following measures were advised:

Local application of healing ointments. Regular dressing and cleanliness of the wound until full recovery.

Surgical Management of Haemorrhoids According to Abū Al-Qāsim Al-Zahrāwī

1. *'Amal al-Qaṭ'* (Haemorrhoidectomy)

a) Internal Haemorrhoids

- The patient is instructed to bear down for exposure.
- Haemorrhoids are seized with hooks (*ṣunnāra*) or fingernails and excised near the root.
- Hemostasis is achieved by either sprinkling caustic powder (*dharūr*) or cauterisation (*Kayy*) with a heated iron.

b) External Haemorrhoids

- Simpler procedure — the mass is grasped and cut using a knife or scissors.
- Cautery is then applied to prevent haemorrhage.

2. *'Amal al-Khaẓam* (Transfixation / Ligation of Pile Mass)

- Adopted when the patient declines excision.
- A silk thread is passed through the base of the haemorrhoid using a needle and tied tightly to strangulate the mass. The haemorrhoid sloughs off naturally after necrosis.
- One pile should be left intact to allow evacuation of morbid matter (*mādda fāsida*).

Post-operative care: application of cloth soaked in *Ravghan-e-Ward* (oil of roses) or wax; rest until detachment.

3. *Kayy* (Cauterisation)

- Used for hemostasis after excision or ligation and for chronic cold-type haemorrhoids (*burūda / fāsid akhlāṭ*).

Sites: directly on haemorrhoids, or at systemic points — back, umbilical area, stomach, or spleen — to balance temperament.

Methods:

Hot iron cautery, or Application of hot caustic powders (*dharūr*).

Post-cautery care: application of *Marāhim* (healing ointments) until complete recovery.

Shiqāq al-Maq'ad

(Fissure in Ano)

Definition

Fissure in Ano (*Shiqāq al-Maq'ad*) is a tear or crack (*Shaqq*) at the anal verge, single or multiple, caused by the passage of Hard and dry stool or excessive straining.

Aetiology According to Classical Physicians

(Ibn Hubal Baghdādī, Ibn Sīnā, Jurjānī, and Raban Al-Ṭabarī)

- Causes include dry stool, acrid humours (*akhlāṭ ḥārra*), and irritant discharges.
- Dryness *(Yubūsat)* and excessive heat (*Ḥarārat*) weaken mucosal elasticity, producing fissures.
- Inflammation of anal vessels (*waram-i-maq'ad*) or venous engorgement further aggravates tearing.
- Hot morbid matter *(Mādda Ḥārr)* causes inflammation, while cold matter *(Mādda Bārid*) leads to chronic indolent fissures.

Aḥmad bin Muḥammad Al-Ṭabarī & Ḥakīm Muḥammad A'ẓam Khān

Classified fissures as:

- Hard, greenish, muddy fissures — require potent *marāhim* and medication.
- Soft fissures — manageable with mild ointments.
- Modern contributory factors include a non-fibrous diet, prolonged sitting, dehydration, and secondary occurrence with haemorrhoids or fistula.

Management of Fissure in Ano *(Shiqāq al-Maq'ad)*

Conservative / Medical Management

- *Faṣd* (Venesection) from *Bāsalīq* and *Ṣāfin* veins to relieve venous congestion.
- *Ḥijāma bi'l Sharṭ* (Wet Cupping) at the lower lumbar region for decompression.
- Topical applications: *Marham Kāfūrī* and *Marham Asfīdāj* for soothing and wound healing.

Surgical Management of Fissure in Ano

Ibn al-Quff al-Masīḥī & Abū Al-Qāsim Al-Zahrāwī

If conservative therapy fails, local stimulation or scraping is performed to initiate healing.

Techniques include:

- Rubbing / Scarification – Gentle rubbing around the anus until bleeding starts to stimulate granulation (Ibn al-Quff).
- Scraping – Removal of the indurated surface of the fissure using a scalpel (*Mishrat*) or fingernail, followed by dressing (Al-Zahrāwī).
- Repeat if non-healing, until a raw surface forms and bleeding promotes healthy granulation.

Post-operative care: application of ointment and regular dressings until healing is complete.

Nāṣūr al-Maq'ad
(Fistula in Ano)

Introduction

The word "Fistula" is derived from Latin, meaning an abnormal tube-like or pipe-like passage.

Historical Background

- Hippocrates (460–370 BCE) was the first to describe anal fistula *(Nāṣūr al-Maq'ad)* in his book Corpus Hippocraticum.

- He provided detailed descriptions of the condition and suggested the use of Seton therapy for complicated and high anal fistulas — a technique still in use in modern colorectal surgery.

Contribution of Unani Scholars

- Unani physicians, more than 1000 years ago, had profound knowledge of the anatomy and physiology of the anal sphincters.
- Zakariya Al-Rāzī (865–925 CE) in *Al-Ḥāwī fi'l-Ṭibb* gave an insightful description of the anal sphincters:
- The internal anal sphincter is involuntary in nature.
- It contracts and relaxes automatically, similar to a purse-string, without voluntary control.

Unani Concept of *Nāsūr al-Maqʿad* (Fistula in Ano)

In Unani texts, *Nāsūr al-Maqʿad* is described as a foul, unhealthy wound near the rectum or anal canal, usually secondary to perianal abscess (*khurāj ḥawl al-maqʿad*).

It is characterised by:

- Persistent discharge of pus or serosanguinous fluid.
- Pain and burning in the anal region.
- Chronic non-healing nature (*ʿasīr al-indimāl qarḥa*).

Views of Early Unani Physicians

Ibn Hubal Baghdādī (1122–1213 CE)

Defined fistula as a deep, chronic wound in the anal region arising after abscess rupture.

Pathogenesis:

- Begins as an abscess that, after bursting, forms a sinus tract.
- Continuous discharge and air entry hinder healing.
- In severe cases, the opening widens, allowing faecal leakage.

Abū Al-Qāsim Al-Zahrāwī (Albucasis, 936–1013 CE)

Clinical Features and Types

Fistulae occur near the anus or perineum, single or multiple, with discharge of thin pus or watery fluid.

Divided into:

Perforating fistulae: communicate with the rectum; may allow passage of faeces, flatus, or worms.

Non-perforating fistulae: no internal connection; detected by probing with bronze or lead probes.

Complex Variants

Some fistulae extend to the bladder, urethra, coccyx, or hip joint, causing urinary leakage, bone pain, and chronic pus formation. Such deep, perforating types are deemed incurable.

Etiopathogenesis

The primary cause of *Nāsūr al-Maqʿad* is *khurāj ḥawl al-maqʿad* (perianal abscess). When this abscess ruptures spontaneously or is improperly drained, a tract remains that evolves into a fistula.

Pathophysiological Concept in Unani Medicine

The rupture of the perianal abscess creates a link between the internal rectal mucosa and external perianal skin.

Healing becomes difficult due to:

- Persistence of morbid matter (*mādda fāsida*),
- Moisture and air contact,
- Continuous pus discharge.

The lesion thus becomes *ʿasīr al-indimāl* (chronic non-healing tract), forming a typical *nāsūr* (fistula).

Classification of *Nāsūr al-Maqʿad* (Fistula in Ano)

Broad Classification in Unani Medicine

a) *Nāsūr Ghayr Nāfidh* (Non-Perforating / Blind Sinus)

Defined as a tract having only an external opening without internal communication. Characterised by chronic discharge and persistence, but considered easily treatable. It is not a true fistula, but rather a blind sinus.

b) *Nāsūr Nāfidh* (Perforating / True Fistula)

Consists of both external and internal openings connected by a tract. Represents a true fistula, more chronic and difficult to manage than *Nāsūr Ghayr Nāfidh.*

Subtypes of *Nāsūr Nāfidh* According to the Site of Internal Opening

a) Fistula with Internal Opening Below the Anal Sphincter

- The internal opening lies below the voluntary anal sphincter.
- Treatable type, though healing is slow and prolonged.

b) Fistula with Internal Opening Above the Anal Sphincter

- The internal opening lies above the sphincter muscles.
- Considered most complex, with chronic course, high recurrence, and risk of incontinence or persistent discharge.

Management of *Nāsūr al-Maq'ad* (Fistula in Ano) According to Ibn Hubal Baghdādī

Conservative / Medical Management

In superficial fistulae limited to the anal margin without deep penetration, Cause minimal harm and can be managed conservatively.

The tract should be gently pressed to expel discharge. A slender suppository (*Shiyāf*) is prepared by wrapping a thin wick around a probe, soaked in old ghee (clarified butter), and inserted into the fistula.

If insertion is not possible, apply drops of medicated ghee into the tract twice daily for three days. This helps in drying and gradual healing of the sinus.

Surgical Management for Suppurative or Progressive Fistula

When the fistula discharges foul-smelling pus or shows a tendency to spread or destroy tissue, it should be excised with sharp surgical instruments before further progression.

If located near the anal margin and resistant to drugs, the tract may be surgically opened to promote early healing.

Contraindications for Surgery

Excision should not be attempted in the following conditions:

If the fistula extends to the bladder neck or thigh muscles, treat only with medicines. If the tract opens into the rectum but lies within the sphincteric muscles, surgery must be avoided, as:

- It may damage the anal sphincter.
- Causes incontinence (loss of stool control).

Surgical Management of *Nāsūr al-Maqʿad* in Unani Medicine

1. Seton Therapy *(Khaẓam)*

Historical Background

- One of the oldest methods for anal fistula, first advised by Hippocrates.
- Later refined by *Zakariya Al-Rāzī*, who introduced the use of setons in surgery.
- Later, the great Arabic scholar Zakariya Al-Rāzī (Rhazes) was credited as the first to use setons in surgery.

Nature of Setons

Setons may be made of silk, linen, nylon, or ligature threads, similar to medicated threads (Kshara Sutra) in Ayurveda.

Indications

- High or intersphincteric fistulae.
- Cases where fistulotomy risks sphincter damage.

Mechanism and Benefits

- Cutting effect: Gradual division of tract (3 weeks–1 year).

- Drainage effect: Continuous pus evacuation, preventing abscess formation.

2. *ʿAmal al-Kharam* (Modified Seton / Cutting Thread Technique)

Historical Background

Described by Abū Al-Qāsim Al-Zahrāwī as an advanced form of Seton therapy, similar to Kshara Sutra, using a special eye-ended malleable instrument for thread passage.

Indications

High or multi-tracked fistulae and complex cases.

Operative Steps

- **Preparation:** Clean the tract with *arq-e-gulab (rose water)* and trace its full course.
- **Thread Insertion:** A silk thread mounted on the instrument is passed from the external to the internal opening, then tied and left for 2–3 days.
- **Debridement:** The thread is untied, rubbed to refresh the tract, and replaced. Repeated until the tract is completely divided and heals naturally.

Postoperative Care

Dressing with *egg yolk and Ravghan-e-Gul*; instillation of *Shiyāf Abyaḍ* for healing.

Concept of Loose Seton (Modern Parallel)

A loosely tied silk ligature around the sphincter allows continuous drainage and fibrosis without cutting.

3. Cauterisation (Kayy)

Destruction of tissue by heat, freezing, electricity, or caustic chemicals to stop bleeding or infection.

Unani Perspective of Kayy (Cauterisation)

Three forms recognised:

- Thermal cautery *(Kayy bi'l Nār)*

2. Freeze cautery (rare)
3. Chemical cautery *(Al-Kayy bi'l Adwiya al-Muḥarriqa)*

In *Nāsūr al-Maqʿad*, only thermal and chemical cautery were applied.

Chemical Cautery (*Kayy bi'l Adwiya al-Muḥarriqa*)

Single (*Mufrad*) Drugs:

Naushadar, Hadtaal, Gandhak, Zangar, Para, Choona, Neela Thotha, Suhaga, Sindoor, Phitkiri, Shingarf.

Compound (*Murakkab*) Drugs:

Sheyafe Ghurab, Ravghan Nasoor, Marham Zangar.

Therapeutic Role

Caustic agents (*Muḥarriq, Akkāl*) remove unhealthy granulation tissue, converting it into a fresh wound for healing.

Followed by application of: *Munbite Lahm* (flesh-generating), *Mudammil Qurūḥ* (wound-healing), *Musakkin, Muḥallil, Ḥābis* agents.

Post-Cautery Healing Drugs

Kundur, Murr Makki, Damul Akhawain, Sibr Zard, Zafran, Anzroot, Gulnar, Mazu, Mom Safed, Post Anar, Safeda Kashghari.

Thermocautery *(Kayy bi'l Nār)*

Indications

Used when chemical cautery fails; preferred for high anal fistulae. Detailed by Abū Al-Qāsim Al-Zahrāwī.

Operative Technique

- Heat the trocar until red-hot. Insert it into the tract and rotate to destroy diseased tissue.
- Remove and clean; pack with *Ravghan* (clarified butter) to soften

tissues.

Postoperative Management

Dressings with *Mudammil Qurūḥ*, *Musakkin*, *Muḥallil*, and *Munbite Lahm.*

Fistulotomy and Fistulectomy (*ʿAmal al-Fatah / ʿAmal al-Qaṭaʿ*)

Fistulotomy: Laying open the fistulous tract for healing from depth outward.

Fistulectomy: Complete excision of the tract, allowing healing by secondary intention.

Historical Significance

Recognised since the Muslim surgical era as the most effective technique for *Nāsūr Nāfidh* (low anal fistula).

Classical Unani surgeons emphasised complete exposure of the tract to avoid recurrence.

Indications

- Low anal fistulae (below the sphincter complex).
- Simple, single-tract fistulae.

Contraindications

- High anal or intersphincteric fistulae.
- Cases at risk of faecal incontinence due to sphincter division.

Operative Technique

Positioning:

Patient in lithotomy position (supine, legs elevated).

Tract Identification:

Fistula cleaned under anaesthesia. A blunt probe passed from the external to the internal opening.

Incision / Excision:

Fistulotomy: Tract incised along the full length and laid open.

Fistulectomy: Entire tract excised and removed.

Wound Care:

Granulation tissue debrided to form a healthy wound bed. And packed with cotton soaked in Unani formulations: *Mudammil Qurūḥ* (wound healers), *Muḥallil* (resolvents/anti-inflammatory), *Ḥābis* (styptic/haemostatic),

Wound left open to heal by secondary intention.

Combined Procedure *('Amal al-Murakkab)*

A staged or combined approach using two or more techniques, described by Abū Al-Qāsim Al-Zahrāwī for complex fistulae.

Rationale:

- The anal sphincters are autonomically controlled and not voluntary.
- Their division during surgery may cause faecal incontinence; hence, staged or combined methods preserve continence.

Indications:

- High or complex fistulae (internal opening above sphincter).
- Multiple tracts or associated systemic disease (e.g., Crohn's, tuberculosis).

Operative Strategy:

Treatment is individualised based on:

- Patient's condition
- Sphincter involvement
- Type and complexity of tract.

Surgical Management of Fistula in Ano According to Al- Majūsī and Al-Zahrāwī

Untreatable and Operable Types

According to Al-Majūsī, fistulae extending to the urinary bladder, rectum *(ma'a mustaqīm),* or bone, and those with hidden or multiple tracts are *'Asīr al-'Ilāj* (incurable).

In such cases, surgical intervention is contraindicated to prevent sphincter laxity (*Istirkhā'*), loss of continence, and uncontrolled stool passage.

Superficial or non-perforating fistulae not reaching deep structures are curable and may be treated surgically with proper technique and instrument use.

Operative Technique According to *Al-Majūsī,*

Positioning: Patient placed supine.

Tract Identification:

- A scalpel (*al-Mibḍa'*) or probe is inserted into the external opening to trace the tract.
- The surgeon's finger is placed in the rectum to detect communication—if palpable, the tract is perforating (inoperable); if not, it is superficial (operable).

Incision & Debridement:

- Non-perforating tracts are laid open completely and necrotic tissue removed using scissors or forceps.
- Instrument *Minjal* recommended for deep exploration.

Dressing & Wound Care:

- Initial packing with cotton for 24 hours, followed by *Marham Bāsalīqūn*.
- If inflammation (*waram ḥārr*) develops → apply cooling poultices (*ḍimād*), then resume *marham bāsalīqūn* for healing.

Surgical Management According to Al-Zahrāwī

Abū Al-Qāsim Al-Zahrāwī in *Kitāb al-Taṣrīf* detailed various operative options for *Nāṣūr al-Maq'ad* (Perianal Fistula), emphasising that no single procedure is appropriate for all types of fistulae. The techniques include:

- Fistulotomy (Lay open the tract).
- Fistulectomy (Complete excision of the tract).
- Cauterisation *(Kayy)* of the fistulous tract.
- *ʿAmal al Kharm* (thread/Seton-like technique).

General Operative Principles

Positioning: Supine, legs raised and flexed.

Probe Examination: A bronze probe or leaden probe used to trace the tract.

Assessment:

- If the probe touches the surgeon's finger per rectum, → perforating and be incurable.
- If separated by a membrane → non-perforating and operable.

Surgical Techniques According to Al-Zahrāwī

1. Cauterisation *(Kayy)*

- Applied using heated metal (Thermocautery) to burn and destroy the unhealthy tract, converting it into a fresh wound.
- Promotes healing through the formation of healthy granulation tissue.

2. Lay-Open Technique (Fistulotomy / *ʿAmal al-Fatah)*

- The fistulous tract is incised along its full course under probe guidance.
- Healing agents (*mudammil qurūḥ, muḥallil, ḥābis*) are applied.
- Care is taken not to extend the incision beyond necessity to prevent faecal incontinence.

3. Thread Technique (Seton / *ʿAmal al-Kharm*)

- After clearing the tract, a silk-threaded probe is passed through the internal and external openings. Both ends are tied and left in place for 1–2 days until the tract is gradually divided.

- Wound is then dressed with healing ointments until recovery.

Prognosis and Surgical Philosophy

Both Al-Zahrāwī and Al-Majūsī emphasised that no single method suits all fistula types. The main surgical objective is to obliterate the tract while preserving continence.

Failure to completely remove the tract results in recurrence, while excessive cutting risks permanent incontinence.

Khurūj al-Maqʿad

(Rectal Prolapse)

Definition

In Unani medicine, *Khurūj al-Maqʿad* refers to the protrusion of the rectum through the anal opening due to *Istirkhā'* (laxity) of the *'Aḍala al-Mumsika* (anal sphincter).

This occurs when excessive *ruṭūbat* (moisture) and morbid secretions weaken rectal musculature, causing prolapse.

Aetiology *(Asbāb)*

According to classical Unani sources, *Khurūj al-Maqʿad* results from:

- *Muzmin Waram* (chronic inflammation) and *Qurūḥ* (ulcers).
- *Bawāsīr* (haemorrhoids), causing prolonged straining.
- *Ḍuʿf* (muscular weakness) of the anal sphincter.
- Excess *Ruṭūbat* leading to sphincter relaxation.
- Neurological weakness of anal nerves.
- Children: congenital muscular underdevelopment.

Management of Rectal Prolapse

General Principles

- Strengthen *'Adala al Mumsikah* (sphincter muscles).
- Reduce *Ruṭūbat* and restore muscle tone.
- Avoid constipation, diarrhoea, and excessive straining.

Medical Management

Local Applications *(Ḍimād / Duhn)*:

Use *Qābiḍ* (astringent) and *Mujaffif* (desiccant) drugs like *Mazu* (oak galls), *Post-e-Anar, Gulnar* (pomegranate flower), *and Safeda Kashghari.*

Suppositories *(Shiyāf)*:

Prepared from *Qābiḍ* and *Mujaffif* agents to strengthen rectal walls.

Diet & Regimen *(Ghidhā' wa Riyāḍat)*:

Avoid moist, heavy, flatulent foods; prefer a dry, light, easily digestible diet to prevent straining.

Manual Reduction

In early cases, the prolapsed rectum is manually repositioned after lubrication with *Ravghan-e-Banafsha* or *Ravghan-e-Zaitun.*

Bandaging or gentle support is applied to prevent recurrence.

Surgical Management

Cauterisation *(Kayy)*:

Applied around the anal verge to shrink and strengthen tissues.

Suturing / Ligation:

Used in severe or recurrent prolapse to tighten sphincter muscles.

Caustic Agents *(Dharūr-e-Muḥarriq)*:

Applied if prolapsed tissue becomes gangrenous to remove necrotic parts and promote healing.

Dubayla-i-Maq'ad

(Perianal Abscess)

Introduction

In Unani medicine, *Dubayla-i-Maq'ad* is defined as an inflammatory swelling around the anus, often associated with *Bawāsīr* (haemorrhoids) or *Nāsūr* (anal fistula), but it may also occur independently.

If neglected, it may rupture spontaneously and progress to *Nāsūr-e-Maq'ad* (chronic anal fistula).

Etiology

The principal causes include:

- Secondary infection of *Bawāsīr* or *Nāsūr.*
- Complications following anal surgery.
- Excess *Ḥarārat (heat)* and *Ruṭūbat (Discharge)* in anal vessels, leading to suppuration.

Principle of Management

According to *Buqrat* (Hippocrates), perianal abscesses must be incised early rather than allowed to ripen fully.

Delayed intervention causes deep-seated pus and leads to *Nāsūr-e-Maq'ad* (fistula formation).

Therapeutic Measures

- In the early stage, promote maturation using warm fomentation.
- When fluctuant: perform early incision *('amal-e-baṭṭ)* for pus evacuation.
- After incision: apply *mujaffif* (desiccant) and *mudammil-e-qurūḥ* (wound-healing) medicines.
- Timely drainage prevents conversion into *Nāsūr-e-Maq'ad.*

Maq'ad Ghayr Mathqūb

(Imperforate Anus / Anal Atresia)

Introduction

Maq'ad Ghayr Mathqūb is a congenital or acquired obstruction of the anal opening.

In congenital cases, the anus is closed by a fine membrane; in acquired forms, closure results from scarring *(indimāl-i-qarḥa)* or healing after *Dubayla-i-Maq'ad* (perianal abscess).

Classical Unani surgeons, including Abū Al-Qāsim Al-Zahrāwī, 'Alī ibn 'Abbās Al-Majūsī, and Ibn al-Quff, described its clinical recognition and surgical correction.

Etiology *(Asbāb)*

1. *Khilqī* (Congenital):

Absence of the anal orifice due to a thin, obstructing membrane.

2.*Iktisābī* (Acquired):

Closure from scarring, granulation, or post-abscess fibrosis around the anal region.

Surgical Management in Classical Texts

Neonatal / Congenital Cases

- In newborns, if the anus is closed by a membrane, the *Qābila* (midwife) should first attempt gentle perforation with her finger.
- If ineffective, a small incision with a scalpel *(Mibḍa')* is made to establish the anal opening.

Caution: avoid injury to the *'aḍala mumsika* (anal sphincter muscle) to prevent incontinence.

Acquired / Secondary Cases

- When the anal canal closes due to *indimāl-i-qarḥa* (cicatrization of wound), it is reopened by surgical incision (*Amal-e-Baṭṭ*) to restore passage

- The wound is managed with *mudammil-e-qurūḥ* (healing ointments) to promote granulation and prevent re-closure.

Prevention of Re-Closure (Maintenance of Patency)

- A leaden or glass cannula (tube) is inserted for several days to maintain patency of the newly created opening.
- The tube is removed during defecation and reinserted afterwards until epithelialization completes.

Postoperative and Antiseptic Care

- Following incision, irrigation with wine (for antisepsis) is advised, followed by dressing with sponges or wool soaked in wine.
- Bandaging is applied firmly to approximate wound edges, and daily dressing changes continue with *marham* (healing ointment) until complete recovery.

Ḥuqna (Enema)

Āla-i-Ḥaqn / Miḥqana (Enema Instruments)

Miḥqana Raqqiya (Leather Bag)

The earliest instrument for administering *Ḥuqna* was made of leather with an attached nozzle for fluid delivery.

Zarrāqa (Copper Syringe)

A copper device with a straight, uniform nozzle on one side for deeper and stronger injection of medicated fluid.

Preferred Nozzle Design

- Divided into two unequal parts — *two-thirds* on one side and *one-third* on the other.
- The partition near the lower part allows the upper one-third portion to open into the two-thirds portion
- The bag is attached to the lower end of the nozzle.

Mechanism of Action

The design ensures:

- Smooth passage of medicated fluid into the intestines.
- Release of gases from a small side opening, preventing bloating, discomfort, and reflux during administration.

Tariqa-i-Ḥuqna (Method of Enema Administration)

Position of the Patient

- Kneeling position is ideal for intestinal pain, as it facilitates deeper distribution.
- If pain is in the back or kidneys → patient lies supine.
- If right-sided → patient lies on right side; if left-sided → on left side.

Depth of Administration

- The *Zarrāqa* delivers medicine deeply into the intestines; excessive pressure may push fluid beyond the affected site — use gentle control.

Temperature of the Solution

- Lukewarm solution ensures better absorption, prevents colic, and minimizes mucosal irritation.

Lubrication: The nozzle and anal opening are lubricated with *Qayrūṭī*. Alternatively, the little finger may be lubricated and inserted gently before the nozzle to relax the *ʿaḍala mumsika* (anal sphincter).

Surgeries of Urological Diseases

Ḥaṣā al Bawliya(Urolithiasis)

Ḥaṣā al-Kulya, Ḥaṣā Al-Ḥālibayn, Ḥaṣā al-Mathāna, Ḥaṣā al-Iḥlīl

(Nephrolithiasis, Ureterolithiasis, Cystolithiasis, Urethral Calculi)

Historical Background

Urolithiasis is among the oldest recorded diseases. In 1901, E. Smith discovered a bladder stone from a 5000-year-old mummy dated 4800 BC in El Amrah, Egypt.

Ancient Mesopotamian texts (3200–1200 BC) described urinary calculi and recommended *Papaver somniferum L.* and *Cannabis sativa L.* for pain and bleeding relief.

During the Greek period, Hippocrates (460–370 BC) stated in his Oath:

"I will not cut for calculus… I will leave this operation to be performed by practitioners."

highlighting early surgical recognition of urolithiasis.

Contributions of Classical Unani Physicians

Al-Razi (Rhazes, 864–930 AD)

In *Al-Ḥāwī fi al-Ṭibb*, Al-Razi elaborated the anatomy, physiology, and diagnosis of urinary tract diseases. He noted:

"Pain of the kidney stone is posterior and localised, unlike the generalised pain of abdominal colic."

He introduced preoperative enema and meatotomy for impacted urethral calculi and recognised that pain worsens when calculi pass through the ureters.

Al-Razi also described perineal lithotomy, similar to Paul of Aegine and devised surgical tools:

- *Almajarra* (spoon-like dragger) for calculus extraction,
- *Alkalbatain* (arrow-extractor forceps),
- Flexible lead urethral catheters with side-eyelets.

He emphasised careful removal over large incisions and considered breaking the stone inside the bladder safe when controlled.

Al-Rāzī, in his book named *Al-Hawi fi al-Tibb* (part 7, book I), precisely explained the anatomy, physiology, and pathophysiology of urinary tract diseases, especially the diagnosis and management of urolithiasis.

He stated, "The site of the pain is important: in abdominal colic, the pain is more generalised and tends to be anterior, while in kidney stones, the pain is more limited and tends to be in the back"

Al-Rāzī, for the first time, introduced preoperative preparation of the patient by an enema and meatotomy for impacted urethral calculi. He believed that "pain becomes worse when the calculi are passing through the ureters; otherwise, patients just 'feel heaviness in the flanks."

The contribution of Al-Rāzī in the field of surgery for the management and treatment of urolithiasis is very important.

Rhazes used *Almajarra* (dragger), an instrument like a small spoon, called, and calculus would be scooped out; he also used *Alkalbatain*, which was similar to the arrow extractor forceps.

In *Al-Hawi Fi-Tibb*, he described perineal lithotomy almost in the same manner as that carried out by Paul of Aegina· condemned the operation of cutting on kidney stones, but approved it in bladder stones.

He, for the first time, introduced preoperative preparation of the patient by an enema and meatotomy for an impacted urethral calculus. Rhazes devised various urological instruments, namely pliable lead urethral catheters, and replaced the traditional openings at the catheter tip with eyelets on the sides. Before Rhazes, it was believed that breaking the calculus inside the bladder to facilitate its removal could be dangerous; therefore, it was customary to extract these calculi through large incisions.

Al-Zahrāwī (Albucasis 930 - 1013 AD)

He shared many specially designed, practically applied surgical equipment for urolithiasis management, which provided the basis to develop modern surgical equipment later on. Al-Zahrāwī was the first one to utilise forceps to remove bladder calculi. Before him, the calculus would be extracted by an instrument like a small spoon called Almajarra (dragger), and it would be scooped out.

Invented a novel lithotomy scalpel, called *Nechil*, with two shārp cutting edges; first to use a tool to confirm the presence of the stone before proceeding with the perineal cystolithotomy operation; introduced the 2-stage bladder stone operation in complicated cases.

Ibn Sina (Avicenna, 980–1037 AD)

In *Al-Qānūn fi'l-Ṭibb*, Ibn Sina detailed the anatomy and physiology of the renal system, causes of *ḥaṣā*, and its medical and surgical management.

He observed that:

"Bladder calculi are larger and harder than kidney calculi, often yellow to black, occasionally grayish-white... They occur mostly in thin people, whereas kidney calculi develop in the obese."

His clinical differentiation between *ḥaṣā al-kulya* and *ḥaṣā al-mathāna* paralleled modern urological observations.

Ibn Zuhr (Avenzoar, 1091–1162 AD)

In *Kitāb al-Taysīr fi'l Mudāwā wa'l Tadbīr*, Ibn Zuhr explained diagnostic features and surgical litholysis.

He stated:

"When urine turns thin like water in a healthy person, it indicates stone formation."

He described using a fine probe tipped with a diamond piece to crush the calculus inside the urethra.

Muḥadhdhab al-Dīn Al-Baghdādī (1117–1213 AD)

In *Kitāb al-Mukhtārāt fi'l Ṭibb*, he recorded the epidemiology of urinary stones, stating:

"Kidney stones occur mostly in aged men, while bladder stones are common in boys—even infants due to excessive curdling of milk."

He observed that kidney stones prevail in the obese, bladder stones in the slim, and rarely in females.

Pathophysiology of *Ḥaṣā al-Bawliya* (Urolithiasis)

Urolithiasis originates from thick and viscous waste material. When excessive and abnormal heat acts upon this material, it dries and hardens into gravel and stones. Gravel forms from thinner waste that is partially excreted through urine, but when some particles remain, they fuse and enlarge, resulting in stone formation.

Clinical Features of *Ḥaṣā al-Kulya* (Renal Calculi)

- **Pain:** Severe flank pain, worsened by movement.
- **Urinary Signs:** Passage of gravel, burning urination, and intermittent obstruction.
- **Associated Symptoms:** Colicky pain radiating to the flanks and shoulder, with nausea and vomiting.
- **Haematuria:** Presence of blood in urine due to ureteral injury.

Clinical Features of *Ḥaṣā al-Mathāna* (Vesical Calculi)

- **Urine Appearance:** Whitish or greyish urine, sometimes watery or oily.
- **Gravel:** May appear before stone formation.
- **Number & Size:** Single or multiple stones; large stones may obstruct the outlet.
- **Mobility:** Stones may move freely or adhere to the bladder mucosa.

Symptoms of Stone Migration (Kidney → Bladder)

- Pain begins in the suprapubic region.
- Pain gradually shifts downward.
- Relief of pain indicates the stone has reached the bladder.

Predisposing Factors of *Ḥaṣā al-Kulya and Ḥaṣā al-Mathāna*

***Ḥaṣā al-Kulya* (Renal Calculi)**

- Smaller in size; common in adults.
- Caused by *balgham* (phlegm) and *ghalīẓ ruṭūbat* (thick humours).
- Weak expulsive power leaves residues that solidify in the kidneys.
- Occurs mostly in obese individuals due to *burūdat wa yubūsat* (cold and dry temperament), narrowing the *al-ḥālibayn* (ureters).

***Ḥaṣā al-Mathāna* (Vesical Calculi)**

- Larger stones are common in children.
- Children's wide ureters and strong *quwwat dāfi'a* (expulsive force) drive residues into the bladder, where *sū' al-haḍm* (poor digestion) and excessive heat form stones.
- Common in lean individuals.
- Rare in females due to a short and wide urethra, allowing easy excretion of wastes.

Management of *Ḥaṣā al-Bawliya* (Urolithiasis)

According to Ibn Sīnā (Avicenna, 980–1037 AD)

Ibn Sīnā described detailed operative principles for *Ḥaṣā al-Mathāna* (bladder calculus) management.

He advised that small calculi can be expelled by manual pressure, whereas larger stones require incision and extraction using grasping pincers (forceps).

In cases of very large stones, the calculus should be crushed gradually and removed piece by piece, ensuring no fragment remains, since even the smallest residue can regrow into a new stone.

He condemned cutting operations for kidney stones *(ḥaṣā al-kulya)* but approved surgery for bladder stones *(ḥaṣā al-mathāna),* following Al-Rāzī's recommendations.

Ibn Sīnā emphasised that lithotomy should be reserved for cases where other methods fail to dislodge the calculus. He recommended the perineal approach (perineal urethrostomy) and highlighted the surgical anatomy, warning of proximity to the vasa deferentia, prostate gland, and neurovascular bundle.

He used grasping forceps for stone removal and described a technique similar to modern Babcock forceps to prevent calculus migration. He also discussed cystotomy complications and emphasised complete extraction of all fragments to prevent recurrence.

According to Muḥadhdhab al-Dīn Al-Baghdādī (1117–1213 AD)

In *Kitāb al-Mukhtārāt fi'l Ṭibb,* he discussed surgical management of *ḥaṣā al-kulya* (renal stones) and described lumbotomy and subcostal approaches but personally discouraged their use due to high operative risk.

He only approved surgical intervention in *ḥaṣā al-mathāna* (bladder stones), considering it safer and more effective.

Surgical Management of *Ḥiṣāt al-Mathāna* (Bladder Stone)

Indications

- When pharmacological treatment fails, surgical removal is indicated.
- Surgery is easier in children due to soft and moist tissues and rapid healing.
- In adults, the procedure is moderately difficult; in the elderly, it becomes challenging due to dryness and rigidity, and healing is often delayed.
- Larger stones are easier to extract because they settle at the bladder base and are easier to locate and grasp.

Medical therapy should always be attempted first; surgery is reserved for cases where life or function is threatened.

Preoperative Care:

Warm bath and massage with oil to relax tissues; catheterisation

(*Qāthāṭīr*) if required.

Positioning:

Patient seated on a chair; knees held by an assistant; tilted slightly to the opposite side of the stone.

Localization:

Palpate rectally in men, children, or virgins; vaginally in married women. And push the stone gently toward the incision site.

Operation:

A small incision is made at the bladder neck to ensure quick healing. And Finger introduced to guide and deliver the stone.

If large, crush with forceps and remove fragments completely.

Postoperative Care:

Warm bath, fomentation, and oil massage; continue wound dressing till healing.

According to Ibn al-Quff al-Masīḥī

Preparation:

Enema for bowel clearance; patient instructed to jump or shake to move the stone toward the bladder neck.

Position:

Sitting upright, knees flexed, hands on knees.

Localization:

Palpate the perineum; rectal examination with oiled finger (index in children, middle in adults).

Incision:

Oblique incision between anus and scrotum, slightly left of midline, guided by rectal finger. The assistant retracts the testes during incision.

Extraction:

Stone removed by finger pressure or with a probe (*al-mirwad*). Large stones are crushed using toothed forceps (*kalbatayn*). Ensure no fragment remains to prevent recurrence.

According to 'Alī ibn 'Abbās Al-Majūsī(Haly Abbas, 930–994 CE)

Preparation:

Patient seated on assistant's lap; gently shaken or made to jump and rotate to help the stone descend to the bladder neck.

Position:

Sitting upright with abducted thighs and hands on knees for bladder tilt.

Localization:

Palpate externally; if not palpable, insert a rectal finger to push the stone toward the perineum.

Incision:

Make an oblique perineal incision between the anus and scrotum; keep it wide externally and minimal internally.

If possible, expel the stone by rectal pressure; otherwise, use an instrument for extraction.

Postoperative Care:

Dress wound with *dharūr aṣfar*, *Kundur*, *Sibr*, and *Dam al-Akhwain*; bandage securely.

Surgical Management of *Ḥaṣā al-Iḥlīl* (Urethral Stone)

Indication:

When a small stone lodged in the urethra cannot be expelled naturally, a surgical incision is required.

Incision Site:

Made exactly at the point where the stone is palpable, from the underside of the urethra.

Precautions:

Tie the urethra at two levels —

- Above the stone to prevent retrograde movement,
- Below the stone to stabilise it.

The bandage must be external to ensure proper realignment during healing.

Postoperative Care:

After extraction, remove the bandage, cleanse the wound, and apply *Munbit-i-Laḥm* (flesh-generating medicine) for complete healing.

Iḥtibās al-Bawl / ‘Usr al-Bawl

(Urinary Retention and Dysuria)

Etiology

Urinary retention or dysuria may occur due to:

- **Diseases of the ureters:** The bladder remains empty; heaviness is felt in the back.
- **Displacement of the bladder:** Retraction or upward movement causes back heaviness.
- **Obstruction:** Due to stricture, swelling, stones, pus, blood clots, or temperature-induced narrowing.
- **Bladder pathology:** Inflammation (*waram al-mathāna*) or weakness (*istirkhā’*) of bladder muscles.
- **Muscular spasm:** Prolonged retention may induce reflex spasm.
- **Reflex causes:** From intestinal flatulence, testicular displacement, or abdominal swellings obstructing the bladder outlet.

According to Abū Al-Qāsim Al-Zahrāwī:

Iḥtibās al-Bawl occurs due to obstruction such as a stone, pus, blood clot, or fleshy tumour.

Clinical Features

- Ureteric cause: Bladder remains empty with heaviness in the back.
- Urethral cause: Full bladder with suprapubic pain and tension.

- Calculus-related: Symptoms of *ḥaṣā al-bawliya* present.
- Pus or blood clot: Indicates a wound or ulcer in the kidney or bladder.

Management of Urinary Retention

Conservative Management

When obstruction occurs at the *fam al-mathāna* (neck of the bladder) due to:

- Thick humours (*khilṭ ghalīẓ*),
- Blood clots, or
- Small impacted calculus

And *mudirr-i-bawl Adwiya* (diuretics) fail, catheterisation *(al-qāthāṭīr)* is indicated for urine evacuation.

Al-Zahrāwī's Technique:

If a stone is lodged in the bladder neck, seat the patient squatting, place a man on his back to press the abdomen, and have the patient hold his breath to increase intravesical pressure.

If unsuccessful and retention persists, perform catheterisation using the proper instrument.

Catheterisation *(Al-Qāthāṭīr)* in Urinary Retention

Used for evacuation of urine when obstruction occurs at *fam al-mathāna*, caused by clots, thick humours, small calculi, or urethral strictures, and when diuretics fail.

Instrument *(Al-Qāthāṭīr)* Structure and Design

- **Material:** Silver, gold, copper, or leather coated with *Garri al-Samak* (fish glue).
- **Length:** Equal to or slightly longer than the penis; adjusted for age.
- **Tip:** Shaped like a small cup (*Sakarja*) for smooth insertion.
- **Holes:** Multiple openings to allow urine flow even if one is blocked.

Advantages of Silver Catheters:

Soft, flexible, smooth, and durable; follows natural urethral curvature and minimises trauma.

Ibn al-Quff's View:

Prefers silver catheters for flexibility and hygiene, with multiple holes for continuous drainage.

Ibn Sīnā's Contributions

Ibn Sīnā was among the first to design soft and malleable catheters made from leather or silver. He recommended:

Multiple openings for dual drainage and drug administration. Smooth structure to avoid repeated insertion.

Use in *iḥtibās al-bawl* due to *ḥaṣā* or *khilṭ ghalīẓ*, ensuring patient comfort and safety.

Catheterisation *(Al-Qāthāṭīr)* Technique in Classical Unani Surgery

According to Ibn Hubal Al-Baghdādī

Patient Positioning

The patient is seated with back support, resting on the coccyx. The *Al-Qāthāṭīr* is prepared for use.

Preparation of the Catheter

Its length and thickness should match the patient's urethra. The surface is lubricated with jasmine oil and raw wax resin, and softened by gentle heat if needed.

Insertion Technique

The catheter is inserted gently to avoid scratching the urethral lining. The urethra is straightened toward the navel, and the catheter is advanced gradually, one or two finger-depths at a time.

When the catheter reaches the bladder, the pain of *iḥtibās al-bawl* subsides.

Final Steps

The urethra is bent downward; the wool thread attached to the catheter is pulled to allow urine or pus to drain. If an obstruction, such as a *Ḥaṣā* (stone), blocks the outlet, the catheter helps dislodge it.

According to Ibn al-Quff al-Masīḥī

Preparation of the Catheter

Lubricate the catheter with violet oil (*Ravghan-e-Banafsha*), butter, or egg white.
A thread is passed through the lumen, with cotton tied to its end to serve as a guide plug.

Patient Preparation

Clean the genital area with warm water; lubricate the catheter.

Insertion Technique

Insert the catheter slowly into the urethra. When it reaches the penile root, lift the penis toward the navel to straighten the path. Then guide it downward until the bladder is reached — signalled by a feeling of release.

Final Steps

Pull the thread to remove the cotton plug and allow urine to flow. If urine flow stops prematurely, repeat insertion two or three times until full evacuation occurs.

According to 'Alī ibn 'Abbās Al-Majūsī

Patient Preparation

Seat the patient comfortably, apply oil (*ravghan*) to the penis, and cleanse with warm water.

Catheter Preparation

Use a catheter with a small perforated tip and lubricate it with *Ravghan-e-banafsha*.

Insertion Technique

Insert the catheter straight to the penile base, then lift the penis upward toward the navel to align the urethral curve.

Guide it gently downward toward the anus until it enters the bladder — confirmed by a sensation of hollow space.

Urine Drainage

Pull the thread to remove the inner wool plug and withdraw the catheter, allowing free urine flow.

Post-Procedural Care

If minor bleeding occurs, inject a medicated solution using *shiyāf abyaḍ* (healing suppository) to soothe irritation and promote mucosal healing.

According to Abū Al-Qāsim Al-Zahrāwī

Catheter Preparation

Attach a small wool plug at the end of a double thread inside the catheter and lubricate with oil, butter, or egg white for smooth entry.

Patient Preparation

Seat the patient comfortably, cleanse the urethral area, and apply warm oil (e.g., olive oil).

Insertion Technique

Insert the catheter gently into the urethra until its root; tilt the penis upward to straighten the path, then guide it downward to reach the bladder. The patient's sense of relief confirms entry into the hollow space.

Pull the thread to release the wool plug and allow urine to drain. Withdraw the catheter slowly, repeating if needed until complete evacuation.

Zarrāqa (Bladder Irrigation)

(Syringe Use in Unani Surgery)

***Zarrāqa* (Syringe / Injector)**

Zarrāqa is an instrument consisting of a tube with a nozzle and piston or bulb used for drawing and ejecting liquids in a fine stream. It is employed to irrigate or instil medicated fluids into body cavities such as the bladder or to inject or withdraw substances.

In Unani medicine, *Zarrāqa* (Irrigation of the Bladder) refers to instilling medicinal preparations directly into the bladder (*mathāna*) using a specialized instrument, particularly when oral or systemic medications prove ineffective.

Description by Abū Al-Qāsim Al-Zahrāwī (Albucasis, 936–1013 CE)

Al-Zahrāwī described bladder irrigation for cases of ulceration *(qarḥa),* pus, or clotted blood within the bladder. He advised using *Zarrāqa* to introduce medicated solutions directly into the cavity, enabling local healing when systemic drugs fail.

Indications of *Zarrāqa* (Bladder Irrigation)

Zarrāqa is indicated in:

- *Qarḥa-e-Mathāna* (Bladder ulcer) causing chronic burning micturition.
- *Waram* (Inflammation) or *Qarḥa* (Ulceration) from *mādda-e-ḥārrra* (Acrid humours).
- Failure of decoctions (*joshanda*) or oral therapies.
- Presence of pus, blood clots, or gravel in the bladder.
- Requirement of direct instillation of soothing drugs (*Adwiya-e-musakkina*).

Instruments for *Zarrāqa (Āla-i-Ḥaqn-i-Mathāna)*

1. Catheter *(Al-Qāthāṭīr)* Used as a Syringe

- A hollow *Al-Qāthāṭīr* serves dual purposes—draining and instilling medicine.

- Its outer end is attached to a medicinal bag; squeezing the bag propels the liquid into the bladder through the tube.

2. Special Syringe *(Zarrāqa)* Design

- Constructed with a wide tube (admitting a thumb) joined to a narrow tube matching the urethral diameter.
- Fitted with a piston *(Madfa)* equal to the wide tube's bore.
- Preferred material: Ivory *(Hajar-e-'Āji)* for smoothness and durability.
- The narrow tube is lubricated (*tadhīn*) and gently inserted into the urethra. The penis is elevated toward the navel to straighten curvature, then lowered to advance the tube.
- The wide tube is filled with soothing medicine (*Adwiya-e-musakkina*), which is pushed into the bladder using the piston.

Surgeries of Penis, Scrotum, and Testis

Surgeries of the Penis

Sū'-i-Waz' Fam-i-Iḥlīl

(Hypospadias)

Definition

Hypospadias is a congenital anomaly in which the urethral opening *(Fam-i-Iḥlīl)* is located abnormally on the ventral surface of the glans penis or along the penile shaft instead of the tip.

Clinical Impact on Fertility

Some men become infertile as their urethral meatus lies below the glans rather than centrally. Consequently, semen is not ejaculated straight into the uterus, leading to failed fertilisation.

Effect on Urination

The urinary stream deviates downward, preventing urination in a normal forward direction.

Surgical Management of Hypospadias

Ibn Hubal Al-Baghdādī's Surgical Approach

Surgical Technique

Positioning: The patient is kept standing for better access.

New Opening Creation: The penis is stretched, and an incision is made on its ventral surface to form a new midline urethral opening.

Urethral Alignment: The incision is adjusted to align the new opening with the natural urethral canal for a straight urinary stream.

Stent Placement: A fine glass probe or stylus is inserted to maintain patency during healing.

Hemostasis: Persistent bleeding is controlled with fine cauterisation.

Postoperative Care: Wound-healing medicines are applied; the stent remains in place until healing is complete to avoid reclosure.

'Alī ibn 'Abbās Al-Majūsī's Surgical Approach

Positioning: The patient lies supine (on the back) for better exposure.

Excision Technique: The glans is pulled forward, and an oblique excision is made around the corona to shape a central, anatomically correct meatus.

Restoration of Anatomy: The remaining tissue is contoured to resemble a normal glans.

Hemostasis: Managed by hemostatic agents or fine cauterisation if required.

Postoperative Measures: The new meatus is regularly monitored to prevent narrowing or closure.

Urethral Atresia

(Absence of External Urethral Meatus)

Definition

Urethral atresia is a congenital anomaly characterised by the complete absence of the external urethral opening (meatus) at birth, which prevents normal passage of urine.

Surgical Management

Classical Unani surgeons advised creating an artificial urethral opening, resembling a modern perineal urethrostomy procedure.

Surgical Technique

Incision at Anatomical Site: When the natural meatus is absent, an incision is made at its normal anatomical position.

Initial Patency: The incision is left open for about one hour to stop bleeding and allow the tissue to remain patent.

Insertion of Glass Probe: A fine glass probe or stylus is gently inserted into the urethra through the new opening and fixed securely.

Maintenance: The probe is kept in place for 3–4 days to maintain patency and prevent closure.

During Urination: The probe is temporarily removed for urination and reinserted afterwards until complete healing is achieved.

Al-Taṭhīr

(Circumcision)

Introduction

Taṭhīr is the term used for the surgical procedure known as circumcision. The word "circumcision" comes from a Latin word, circumcidere, which means to cut around. In Arabic, it is also known as *Al-Ṭuhur* or *Al-Ṭahira*, meaning purification.

Historical background

It is not clearly known how this practice came into existence. Many theories and explanations have been put forward to answer this question.

An English Egyptologist, Sir Graham Elliot Smith, suggested that it was the features of a heliolithic culture about 15000 years ago. The earliest Egyptian mummies of approximately 1300 BC were circumcised.

In biblical times, the ritual of circumcision in newborns was performed by their mothers, but gradually it was taken over by a *Mohel,* a man who had the requisite religious and surgical knowledge.

Circumcision in the Unani System of Medicine

Abū Al-Qāsim Al-Zahrāwī on Circumcision

Observations and Principles

Abū Al-Qāsim Al-Zahrāwī provided one of the earliest detailed surgical descriptions of circumcision.

He emphasised safety, precision, and infection control—principles consistent with modern surgical practice.

Preoperative Preparation

Al-Zahrāwī advised marking the prepuce before excision to prevent excessive removal and ensure symmetry.

He recommended thorough cleansing of the prepuce, glans, and urethral meatus to avoid postoperative infection.

Preferred Technique

Excision with Scissors: Al-Zahrāwī preferred scissors over a knife for controlled removal of the prepuce.

Suturing: Cut edges should be approximated and sutured with thread to promote healing and minimise complications.

He noted that the prepuce is double-layered and warned that using a knife could leave inner layers uncut, risking incomplete circumcision or urethral injury.

He also condemned unhygienic methods such as circumcision with thumb nails due to infection risk.

Al-Zahrāwī's Operative Technique

Operative Steps

Two ligatures are tied:

- First thread proximal to the glans.
- Second, just distal to the first.
- This demarcation ensures accurate excision.

Surgical Excision

The foreskin is excised between the two threads while the proximal thread is held firmly. After excision, the cut edges are opened with forceps to expose the glans.

Immediate Postoperative Care

A wet bandage is applied, and fine ash of *Abresham* (Bombyx Mori) is dusted on the wound for hemostasis and healing.

Management of Postoperative Swelling

If oedema develops below the glans:

- An ointment of *qābiz dharūr* (astringent powder), egg yolk, and *arq-e-gulāb* (rose water) mixed with *ravghan-e-gul* (rose oil) is applied for two days.
- If swelling persists beyond three days, further manipulation should be avoided until inflammation subsides.

Ibn-al-Quff's Methods of Circumcision

Ibn al-Quff Masīḥī (1233–1286 CE), one of the renowned medieval surgeons, described four distinct techniques of circumcision. His emphasis was on protecting the glans penis during the procedure and ensuring complete removal of the prepuce.

1. First Method: Circumcision with *Mishdākh* (Protective Ring)

In this technique, the prepuce (foreskin) is passed through a small protective ring *(Mishdākh)*.

- The ring is positioned to encircle the prepuce and protect the glans.
- The prepuce is then excised with a knife.
- The main purpose of using the ring is to shield the glans from accidental injury during the excision.

2. Second Method: Rolling Ring Technique

This method involves:

- Rolling a ring over the glans and shaft of the penis underneath the prepuce.

- The ring acts as a rigid barrier to protect the glans.
- The prepuce is then excised safely with a knife, minimising the risk of urethral or glans injury.

3. Third Method: Thread-Tie Technique

This is a simpler method in which:

- A thread is tied tightly over the prepuce just proximal to the tip of the glans.
- The prepuce is then excised distal to the tied thread.
- This technique ensures a relatively bloodless field by acting as a temporary ligature.

4. Fourth Method: Circumcision with *Mirwad* (small probe) and *Mishdākh*

This is the most elaborate method described by Ibn-al-Quff:

- A device called *Mirwad* (small probe/with blunt edges) is inserted into the prepuce.
- *Mishdākh* is then placed between the prepuce and the *Mirwad* (small probe), acting as a protective separator.
- The prepuce is excised, and ash of dry pumpkin is sprinkled over the wound to stop bleeding.
- The dressing is completed with *dharūr* (a medicinal powder with hemostatic properties, i.e.*Ḥābis-al-Dam*).

Surgeries of the Scrotum

Qurū, Qīla, Udhra, and Fatq

Concept and Terminological Differences

When the *A'mā'* (intestine), *Al-Tharb* (omentum), *Rīḥ* (gas), or *Mā'iyyat* (fluid) descends into the scrotal sac, the condition is termed *Qīla, Udhra,* or *Qurū.*

In contrast, *Fatq* (hernia) is a general condition in which an internal organ or tissue protrudes through a natural or pathological opening in the *ṣifāq* (peritoneum). The protrusion may descend into the scrotum or remain in another region.

Scholars distinguish as follows:

- When the peritoneum ruptures and an organ protrudes → *Fatq* (hernia).
- When the organ descends through a natural or congenital opening like the *kanj-e-rān* (inguinal canal) → *Qīla, Udhra,* or *Qurū.*

Subtypes of *Fatq* (Hernia)

1. ***Fatq Urbī-o-Rābī* (inguinal hernia not reaching scrotum)**

   Occurs when the peritoneum near the inguinal canal ruptures; the organ descends but does not enter the scrotum.

2. ***Qīla* (inguinoscrotal hernia)**

   When the organ descends into the scrotal sac. Based on the content:

- ***Qīla Al-Tharbiyya*** – containing omentum (omentum hernia)
- ***Qīla A'mā'*** – containing intestine (intestinal hernia)
- ***Qīla Rīḥiyya*** – containing gas (gaseous hernia)
- ***Qīla Mā'iyya*** – containing fluid (hydrocele-like hernia)

Difference Between *Qīla* and *Qurū*

***Qīla* (hernia)**:

Refers to the protrusion of an internal organ, usually the intestine, through a weak spot in the abdominal wall. Variants include *Qīla Mā'iyya* (fluid-filled) and *Qīla Laḥmiyya* (fleshy hernia).

***Qurū* (solid tumour or swelling)**:

Denotes a localised solid lump or mass, either ḥard or soft, corresponding to indurated or tumorous swellings.

Subtypes include *Qurū Mā'iyya* (cystic swelling) and *Qurū Laḥmiyya* (fleshy tumour).

Terminological Note:

While *Qīla* and *Qurū* are sometimes used interchangeably in classical texts, *Qīla* denotes a protrusion of an organ or content, whereas *Qurū* represents a solid swelling or tumour.

Types of *Qaru / Qīla*

Five Types According to Classical Unani Literature

1. Hydrocele *(Quru Mā'ī)*
2. Scrotal Mass or Tumour *(Quru Laḥmī)*
3. Intestinal Hernia / Enterocele *(Quru Mi'wī)*
4. Physocele *(Quru Rīḥī)*
5. Varicocele *(Quru Dawālī)*

Qurū Mā'ī / Qīla Mā'ī (Hydrocele)

Definition

Hydrocele *(Qurū Mā'ī / Qīla Mā'ī)* is the accumulation of watery fluid within the sac of the testis or tunica vaginalis *(ṣifāq)* surrounding the testes. Occasionally, the collection occurs within the specific membrane of the testis itself.

The primary causative factor is weakness of the testes, leading to improper transformation of blood, often following trauma or injury. The fluid may appear yellowish, reddish, or dark.

Abū Al-Qāsim Al-Zahrāwī described *qīla mā'ī* as the collection of fluid within the white membrane beneath the scrotal skin.

Clinical Features

- When fluid collects in the scrotal sac, swelling is rounded and spherical; the testes become obscured by fluid.
- When fluid accumulates in the tunica vaginalis *(ṣifāq)*, the testes feel soft with palpable fluctuation.
- When fluid gathers within the inner membrane, a separate, rounded mass appears beside the normal testes.

Types of *Qīla al-Mā'* (Hydrocele)

1. *Qīla al-Mā'* in the Scrotal Sac

Occurs when fluid accumulates within the coverings of the testes *(al-Unthayayn)*.

- Swelling resembles a water-filled leather bag with a shiny surface.
- On puncture, large amounts of fluid drain out but may reaccumulate. The fluid often descends from the upper organs.[7]

2. *Qīla al-Mā'* within the Testes Itself *(Nafs Al-Khuṣya)*

- The testes enlarge and become hard, unlike the first type, where the scrotal sac distends while the testes remain normal.
- The collected fluid *(mā'iyyat al-dam)* is the serous part of blood; when excessive, it hardens.
- Condition is usually painless as the glandular tissue lacks sensation.

Management of *Qīla Mā'ī / Qurū Mā'ī*

Initial management aims at fluid absorption and removal through

Faṣd (phlebotomy) and application of *ḍimādāt* (local poultices) to reduce swelling.

Surgical Management of Hydrocele *(Qīla Mā'ī / Qurū Mā'ī)*

Indication

When conservative therapy fails, fluid persists in the scrotal sac, tunica vaginalis, or testicular membrane.

Operative Technique

- Patient lies supine on an elevated surface. Scrotum supported by cloth or sponge.
- Surgeon sits on the left, assistant on the right to stabilise the genitals.

Incision and Drainage:

- A midline incision near the pubic region using a broad scalpel.
- For central hydroceles, an incision is made obliquely.
- Accumulated fluid is completely drained.

Use of Instruments and Closure:

- *Ṣunnāra* (hooks) used to retract edges. After drainage, the wound is sutured, and *ḥābis al-dam adwiya* (hemostatic powders) are applied.

Deeper Hydroceles (in Tunica Vaginalis or Inner Membrane)

If fluid lies deeper, incision is extended, hooks are applied for retraction, and the same method is followed for drainage and closure.

Surgical Technique According to 'Alī ibn 'Abbās Al-Majūsī

Positioning:

Patient lies on a wooden platform (shop-bed) with cushions beneath buttocks; a soft pad supports the scrotum. The surgeon sits on the left, the assistant on the right.

Incision:

A straight incision is made along the midline of the scrotum to reach the thin membrane of the testes. If the fluid is within the tunica vaginalis, the incision extends over the sac.

Evacuation and Excision:

The sac is exposed, small incisions are made, and fluid is evacuated. The sac is then grasped with forceps and excised from thin regions, leaving the *ṣifāq* (membrane) clean.

Closure and Healing:

Earlier surgeons sutured the wound and applied powders; later, *Munbit-i-Laḥm* (flesh-promoting medicines) were used without suturing.

Surgical Treatment of Hydrocele *(Qīla Mā'iyya)* According to Al-Zahrāwī and Later Surgeons

Operative Method by Al-Zahrāwī

Preparation and Incision

Al-Zahrāwī advised using a broad scalpel to make a longitudinal incision in the scrotum, extending from the midline toward the pubic region, parallel to the median raphe. The incision should be deep enough to reach the tunica albuginea, taking great care to avoid injury to this delicate layer.

Dissection and Drainage

Dissection should be performed only on the adherent side of the testes. After reaching the hydrocele sac, a wide opening is made to evacuate the accumulated fluid (Mā'). The wound edges are retracted with hooks *(Ṣunnāra),* elevating the membrane while preserving the overlying skin.

Excision of the Sac

Al-Zahrāwī emphasised complete excision of the sac, either in one piece or in sections, particularly from the side walls. He warned that incomplete removal may lead to recurrence of the hydrocele.

Management and Closure

If the testes protrude during the operation, they must be repositioned carefully before suturing the wound. Standard wound dressings are applied until healing is complete.

Cautery Method *('Amal bil-Kayy)*

Application of Heated Cautery

As an alternative to incision, Al-Zahrāwī proposed cauterisation using a heated knife-edged cautery, applied to the scrotal skin until the white hydrocele membrane is exposed.

Perforation and Evacuation

A second heated cautery is used to perforate the membrane, allowing complete drainage of the fluid.

Excision with Cautery

The membrane is stretched with hooks and gradually excised using the cautery. The process continues until the entire sac is removed, ensuring that the testes are not touched directly by the hot instrument.

Advantages of Cautery

Al-Zahrāwī noted that cautery is safer than incision because it minimises bleeding and reduces the recurrence of hydrocele.

Cauterisation, according to Ibn Hubal Al-Baghdādī

Ibn Hubal described cauterising the testicle with a round cauterising iron, performed once or repeatedly. In some cases, the overlying skin is removed, and the testes itself cauterized.

Opinion of Abū al-Ḥasan Al-Ṭabarī

Al-Ṭabarī reported differing views among physicians — some supported cauterisation to induce fibrosis and prevent fluid reaccumulation, while others opposed it, believing the fluid would naturally drain without intervention.

Qurū Laḥmī (Scrotal Mass or Tumour)

Description

Qurū Laḥmī refers to a fleshy growth *(al-Laḥm al-Zā'id)* forming around the testicles. The swelling is usually firm and may become indurated (stone-like ḥardness) over time, sometimes leading to degenerative complications.

Opinion of 'Alī ibn 'Abbās Al-Majūsī (Haly Abbas)

According to Al-Majūsī, several abnormal masses can arise around the testicles, appearing firm, elevated, and often associated with severe or even fatal pain.

Medical Management of *Qurū Laḥmī*

The treatment resembles that of other ḥard swellings, focusing on *faṣd* (venesection) and *istifrāgh* (evacuation therapies). Local applications include *fenugreek, linseed, chamomile, myrrh, mi'ah, marham dakhiliyun,* and emollient ointments. Induced vomiting is also considered beneficial.

Surgical Management of *Qurū Laḥmī*

General Surgical Approach

Earlier Greek physicians discouraged surgery due to high mortality risk, but later Unani surgeons performed excision with caution:

- Patient placed supine.
- Longitudinal incision made along the scrotal raphe up to the tunica vaginalis. If the mass involves the testes, incision is extended to the tunica albuginea. The fleshy mass was excised carefully.
- *Ḥābis al-Dam* (hemostatic powders) applied.

Postoperative management followed principles for *Qurūḥ* (chronic ulcers).

Operative Technique According to 'Alī ibn 'Abbās Al-Majūsī

Positioning and Initial Incision

The patient is first seated before the surgeon, then placed supine. An incision is made over the rounded part of the testes, deep enough to reach the *jild-e-khuṣya* (tunica covering the testes).

Tumour Adherent to Testes

If the tumour adheres to the testes, the tunica is incised similarly to the procedure for *qurū mā'ī* (hydrocele). Earlier physicians discouraged this due to the risk of severe haemorrhage, but later surgeons adopted it cautiously.

Method of Later Physicians

When the growth occurs between *'urūq sakīna* (vessels), the *Khuṣya* (testes) is drawn upward and exteriorised. If the testes are directly attached to the mass, both are excised together.

If the tumour lies behind the testes, all surrounding tissues and the testes must be removed completely to prevent recurrence.

Qurutain (Calcified Tumours)

Nature and Differentiation

Some Qurū Laḥmī undergo calcification and become Qurutain, forming within the *khuṣya* or its tunica.

They differ from *qurū laḥmī* in:

- Degree of ḥardness
- Extent of elevation
- Irregular shape

Treatment

The treatment parallels that of *qurū laḥmī*, involving surgical excision followed by appropriate wound management.

Qurū Mi'ā'ī / Qurū Mi'wī

(Intestinal Hernia / Enterocele)

Definition

Qurū Mi'ā'ī (Intestinal Hernia) occurs when the *Ṣifāq* (peritoneum) ruptures or stretches, allowing part of the intestine *(A'mā')* to descend into the *kisah al-khuṣyatayn* (scrotal sac), resembling the testes. In some cases, the *Tharb* (omentum/mesentery) also descends, causing severe pain and discomfort.

'Alī ibn 'Abbās Al-Majūsī described two principal forms:

1. Rupture of the peritoneum – incurable.
2. Stretching without rupture – treatable by surgical intervention using iron instruments.

Causes *(Asbāb)*

- *Ḍarba* (trauma) to the abdomen.
- Excessive strain from lifting, shouting, or jumping.
- Gradual accumulation of *ruṭūbat muzliqa* at the site.
- Sudden onset follows trauma; gradual development occurs with fluid accumulation or prolonged strain.

Clinical Features

- Swelling palpable in the scrotum, reducible when lying with legs raised.
- Gurgling sound *(Qarāqir)* if air is trapped.
- Commonly involves the *al-a'war* (caecum) due to its loose attachment.
- If the *Tharb* (omentum) descends, swelling is smaller, firmer, and less reducible.
- Omental hernia develops slowly; intestinal hernia often presents

suddenly.

- Large omental hernias fill the entire scrotal sac and are difficult to treat.

Surgical Management of *Qurū Mi'ā'ī / Qurū Mi'wī*

Patient Positioning and Initial Procedure

- Patient placed supine, legs raised.
- Manual reduction of the intestine attempted first. The assistant lifts the inguinal skin ('Arbi area).
- Transverse incision made across the region (some prefer vertical). Incision widened to allow the *khuṣya* (testes) to be exteriorised.

Exposure and Separation

- Once the *Ṣifāq* (peritoneum) is exposed, the index finger is introduced beneath it. And adhesions between the intestine and testes are carefully separated.
- The surgeon elevates the peritoneum and testes while ensuring no intestinal loops remain adhered. If any loop is found gently repositioned into the abdomen.

Closure and Excision

- Using a curved needle and double silk thread, sutures are placed in a cruciate pattern (four stitches). Additional stitches are added two finger-breadths apart for reinforcement.
- Redundant peritoneum is excised circularly, leaving a small margin.

Drainage and Dressing

- A small drainage incision made below the testes.
- Wool soaked in oil is applied, followed by bandaging for healing.

Surgical Treatment According to 'Alī ibn 'Abbās Al-Majūsī

Procedure

- Patient lies on the back; the assistant pulls the groin skin upward.
- A transverse incision is made and deepened to expose the *ṣifāq* (peritoneum).
- Adhesions and omental tissue are dissected using sharp instruments. The index finger is introduced between the peritoneal layers to separate tissues from the testes.
- The intestine is gently returned to the abdomen.

Closure of Peritoneal Defect

- A thick, doubled thread is passed through the peritoneum and tied in a cross-fashion, preventing vessel bleeding and recurrence. A second layer of sutures strengthens closure.
- Redundant peritoneum and, if necessary, the affected testes are excised.

Drainage and Dressing

- A small scrotal incision provides drainage of blood and pus. A seton wick is inserted, and rose-oil–based dressings are applied.
- The wound is managed similarly to *Qurū Mā'ī* (hydrocele).[3]

Management of *Fatq* (Hernia) According to Ibn Hubal Al-Baghdādī

When a *fatq* (hernia) results from rupture of the *ṣifāq* (peritoneum), complete healing is rare. Strengthening *Ḍimādāt* (plasters) and tight bandaging are recommended; however, the best treatment is *'Ilāj bil-Kayy* (cauterisation).

Reduction Technique

If the *A'mā'* (intestine) or *Tharb* (omentum) descends into the *al-ṣafan* (scrotum):

- The patient lies supine with legs elevated.
- The herniated part is pushed gently upward. If difficult, Warm

baths or compresses are applied. In resistant cases, the patient's legs are lifted and shaken to aid in reduction.

- A tight bandage is then applied to support the region.

Cauterization *('Ilāj bil-Kayy)*

When medications fail, and there is a risk of further descent of intestine or omentum, cauterisation at the site of *fatq* is performed. It helps dry excessive Discharge, strengthen tissues, and prevent recurrence. [1]

Qīla Rīḥī / Qurū Rīḥī (Physocele)

Definition and Concept

Physocele *(Qīla Rīḥī / Qurū Rīḥī)* refers to a scrotal swelling caused by the accumulation of air or gas rather than fluid. According to Unani physicians, it develops when *Ruṭūbat* (bodily fluids) undergo decomposition, producing *riyāḥ ghalīẓa* (thick vapours) that descend through the inguinal canal and collect within the scrotal sac.

Differential Diagnosis between Hydrocele *(Qīla al-Mā')* and Physocele *(Qīla al-Rīḥ)*

1. **Nature of Content**

- In *Qīla al-Mā'* (Hydrocele), the swelling contains fluid *(mā')* collected within the tunica surrounding the testes.
- In *Qīla al-Rīḥ* (Physocele), the swelling contains air or gas *(rīḥ)* formed due to the decomposition of bodily humours.

2. **Consistency and Weight**

- Hydrocele appears heavy, tense, and fluctuant on palpation.
- Physocele feels light, soft, and compressible, often described as an air-filled bag.

3. **Response to Pressure**

- In a hydrocele, compression does not change the swelling; fluid remains static without sound.

- In a physocele, pressure produces a gurgling or crackling sound *(Qarāqir),* and the air shifts upward, temporarily flattening the scrotum.

4. **Reducibility**

- The swelling of a hydrocele is non-reducible; it remains distended even after pressure is applied.
- The swelling of a physocele is easily reducible, as air returns to the abdomen and may reaccumulate later.

5. **Change with Position**

- Hydrocele may show a slight variation in size when the patient lies down.
- Physocele remains unchanged in both standing and lying postures.

6. **Associated Sensation**

- Hydrocele presents a sensation of heaviness in the scrotum.
- A physocele gives a feeling of emptiness or lightness after pressure is applied.

7. **Diagnostic Sound**

- Hydrocele: Silent on percussion.
- Physocele: Produces resonant or tympanic sound due to entrapped air.

Clinical Features

- Swelling is light, soft, and easily reducible.
- Compression produces gurgling *(qarāqir)* due to trapped air.
- Swelling remains unchanged in standing or lying posture, unlike *Udhra Mu'aiyya* (enterocoele) or *Udhra al-Tharbiyya* (omental hernia).

Unani Therapeutic Approach

Unani scholars emphasised non-surgical, conservative management in *qīla rīḥī*:

- *Takmid* (fomentation): Hot decoctions of *Darmana Turki* (Artemisia maritima), *Pudina* (Mentha piperita), and *Sa'tar* (Origanum vulgare) applied on cloth to the affected area.
- *Dalk Khafīf* (gentle massage): Helps *ikhrāj-il-rīḥ* (expulsion of entrapped gas) and reduces tension in the scrotum.

Surgical and Cauterisation Methods

Although rare, some early physicians adopted invasive methods when conservative measures failed:

Surgical approach: Incision of the scrotal sac, removal of the underlying membranous covering, and suturing of edges to prevent further air accumulation.

***Kayy* (cauterisation):** The testes were pulled downward, and the inguinal passage cauterised to seal the air tract, while keeping the skin intact.

Dawālī al-Ṣafan / Qurū Dawālī / Qīla Dawālī (Varicocele)

Definition

Varicocele *(Dawālī al-Ṣafan / Qurū Dawālī / Qīla Dawālī)* is characterised by abnormal dilatation and tortuosity of the veins of the pampiniform plexus within the scrotum. It manifests as a swelling resembling a cluster of grapes, accompanied by heaviness, relaxation of the testes *(Istirkhā' al-Khuṣya)*, and discomfort during movement or exertion.

Pathophysiology According to Unani Medicine

In *Qīla Dawālī*, the veins of the spermatic cord become dilated and swollen like grape clusters. Unlike arterial dilatation, which subsides on pressure, venous distension persists, as compression fails to empty the vessels.

Management

Conservative management of *Dawālī* follows the principles used for varicose veins of the legs:

- *Faṣd* (venesection) of the affected vein to remove morbid blood.
- *Istifrāgh-e-Sawdā'* (purgation of black bile) using suitable purgatives.
- *Ḍimād* (topical applications) of medicinal pastes containing:
    - *Hulba* (Trigonella foenum-graecum)
    - *Baqla* (Vicia faba)
    - *Ās* (Artemisia absinthium)
    - *Khitmī* (Althaea officinalis)
    - *Muqil* (Commiphora mukul)
    - *Shahm al-Ma'zi* (goat fat)

Additional formulations containing bone marrow, animal fat, or ointments with mineral or silicate components were applied to soften and strengthen local tissues.

Surgical Management in Classical Texts

When medical therapy failed, operative treatment was indicated. The procedure included:

Positioning: The patient was seated so that the testes hung freely.

Incision: The scrotal skin was stretched downward, and a deep incision was made with *al-mibḍa'(*broad scalpel).

Exposure: A *Ṣunnāra* (probe) was used to separate subcutaneous tissues until the spermatic vessels were visible.

Ligation: Dilated veins were isolated and tied at two points—proximal and distal—using a threaded needle. The intervening part was incised to release congested blood.

Healing: Suppuration was encouraged to obliterate the diseased veins, causing them to collapse and prevent recurrence.

Operative Technique According to 'Alī ibn 'Abbās Al-Majūsī

Al-Majūsī described the following surgical steps:

Patient Position: Seated on an elevated surface to allow descent of the testes.

Identification: The spermatic cord was recognised by its firm texture and sensitivity to pressure.

Incision: A parallel deep incision was made over the dilated vessels with *al-mibḍa'*.

Ligation: A double-threaded needle passed through the veins at proximal and distal points; the section between them was incised, and blood evacuated.

Postoperative Care: Managed like *Sill Shiryān* (arterial aneurysm), to promote obliteration of the vein.

In advanced disease involving the entire spermatic cord, orchiectomy with excision of diseased veins was performed.

Surgical Technique by Abū Al-Qāsim Al-Zahrāwī

In *Kitab al-Taṣrīf,* Al-Zahrāwī provided a precise method for *dawālī al-ṣafan:*

Positioning: The patient was seated on a high stool for free suspension of the testes.

Localisation: The suspensor of the testes and vessels near the base of the penis were held firmly by the assistant.

Incision and Exposure: An oblique incision was made along the course of the vessels, exposing the dilated veins.

Ligation and Excision: The exposed veins were ligated at two sites—where dilatation began and ended. The varix was incised transversely, and corrupt blood was drained.

Wound Dressing: Standard postoperative dressing ensured proper healing and reduced the risk of recurrence.

Istirkhā' al-Ṣafan

(Scrotal Redundancy / Scrotal Ptosis)

Clinical Presentation

Istirkhā' al-Ṣafan refers to a condition where the scrotal skin becomes loose, elongated, and pendulous, without involvement of the *khuṣya* (testes), its membranes, or associated vessels and ducts. The laxity results in an undesirable cosmetic appearance but usually does not interfere with physiological function.

Indication for Surgery

Though non-pathological, this condition often causes aesthetic concern or discomfort due to the excessive hanging of scrotal skin. Hence, surgical correction is performed primarily for cosmetic and reconstructive purposes rather than for therapeutic necessity.

Scrotoplasty (Scrotal Reduction Surgery)

Operative Technique

Positioning: The patient is placed in the supine position.

Skin Handling: The redundant scrotal skin is gathered between the surgeon's fingers to estimate the extent of excision.

Excision: The excess skin is removed using *miqrāḍ* (surgical scissors) with careful preservation of underlying structures.

Closure: The wound edges are approximated and closed with silk sutures to ensure proper alignment.

Postoperative Care: *Dharūr Aṣfar* is applied locally to promote healing, prevent infection, and aid cicatrization.

Surgeries for Hernia

Fatq (Hernia)

Definition

Hernia *(Fatq)* is defined as the rupture of the peritoneal covering within the abdomen through which a part of the stomach *(mi'da),* omentum *(al-tharb),* or intestines *(al-am'ā')* protrudes, depending on the site of occurrence.

Types Based on Location

- **Near the cardia *(Hiatus Hernia / Fam al-Mi'da):*** The upper portion of the stomach ascends upward during distension.
- **Above the umbilicus *(Al-Surra):*** A part of the omentum *(al-tharb)* protrudes.
- **In the pubic or inguinal region *('Āna):*** The rectum *(Al-Ma'y al-Mustaqīm)* or the terminal portion of the omentum rises upward.

Aetiology of *Fatq* (Hernia)

Due to Moisture and Tissue Flaccidity

- Excess moisture *(ruṭūbat)* weakens and loosens the tissues.
- This leads to gradual dilatation of peritoneal openings.
- It develops slowly and without pain.

Due to Sudden Rupture (Tear of the Peritoneum)

- Caused by violent exertion such as jumping, straining, or over-distension.
- Appears suddenly with severe tearing pain.
- Sensation resembles salt sprinkled over a wound.

Common causes include:

- Perforation of intestinal walls.
- Strenuous exertion during gastric fullness.

- Weakness of the peritoneal membrane.
- Increased intra-abdominal pressure acting on abdominal organs.

In severe cases, both the peritoneum and the abdominal wall rupture, causing pain and distress.

Management of Hernia

Conservative Treatment

The safest Unani management involves the use of bandaging *(al-ribāṭ)* and topical medicaments *(ḍimād)* prepared from strengthening drugs *(adwiya muqawwiya)* to reinforce the abdominal wall.

Mechanical Support (Truss Application/Abdominal Support)

1. **Long Truss resembling a waist-belt *(Himyan-like Belt):***

- Contains a spherical projection (ball-shaped support).
- Effective for umbilical *(fatq surrī)* and supra-umbilical hernia.
- Worn during daytime like a wide abdominal belt *(mintaqa).*

2. **Circular Truss with knots**

- Ring-shaped with four knots.
- Specially designed for inguinal hernia.

3. **Triangular Truss:**

- Shaped like a scalene triangle *(Muthallath Mukhtalif al-Adhla').*
- Suitable for all types of hernia.

Philosophy of Treatment

The goal of this conservative approach was to prevent further protrusion of abdominal contents, restore support to the weakened abdominal wall, and reduce pain and recurrence.

Fatq Urbī (Inguinal Hernia)

Classical Description

According to Abū Al-Qāsim Al-Zahrāwī, hernia sometimes occurs in the groin *(urbiya / kunjran)* due to weakness and stretching of the membrane in that region. Initially, only a small portion of the intestine may descend into the scrotum and is easily reducible, but with time, the rupture enlarges, allowing both the bowel and omentum to enter the scrotum.

Surgical Management by Al-Zahrāwī

1. **Cauterisation *(Kayy):*** To strengthen and seal the ruptured site.
2. **Excision with Knife:** When cauterisation alone is inadequate.

Operative Technique

- Patient lies supine. and a transverse incision (about three fingers wide) is made across the swelling.
- Subcutaneous layers are dissected until the white fascia at the rupture site is exposed.
- A probe *(Ṣunnāra)* is placed on the protruding fascia and used to reduce it back into the abdomen.
- The edges of the membrane are sutured together over the probe to close the defect. The probe is removed, and the wound is dressed for healing.

Surgical Technique by Al-Majūsī

Incision and Exposure

A transverse incision (about three fingers broad) is made at the root of the thigh.

An assistant holds the wound edges with the omentum-like membrane until the peritoneal layer *(ṣifāq)* is visible.

Reduction and Suturing

The scalpel *(al-mibḍa')* is used to gently displace the intestine inward.

And the edges of the peritoneal rupture are lifted and sutured tightly together to close the defect completely.

Dressing and Support

The wound is covered with a rolling bandage *(Shal)* to secure sutures and support healing.

Fatq Surrī / Nutū' al-Surrī
(Umbilical Hernia)

Causes of Umbilical Swelling

According to Abū Al-Qāsim Al-Zahrāwī, swelling of the umbilicus may occur due to:

- Rupture of the peritoneum, allowing omentum *(al-tharb)* or intestines *(al-am'ā')* to protrude.
- Extravasation of blood from arteries or veins.
- Trapped Gas *(riḥ)* within the umbilical region.

Examination of Umbilical Swelling

1. Due to Ruptured Peritoneum with Omental Prolapse

- Colour resembles the surrounding skin.
- Soft, painless, and slightly movable.

2. Due to Intestinal Prolapse

- More prominent displacement.
- Disappears with pressure but recurs.
- May produce crepitus.
- Increases after exertion or a hot bath.

3. Due to Fluid Accumulation

- Soft swelling, non-reducible, and constant in size.

4. Due to Blood Extravasation

- Swelling appears blackish and tense.

- Pain and discolouration may accompany.

5. Due to Fleshy Overgrowth *(Laḥmīyya)*

- Hard, solid, constant swelling.
- Non-reducible and painless.

6. Due to Gas *(Riḥ)*

- Soft swelling due to trapped air in the tissues.

Umbilical Hernia and Related Conditions

Al-Zahrāwī's detailed differentiation of umbilical swellings reflects a remarkably advanced clinical diagnostic approach, distinguishing between omental, intestinal, fluid, blood, fleshy, and gaseous swellings. His caution against surgical intervention in cases of hematoma or Gas-related swellings demonstrates clinical prudence and aligns with safe, conservative management principles.

1. Omental Hernia *(Al-Tharbi)*

- Soft, painless swelling at the umbilicus, same colour as surrounding skin, slightly mobile.

2. Intestinal Hernia *(Al-Am'ā' i)*

- Swelling reduces on digital pressure but recurs; associated with crepitus; increases after exertion or a hot bath.

Note: Crepitus corresponds to the movement of intestinal gases.

3. Fluid-Related Swelling

- Soft, non-reducible swelling that remains constant in size.

4. Blood Extravasation

- Swelling appears blackish, due to leakage of blood into the tissues.

5. Fleshy Overgrowth

- Solid, hard swelling, constant in size, non-reducible.

6. Gas Accumulation

- Swelling feels soft, variable in nature, caused by trapped Gas.

Treatment Considerations

When the swelling arises from a ruptured peritoneum with omental or intestinal prolapse, surgical or conservative management may be undertaken.

In cases caused by blood extravasation or Gas accumulation, intervention should be avoided, as treatment is considered hazardous and prognostically uncertain.

Management of Hernia *(Fatq)*

General Principles of Treatment

Initial management of a hernia includes:

- Evacuation of morbid humours *(Istifrāgh)* by purgation and eliminative measures.
- Regulation of diet) with reduced food intake.
- Application of binding devices *(ālāt al-fatq)* and strengthening plasters *(ḍimād muqawwiya)* for local support.

Truss Application / Abdominal Support

Bandaging and truss use are the safest and most reliable Unani methods for preventing hernia recurrence.

1. **Long Belt-shaped Truss *(Himiyan-type)***

- Worn like a waist-belt *(Mintaqa).*
- Rounded projection supports the herniated area.
- Used for umbilical *(fatq surrī)* and supra-umbilical hernias.

2. **Circular Truss with Clasps**

- Circular design with four clasps and knots.
- Effective for inguinal hernia.

3. **Triangular Truss *(Muthallath Mukhtalif al-Adhla')***

- Unequal-sided triangular form.
- Adaptable for all types of hernia.

Surgical Management of Umbilical Hernia

According to Al-Majūsī

Indication: When the umbilical protrusion *(nutū 'al-surra)* is due to the descent of intestines *(al-am'ā')* or omentum *(al-tharb)* through the peritoneum.

Operative Steps:

- Patient stands while the operative circle is marked around the swelling, then lies supine.
- A deep incision is made along the circle with a scalpel *(al-mibḍa')*. The swelling is lifted and ligated at its base with cord or thread.
- The incision is slightly enlarged to examine contents; if the intestine is caught, the ligature is loosened, the intestine reduced, and excess omentum excised.
- Care is taken to preserve vessels *('Urūq Sākina wa Jahinda)*.
- Crosswise sutures are placed with two needles at four points for necrosis and sloughing.
- After tissue separation, healing agents *(adwiya munbit-i-laḥm)* are applied.

Special Considerations:

- If caused by *Laḥmīyya* or *Ruṭūbat*, excise the abnormal mass and apply granulation-promoting drugs.
- In arterial *(Shiryān)* or venous swellings, extreme caution is required.

According to Abū Al-Qāsim Al-Zahrāwī

Surgical Management of Umbilical Hernia:

- Patient holds breath standing; a circle is marked around the umbilicus.
- Patient laid supine; a circular incision made along the marking.
- Swelling is elevated with a hook and ligated at the base with strong silk or thread. The swelling above the ligature is opened and examined. If bowel *(al-am'ā')* is trapped, the knot is loosened and bowel returned; if omentum *(al-tharb)* is present, excess is excised.

Surgical Management of Umbilical Haemangioma:

- Affected vessel is tied firmly. And two needles with ligatures are inserted crosswise (cruciate) through the swelling. Ligatures are left to induce necrosis, after which tissue sloughs off.
- Wound is dressed with healing ointments until full recovery.

Surgical Management of Umbilical Granuloma:

- Excess tissue excised and fluid drained. Wound treated with stimulating dressings *(adwiya muḥarrika)* to promote granulation.

Surgeries in Obstetrics and Gynaecology

Surgeries in Obstetrics

Ikhrāj al-Janīn al-Mayyit

(Extraction of Dead Fetus)

Clinical Context

When labor becomes obstructed, and all medical or manipulative measures fail, surgical intervention may be considered for *Ikhrāj al-Janīn al-Mayyit.*

Contraindications for Surgery

Surgical procedures are contraindicated in women showing extreme weakness, indicated by:

- Fainting spells or paralysis of limbs.
- Weak or faint response to speech.
- Feeble pulse *(Nabḍ Ḍu'f wa Ṣaghīr).*

In such cases, the use of instruments *(ālāt ḥadīd)* is considered unsafe and must be avoided.

Indications for Surgical Extraction

Surgery is permissible only when:

- The woman retains sufficient strength and vitality.
- Appetite and general health are satisfactory.
- She can endure the operative procedure.

Manual Extraction *(Ikhrāj al-Janīn al-Mayyit bil-Yad)*

When medicinal therapy fails, and the patient remains strong, manual extraction is advised.

Patient Positioning

- The woman is lying supine, with head lowered and feet elevated.
- She is restrained by female attendants or secured with straps to

prevent movement.

Preparation and Cervical Dilatation

- The midwife anoints her hand and the vaginal canal with oil, introducing her fingers gradually to dilate the cervix *(Fatḥ al-Raḥim)*.
- Continuous lubrication ensures relaxation and minimises trauma.

Recognition of Presentation

- **Cephalic:** eyes, mouth, chin, clavicle, ribs, identifiable by touch.
- **Podalic:** pubic bone *('Āna),* ribs, or vertebral column palpable.

Instrumental Application

- The *Ṣunnāra* (hook-like instrument) is guided by the left hand inside the vagina, securing parts of the fetus to facilitate traction.
- If required, *Miftāḥ al-Raḥim* (cervical dilator) is used to widen the passage.

Extraction Technique

- Gentle, rotational traction is applied, avoiding forceful pulling.
- Once one part is expelled, the instrument is advanced further until complete delivery.

Extraction of a Dead Fetus According to Al-Majūsī

Patient Position and Restraint

- The woman lies supine on a flat surface with legs elevated and head lowered.
- One attendant supports the legs; another steadies the chest for complete immobilisation.

Cervical Dilatation and Lubrication

- The midwife dilates the cervix using four fingers coated with *Ravghan-e-Banafsha.*
- The fetal body is also lubricated to minimise resistance.

Instrumental Fixation

Hooks are fixed into various parts of the fetus depending on presentation:

- **Cephalic:** eyes, jaw, neck, scapula, or ribs.
- **Podalic:** pelvis, ribs, or vertebral junctions.

Traction and Separation

- The fetus is extracted gradually with controlled traction, alternating right and left movements for ease.
- The operator inserts lubricated fingers between the uterus and fetus to separate adhesions, facilitating smooth delivery.

Stepwise Extraction

- As each portion emerges, hooks are repositioned higher until the entire fetus is safely expelled.

Destructive Obstetric Procedures (Fetotomy)

Classical Descriptions by ʻAlī ibn ʻAbbās Al-Majūsī and Ibn Hubal Al-Baghdādī

1. Amputation of Fetal Limbs *(Qaṭʻ Aʻḍāʼ al-Janīn)*

- When one or both fetal hands or legs emerge and cannot be repositioned due to constriction, A cloth band is tied to the limb to maintain grip.
- The limb is amputated — hands at the shoulder joint, legs at the hip joint — to facilitate extraction.

2. Craniotomy *(Shaqq Ra's al-Janīn)*

Indication: Fetal head too large to pass through the canal.

Technique:

- A scalpel *(al-mibḍaʻ)* or knife is inserted between the fingers to perforate the skull.
- The forceps *(Kalbatayn)* are then introduced, the cranial bones fragmented, and brain matter evacuated to collapse the skull for delivery.

3. Thoracotomy *(Shaqq Ṣadr al-Janīn)*

Indication: Chest impacted after head delivery.

Technique:

- An incision is made at the strongest part of the chest; thoracic fluids are released, causing collapse and easing extraction.

4. Evisceration *(Shaqq Baṭn al-Janīn)*

Indication: Abdominal distension of the fetus.

Technique:

- The abdomen is incised and the viscera removed to reduce volume, enabling delivery by traction.

5. Controlled Traction

- Fetal feet are grasped or hooked carefully.
- Gentle rotational traction is applied to prevent *Inqilāb al-Raḥim* (uterine inversion).

6. Complete Fetotomy (Sectioning into Pieces)

- When extraction fails, the fetus is divided into smaller parts inside the uterus and removed piecemeal, minimising maternal injury.

Post-Operative Management of the Mother

- Treated as a case of *Waram al-Raḥim* (uterine inflammation).
- Hemostatic and soothing medicines are applied in cases of uterine bleeding.
- Caution is advised throughout to avoid *Inqilāb al-Raḥim* (uterine inversion).

Fetotomy Procedures According to Al-Zahrāwī

1. Craniotomy (Perforation or Crushing of the Head)

Indication: Large head or hydrocephalus obstructing delivery.

Technique:

- A spike-shaped scalpel (*Mibḍa' Shaukiya*) is inserted between the fingers to puncture the skull and release fluids.
- The head may be crushed using the cephalotribe *(Al-Mishdākh)*.
- Forceps *(Al-Kalālīb)* are used to extract fragments and complete delivery.

2. Thoracotomy *(Shaqq Ṣadr al-Janīn)*

Indication: Head delivered, but chest impacted at the clavicles.

Technique:

- An incision is made on the thorax to release internal contents.
- The chest collapses; if not, small pieces of bone or tissue are removed until delivery becomes possible.

3. Evisceration *(Shaqq Baṭn al-Janīn)*

Indication: Fetal abdomen enlarged or dropsical.

Technique:

- The abdomen is opened and all accumulated fluid evacuated.
- Collapse of the trunk facilitates delivery through reduced bulk.

Iḥtibās al-Mashīma (Manual Removal of Placenta)

Indication

After childbirth, if the placenta *(Al-Mashīma)* remains inside the uterus despite delivery of the fetus and the cervical os remains open, manual extraction *(ikhrāj bil-yad)* is required.

Preparation and Lubrication

- The operator's hand is anointed with *ravghan-e-banafsha* (violet oil) or *ravghan-e-kunjad* (Warm sesame oil) for lubrication.
- The lubricated hand is gently introduced into the uterine cavity with care and steadiness.

Technique of Removal

- If the placenta is coiled or folded to one side, it is gently palpated and drawn out.
- If adherent to the uterine wall, the hand is moved slowly in all directions to detach it without force.
- Forceful traction is prohibited to prevent *Inqilāb al-Raḥim* (uterine inversion).
- Gradual alternating movement—right, left, upward, downward—helps in safe detachment and expulsion.

Precautions

- Avoid hurried or careless extraction.
- Do not attempt removal if the cervical os has closed prematurely.
- Ensure complete expulsion, as a retained placenta may decompose *(ta'affun),* liquefy, and discharge later, posing harm to the mother.

Surgeries in Gynaecology

Ratqa, Inghilāq al-Raḥim

(Vaginal Atresia / Imperforate Hymen)

Definition

Al-Zahrāwī: *Ratqa* is a condition in which the pudenda of a woman have no opening or only a very narrow one.

Ibn al-Quff describes *Ratqa* as a condition where the female genital passage is completely closed or extremely constricted.

Al-Majūsī: Defines it as a congenital or acquired obstruction of the vaginal canal or uterine mouth following ulceration or scarring.

Ibn Hubal Al-Baghdādī: Compares *Ratqa* to an imperforate anus in infants — either congenital or due to scar tissue, where a membrane or fleshy mass blocks the vaginal opening, preventing menstruation and intercourse.

Etiology

1. Congenital (*Khilqī*):

- Absence of the vaginal orifice.
- Imperforate hymen completely covering the passage.

2. Acquired (*Iktisābī*):

- Adhesion or scarring following ulcers or trauma.
- Formation of *Laḥmīyya* (fleshy growth) or membranous tissue obstructing the passage.
- Adhesion after ulcers or trauma.
- Growth of fleshy or membranous tissue (thin or thick).
- External or internal blockage of the passage.

Clinical Features

- **Amenorrhea:** Retained menstrual blood refluxes into the veins, leading to systemic illness and discolouration.

- **Dyspareunia and Infertility:** Prevents intercourse and conception.
- **Obstructed Labour:** If conception occurs, delivery becomes impossible, endangering both mother and fetus.
- **Complete Sterility:** In total closure of the passage.

Pathological Variants

According to Al-Majūsī, the obstruction may occur at different levels of the genital tract:

- Depth of the vagina or uterus.
- Roof or upper part of the uterine cavity.
- Middle portion or cervix.

Mode of Closure:

- Adhesion of the vaginal opening.
- Fleshy overgrowth.
- Formation of a membranous barrier.

Descriptions by Al-Zahrāwī and Al-Majūsī

Both scholars agree that *Ratqa* may be congenital or acquired.

- The acquired type results from disease, ulceration, or inflammation, producing a fleshy mass or membrane.
- The obstruction may occur at the fundus, walls of the uterus, or vaginal passage, preventing menstruation, conception, and delivery.

Surgical Management of Vaginal Atresia *(Ratqa)*

Surgical Principles According to Ibn Zuhr

According to Ibn Zuhr, the line of management depends on the nature of the obstruction:

Ratq Laḥmī **(Fleshy Obstruction):** Curable by surgical excision with a scalpel, without harm to the patient.

Ratq 'Aẓmī **(Osseous Obstruction):** Scalpel ineffective; surgery is contraindicated.

***Ratq with Plaster-like Membrane (Gach-type)*:** Surgical operation carries a significant risk.

Surgical Techniques by Al-Zahrāwī and Ibn al-Quff

1. Membranous Obstruction (Thin Membrane)

- Patient positioned supine, legs widely separated. Labia stretched using both thumbs until the membrane ruptures.
- After rupture, wool soaked in oil is applied locally to aid healing.

2. Membranous Obstruction (Thick Membrane)

- Incise with a broad scalpel *(al-mibḍa')* shaped like a myrtle leaf.[5]

3. Fleshy Growth *(Laḥmīyya)*

- Seize with two surgical hooks and excise carefully.
- Haemostatic remedies *(Adwiya Qābiḍa)* are kept ready to control bleeding.

Postoperative Management

- Insert a lead cannula to maintain patency and prevent re-closure.
- Apply a dry linen bandage externally; continue topical healing applications until recovery.

Surgical Technique According to Ibn Hubal Al-Baghdādī

Patient Positioning and Exposure

- Patient seated on a chair, leaning backwards against a support in front of a light for visualisation.
- Thighs flexed toward the abdomen and secured; a midwife assists in identifying the membrane.
- The obstructing membrane is gently drawn forward with a hook for incision.

Surgical Incision

- Incision made transversely to avoid bladder injury *(mathāna)*.

- Moderate incision: a narrow opening hinders delivery; excessive incision may cause inflammation or convulsion.

Adjunct Measures and Postoperative Care

- After incision, apply wool soaked in Warm wine to prevent infection.
- Insert a zinc cannula for 1–2 days to keep the passage open. After removal, apply *marham shāfiya* (healing ointment) until complete recovery.

Surgical Management According to Al-Majūsī

- If adhesion or fusion of the vaginal opening, incise longitudinally using a broad scalpel *(al-mibḍa')* or an instrument used for haemorrhoid/fistula surgery. If fleshy growth *(Laḥmīyya) is* present, grasp with hook or forceps and excise. and if membranous, incise with a scalpel after traction with a hook.
- Apply styptic medicines *(adwiya qābiḍa)* for hemostasis, followed by non-irritant desiccants and *marham munbit-i-laḥm* for granulation.

Postoperative Measures

- If persistent bleeding or pus formation leads to scar tissue, the wound is refreshed with nail or sharp iron and sutured with silk thread.
- Over the sutures, a desiccative powder made of *Kundur* (frankincense), *Shagufa-e-Ward* (rose buds), and *Gulnar Shirin* (pomegranate blossom) is applied to prevent putrefaction and promote healing.

Khurāj al-Raḥim (Uterine Abscess)

General Considerations

According to 'Alī ibn 'Abbās Al-Majūsī, when an abscess develops within the uterus, immediate incision is not advised.

- The uterus *(raḥim)* is a vital organ; hence surgical intervention must be delayed until the abscess matures *(nuḍj)* and the acute inflammation subsides.

- Premature incision may cause serious complications and harm to the patient.

Surgical Technique

Positioning of the Patient

- The woman is placed reclining on her back upon an elevated seat.
- Legs flexed and raised towards the abdomen, arms passed under the knees and tied to the neck to stabilise posture.

Exposure of the Cervix *(Fam al-Raḥim)*

- The midwife *(qābila)* sits on the patient's right side.
- A speculum-like instrument *(miftāḥ al-raḥim)* is inserted and gently rotated to dilate the uterine mouth gradually for visualisation.

Localisation of the Abscess

- Palpation is performed to detect fluctuation and softening.
- The incision site is selected at the softest and most dependent point to allow effective drainage.

Incision and Drainage *(Fatḥ wa Ikhrāj al-Mādda)*

- Using a fine-edged scalpel *(al-mibḍa'),* a small incision is made precisely at the localised site.
- Pus *(Mādda Ṣadīdiyya)* is carefully evacuated until the cavity is empty.

Postoperative Management

A soft wick or gauze soaked in *ravghan-i-ward* (rose oil) is inserted into the abscess cavity.

The free end is left protruding from the cervix to facilitate continuous drainage and easy dressing.

Precaution

If the abscess lies near the cervical os *(fam al-raḥim),* the use of surgical instruments *(ālāt ḥadīdiyya)* is strictly contraindicated, as intervention in this region may cause severe or fatal complications.

Massa al-Raḥim
(Genital Wart / Cervical Wart)

According to ʻAlī ibn ʻAbbās Al-Majūsī, *Maasa al-Raḥim* refers to pustular, nodular, or haemorrhoid-like swellings that appear within the female genital tract. These growths resemble hemorrhoidal protrusions in shape and texture.

Surgical Technique

- The wart or swelling is grasped with a forceps *(kalālīb)* and gently drawn outward.
- It is then excised using scissors *(miqrāḍ)* with precision to avoid injury to the surrounding mucosa.

Postoperative Management

- After excision, tissue-regenerating medicines *(dawā' munbit-i-laḥm)* are applied to stimulate granulation and healing. Desiccant drugs *(Dawā' Mujaffif)* are used locally to dry the wound and prevent recurrence.

BIBLIOGRAPHY

1. Baghdadi IH. Kitab al-Mukhtarat fi al-Tibb. (Urdu translation by CCRUM). New Delhi: CCRUM, Ministry of Health and Family Welfare, Govt. of India; 2007
2. Ameen-UD, Abu al F, Ibn al QM (2013) Kitab-al-umda fil Jarāḥat. CCRUM 2: 231.
3. Majusi ABA. Kamil al Sana'a al Tibbiya (Urdu translation by Kintüri GH). New Delhi: Idara Kitabush Shifa; 2010
4. Razi ABMBZ. Kitab al Hawl fil Tibb (Urdu Translation by Jafri SAH. Siddiqi MY). Part 1, Vol 23. Aligarh: Bahtmam Saba publisher: 1994
5. Al-Zahrawi A. *On Surgery and Instruments (Kitab al-Tasrif, Volume 30).* Translated by Spink MS, Lewis GL. London: The Wellcome Institute of the History of Medicine; 1973.
6. Zuhr I. *Kitāb al-Taysīr fī'l Mudāwā wa'l Tadbīr*. New Delhi: CCRUM, Ministry of Health and Family Welfare, Govt. of India; 1986.
7. Tabri AHABM. *Al-Mu'āljāt al-Buqrāṭiyya* (Urdu translation by CCRUM). New Delhi: Central council for research in Unani medicine: 1997.
8. Razī ABMBZ. Kitab al Fakhir fi'l Tibb (Urdu translation by CCRUM), New Delhi: Ministry of Health and Family Welfare, Govt. of India; 2008
9. Husain MA. *Tibbi Lughat Makhzanul Jawahir.* New Delhi: Central Council for Research in Unani Medicine (CCRUM), Ministry of AYUSH; 2009.
10. Golzari SE, Khan ZH, Ghabili K, Hosseinzadeh H, Soleimanpour H, Azarfarin R, Mahmoodpoor A, Aslanabadi S, Ansarin K. Contributions of medieval Islamic physicians to the history of tracheostomy. Anesthesia & Analgesia. 2013 May 1;116(5):1123-32.

11. Sina ABAI. Al-Qanoon fi't Tibb (Urdu translation Kintüri GH). New Delhi: Idara Kitabush Shifa: 1999

12. Alam MA, Quamri MA, Sofi G. Historical account of endocrinal disorders in Unani medicine. Journal of Basic and Clinical Physiology and PḤārrmacology. 2021 Dec 8;32(6):1013-9.

13. Ansari S, Hussain AB, Shaikh A. Concept of Haemorrhoid (Bawāsīr) and Management in Unani System of Medicine. Res Rev A J Unani, Siddha Homoeopath. 2018;5(2):15–8.

14. Jurjani AHI. Zakhira Khawarizam Shahi (Urdu translation Khan HH). New Delhi: Idara Kitabush Shifa; 2010,

15. Azam Khan M. *Iksir-e-Azam*. New Delhi: Idara Kitab-us-Shifa; 2011.

16. Arzani A. Mizān al-Tibb (Urdu translation by Kabīruddin HM) New Delhi: Idara Kitabush Shifa; 2002,

17. Samarqandi NA. Al Asbab wa-al-alamat. Tehran: Nuskha Khatti: YNM (Rizwan HK. Trajuma SḤārrh Asbāb, Volume.3.. 167–173 p.)

18. (Chandpuri K. Moojizal Qanoon. 2nd ed. New Delhi: Traqi Urdu Beuru; 1988. 352 353 p.)

19. Ḥārrichand Multani. Tajul Haikmat. Lahour: Nadeem Interpresis Lahour; 215–221 p.)

20. Khan MHA. Haziq. Delhi: Jaseem Book Depo; 1983, p. 556

21. Kabiruddin H. *Makhzan al-'Ilaj*. New Delhi: Idara Kitab-us-Shifa; 2010.

22. (Al Zahrāwī AQ. Jarahiyat-i-Zahrāwī.New Delhi: CCRUM; 2012. p.23-4,140,187.Urdu)

23. ; Ali ibn Rabban al-Tabari. Firdaus al-Hikmat (Paradise of Wisdom). Translated and edited by K. Zillur Rahman. New Delhi: CCRUM, Ministry of AYUSH; 2008.

24. Venes D. Taber's cyclopedic medical dictionary. FA Davis; 2009.Page 804, 362.

25. Azizi R, Mohammadipour S. New techniques in anal fistula management. Ann Colorectal Res. 2014 Mar;2(1):e17769.

26. Löffler T, Welsch T, Mühl S, Hinz U, Schmidt J, Kienle P. Long-term success rate after surgical treatment of anorectal and rectovaginal fistulas in Crohn's disease. International journal of colorectal disease. 2009 May 1;24(5):521-6.

27. Syed IB. Islamic Medicine: 1000 years ahead of its time. Jishim. 2002; 2:2-9.

28. Hitti P. The Arabs: A Short History; Henry Regnery, Chicago, 1943, page 143).

29. Bailey H, Bulstrode CJ, Love RM, O'Connell PR. Bailey & Love's short practice of surgery. CRC Press; 2008: 1265, 1268.

30. Hamalainen KJ, Sainio AP. Cutting setons for anal fistulas: high risk of minor control defects. Dis colon rectum 1997; 40:1443-7. 10.)

31. Ritchie RD, Sackier JM, Hodde JP. Incontinence rates after cutting the seton treatment for anal fistula. Colorectal disease. 2009 Jul;11(6):564-71)

32. Sungurtekin U, Ozban M, Erbis H, Birsen O. Loose Seton: A Misnomer of Cutting Seton. Surgical Science. 2016 May 11;7(05):219.

33. Alatab S, Pourmand G, El Howairis MEF, Buchholz N, Najafi I, Pourmand MR et al. National profiles of urinary calculi - A comparison between developing and developed worlds. Iranian Journal of Kidney Diseases. 2016; 10(2):51-61.

34. British Association of Urological Surgeons Limited Ancient Mesopotamia- Surgery, urology and sexology. http://www.baus.org.uk/, 2016.

35. *Ashtiyani SC et al., Iranian Journal of Kidney Diseases, 2011; 5(5): 300–308; 2010; 4(2): 106–110)*

36. *Ashtiyani SC et al., 2010; Abdel-Halim RE, Saudi Medical Journal, 2006;*

27(11): 1631–1641

37. Tefekli A, Cezayirli F. The History of Urinary Stones: In Parallel with Civilization. The Scientific World Journal. 2013; 2013:5.
38. Abdel-Halim RE. Contributions of Muhadhdhab Al-Deen Al-Baghdadi to the progress of medicine and urology. A study and translations from his book Al-Mukhtar. Saudi Medical Journal. 2006; 27(11):1631-1641
39. Abdel-Halim RE. Contributions of Ibn Zuhr (Avenzoar) to the progress of surgery: a study and translations from his book Al-Taisir. Saudi Medical Journal. 2005; 26(9):1333-1339
40. Faridi P, Roozbeh J, Mohagheghzadeh A. Ibn-Sina's life and contributions to medicinal therapies of kidney calculi. Iranian Journal of Kidney Diseases. 2012; 6(5):339-345.
41. *WHO International Standard Terminologies on Unani Medicine, p. 388*
42. Rogers SL (1956) Sex organ mutilation. primitive surgery skills before science. Springfield, Illinois. pp 56-60.
43. Lewinsohn R (1958). Belief in beauty. A History of Sexual Customs. Longmans Green, London.
44. Allan N (1989). Illustrations from the Welcome Institute library. A Polish Rabbi's circumcision manual. Med Hist 33: 247-254.
45. Hay W, Levin M, Deterding RR, Abzug MJ (2012) Current diagnosis and treatment paediatrics. McGraw-Hill Professional, USA.
46. Ameen-UD, Abu al F, Ibn al QM (2013) Kitab-al-umda fil Jarāḥat. CCRUM 2: 2 31.

www.ingramcontent.com/pod-product-compliance
Lightning Source LLC
LaVergne TN
LVHW050927210926
848482LV00013B/561
9798903921737